IMAGES
of America

EAST AND WEST ROCKHILL TOWNSHIPS

I0807665

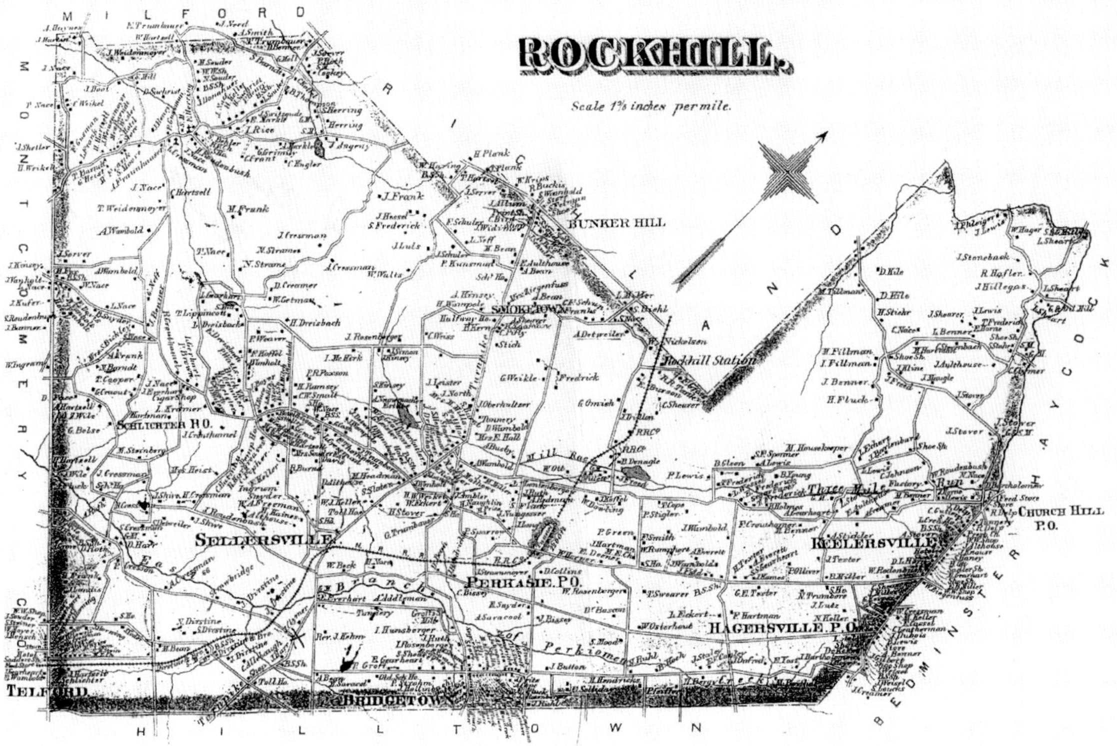

This map, created in 1876, was made by J.D. Scott of Philadelphia and was a combination atlas and map of Bucks County. (Courtesy of West Rockhill Historical Society [WRHS].)

On the Cover: The Guenst Farm on Butter Creek Road is pictured around 1906. The first Charles Guenst came here from Germany in 1898. In 1901, he settled on the Butter Creek Farm. He established not only a sawmill but also a grain mill and a mill for breaking the boulders of Rockhill into smaller stones for road paving. (Courtesy of Charles Guenst.)

IMAGES
of America

EAST AND WEST ROCKHILL TOWNSHIPS

Brenda Phelan

ARCADIA
PUBLISHING

Copyright © 2011 by Brenda Phelan
ISBN 978-0-7385-7537-7

Published by Arcadia Publishing
Charleston, South Carolina

Printed in the United States of America

Library of Congress Control Number: 2010942323

For all general information, please contact Arcadia Publishing:
Telephone 843-853-2070
Fax 843-853-0044
E-mail sales@arcadiapublishing.com
For customer service and orders:
Toll-Free 1-888-313-2665

Visit us on the Internet at www.arcadiapublishing.com

This book is dedicated to the residents, past and present, of East and West Rockhill Townships, for they made its history.

Contents

Acknowledgments		6
Introduction		7
1.	Heart of the Community	9
2.	Education	19
3.	Community	31
4.	Taverns, Mills, and Bridges	69
5.	Grand View Hospital's Beginnings	87
6.	Grand View Hospital into the Future	103
7.	Rockhill's Brush with Fame	113
Bibliography		127

ACKNOWLEDGMENTS

Walter J. Hendricks, MD, author of *A History of Grand View Hospital*, conveyed it best in 1966 when he wrote, "The present is forever in debt to the past, and the past is often obscure. Dates are forgotten, documents lost, and memories fail. Total recall is virtually impossible."

When I undertook this project I was aware that, at the very least, it was going to be a daunting task. Instead, the people of East and West Rockhill made it fun and exciting. I did not write this book—the people of East and West Rockhill did. It is their voices and stories that lie within. I was honored and privileged to be welcomed, not only into their homes, but also into their lives. It has been a privilege to collect the history of the township, and pass it on to the reading public. I will treasure the experience forever.

I wish to thank the executive committee of the West Rockhill Historical Society for supporting this project: Jill Cardell, Petrona Charles, David Collingwood, Fred Diseroad, Eleanora Gruber, Mary Wileman, and all the membership for their help and support. Petrona Charles and David Collingwood, who helped collect images and write text. Thanks to Fred Diseroad for allowing us to use his artwork, as well. Thanks to longtime residents Charlie and Lois Guenst who put up with my endless visits to glean information about the history and people of this area. Special thanks also go to Marty Steely and the Sellersville Museum and staff for allowing access to their archives; Heather Davis, who spent countless hours pouring over Grand View Hospital slides with me, as well as other photographs; author Timothy D. Hufnagle, who spent many hours with me going over text and fact checking, lent his pictures, and contributed to the text. He not only inspired me, but left me awestruck at his endless knowledge. My thanks go to Petrona Charles, who spent countless hours helping to research the history of the township, collecting photographs, and contributing text; the staff at the Jerusalem Evangelical Church for lending their historical information; the staff at Grand View Hospital for the use of their photographs and archives; and to Brenda Birch and Mary DeHaven for historic research and helping to proofread text. We wish also to acknowledge the following, who contributed photographs and history: Rosell L. Leister, Eddie Baker, Eleanora Gruber, David Collingwood, Pastor Steven Hamilton, David Mann, Ben Scholl, Brenda Oelschlager, Richard Warmkessel, Rhoda Clark, Jim Detwieler, Emil Klinger Jr., Ruth Richards, Stella Crouthamel, Lee Felbinger, Whitey Hager, and Emil Klinger. I would also like to thank William F. Byrnes and Tam and April Chau for technical help and support.

I would like to thank everyone for their contributions. This book would not have been possible without your help.

Introduction

Rockhill Township has a very rich and diverse history. Prior to its creation, the land in this part of Pennsylvania was part of a tract of 11,000 acres owned by William Penn. This tract was surveyed in 1708 and was opened to sale and settlement in 1735. History holds that this area was known as "Servants" because William Penn had set the lands aside for indentured servants. By 1740, Rockhill Township had been established, deriving its name from the surrounding rugged terrain, rocky soil, large boulders, and wooded hills. Rockhill Township, at the time of its founding, was the largest township in Bucks County. Some of the first people to reside in this area were the Lenni Lenape Indians. Proof of their residence lies not only in the artifacts that they left behind; some of the earliest churches established in the area, Tohickon Evangelical Lutheran Church, founded in 1743, and the Jerusalem Church, founded in 1826, both have fieldstone rocks marking the gravesites of Native Americans.

The population was 90 percent German by 1798. The majority of these settlers cultivated crops and raised livestock. By 1870, the population was increasing as a result of the Pennsylvania & Reading Railroad, which traveled through communities known today as Sellersville, Perkasie, and Quakertown. Early industries included pottery, brickyards, mills, quarries, tanneries, gunsmiths, and boot and shoe shops.

After an arduous 20-year-long court battle over the lack of road maintenance and the disorganization in the township, the district of Rockhill Township was reorganized. In 1890, it was separated into East and West Rockhill. Both townships saw growth slow as a result of the railroad, which brought business and commerce to Sellersville and Perkasie. In addition, the construction of both Routes 313 and 309 directed traffic away from the little villages that were beginning to thrive in East and West Rockhill. To this day, time seems to have stood still in both townships. They are scenic and beautiful to travel through, and many structures from the past are still standing. There are numerous schoolhouses, covered bridges, mills, and hundreds of homes dating back to the 18th and 19th centuries. One of the most cherished areas is the village of Ridge Valley. It is home to two churches that sit directly across from one another (known as the twin churches), several homes, and a schoolhouse, all from the 1800s, making the valley a historic treasure. In addition, East and West Rockhill Townships have establishments that have been in continuous use for over a century, including Fasageo's (formerly the Almont Hotel), Arielas (formerly the Argus), the White Horse Tavern, and the Naceville Hotel. In the 1800s, these were well-known establishments for people traveling from Philadelphia to Allentown and Bethlehem.

Rockhill was an intricate part of the history of this county. In 1777, the Liberty Bell was carried from Philadelphia to Allentown up Old Bethlehem Pike through Rockhill Township. A portion of that trail was converted to the Liberty Bell Trolley Line, in operation from 1900 to 1951. The North Pennsylvania Railroad came through Rockhill and stopped at the Derstine Station. The station was named after a prominent family that settled in Rockhill in the 1730s and still owns land here. The Derstine station was closed in the early decades of the 20th century.

One of our most prominent and famous citizens was none other than John Fries. He was the instigator in one of only two rebellions to take place in the newly formed country. In 1798, a rebellion against the house tax took place. The Revolutionary War against taxation without representation was still fresh in the minds of the German residents of the area, and they took up arms. John Fries and several other residents tried to thwart the government's attempt to survey houses for tax purposes. Earlier, Fries had been part of the first rebellion, which took place in 1794. Known as the Whiskey Rebellion, residents revolted against the whiskey tax and attacked excise agents. John Fries's residence is believed to be located in West Rockhill Township.

Rockhill was also well known for its church camps and vacation camps. Many people came to this area on weekends trying to get away from city life in Philadelphia. It was not only a vacation spot for the residents of Philadelphia, but also for the local farmers to get a much needed break from all their work. There are many well-documented camps. One of the more famous is Highland Park, which is still operational. Today, the two townships have a growing population of approximately 9,500. Many of the old farms are beginning to disappear as the population increases and technology moves forward.

While this book does not represent a complete history of the area, our hope is to preserve the past in these pages so that future generations will know the trials and tribulations of those who came before them. We continue to strive in our endeavor to collect and preserve the histories of these two enchanting places.

One

Heart of the Community

Many communities in the 18th and 19th centuries did not have church buildings in which to hold religious services. Instead, they would meet in private homes, and if weather permitted, services would be held outside. Often, people would remain after services to socialize and have dinner. The host had to accommodate people during church services and also provide food and drink.

Most community churches were small and plainly decorated and had a cemetery nearby. Families traveled to services by foot, by cart, or by horse and buggy, the men dressed in suits and white shirts and the women in skirts and long-sleeved blouses with shawls and hats. Men were considered the elders and made all the decisions concerning the church. Women were expected to organize social events and provide food. Most churches had their origins in two and three denominations, and as time passed, many branched off and started their own churches. Churches served both religious and educational needs. They were also the original genealogists, keeping all the birth, death, and marriage records.

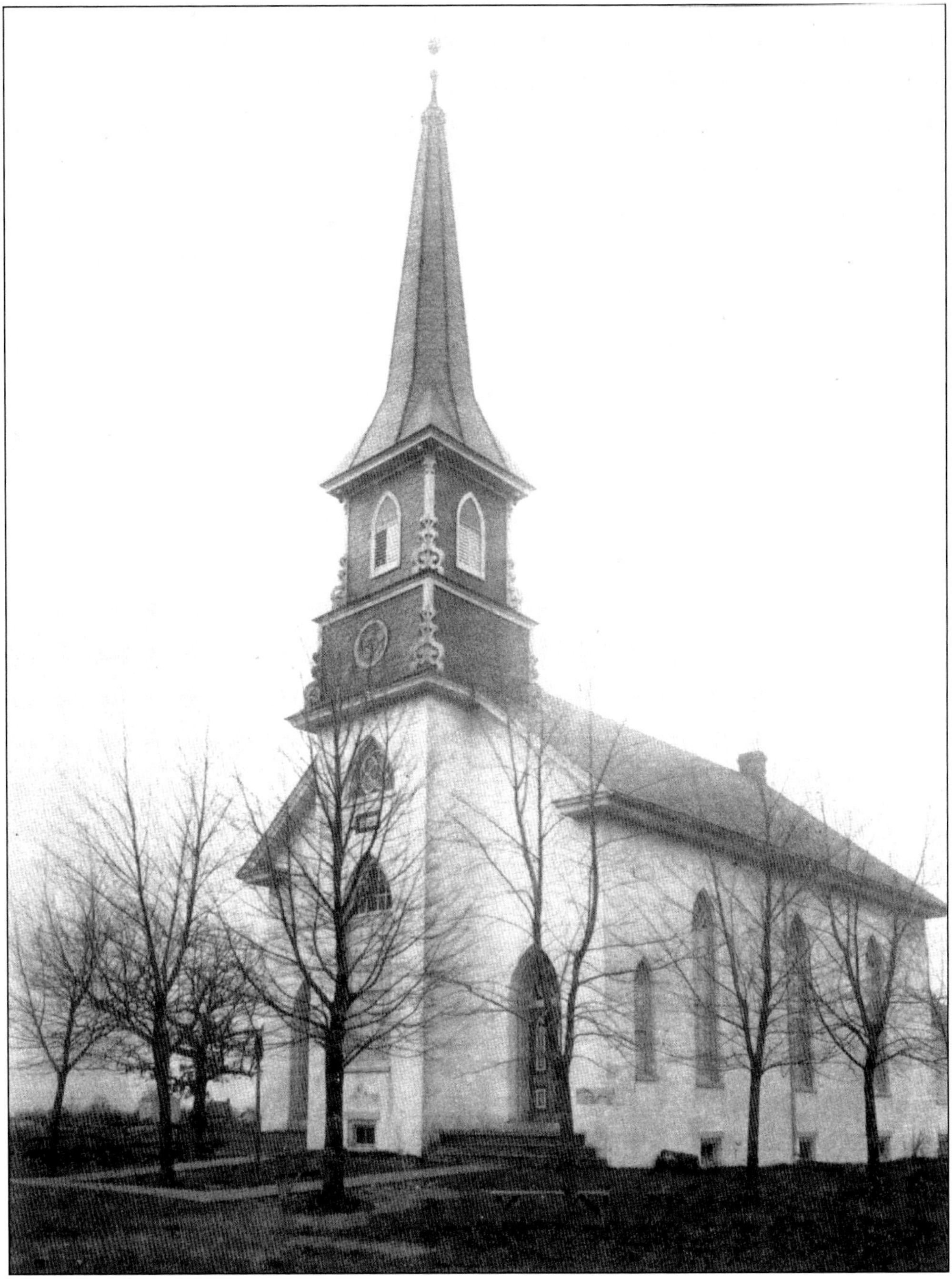

This photograph, taken in the late 1800s, is one of the earliest known pictures of the Lutheran and Reformed Church of Almont, later known as Jerusalem Lutheran Church. Records indicate that Enos Schlichter Sr. donated the land for the church, and as a result, the church was known as Schlichtersville Church for many years. George Getman donated the land for the cemetery. Though the building dates to 1826, tombstones dating back to 1764 and church records indicate that there were religious services held here prior to the construction of the church itself. (Courtesy of Jerusalem Church.)

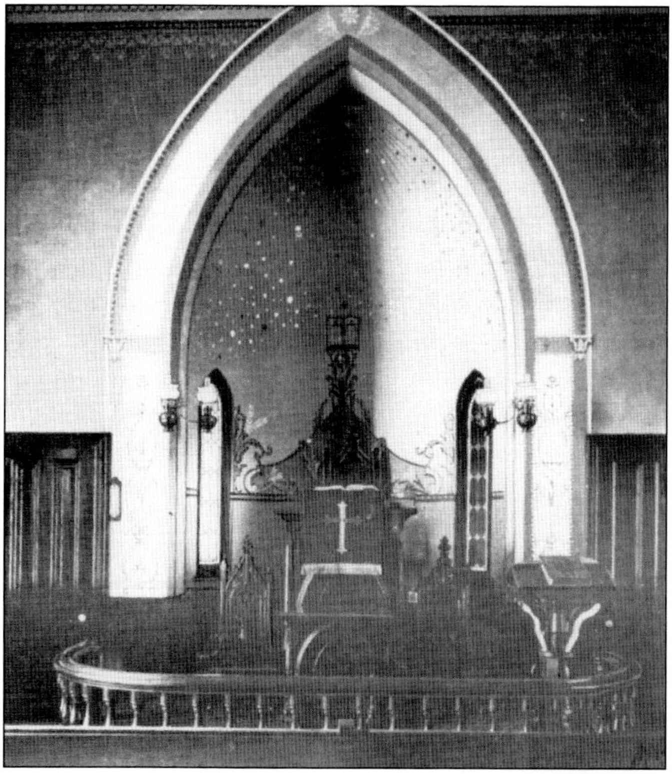

The original interior of the Jerusalem Lutheran and Reformed Church, located on Ridge Road in Almont, is pictured in this c. 1900 photograph. Prior to the building of the structure, Henry Melchior Muhlenburg held church services outside under the old oak tree. During inclement weather, services would be held at a congregant's home. (Courtesy of Jerusalem Church.)

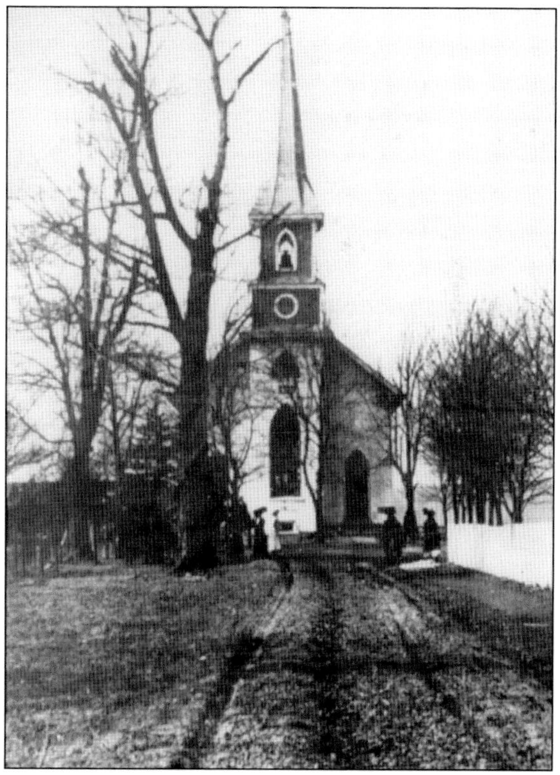

Residents gather for services at the Jerusalem Lutheran and Reformed Church in this photograph, taken prior to 1900. The church originally served three denominations—Lutheran, Reformed, and Mennonite. As the Reformed and Mennonite congregations dwindled in the late 1800s, this became Jerusalem Lutheran Church. (Courtesy of Jerusalem Church.)

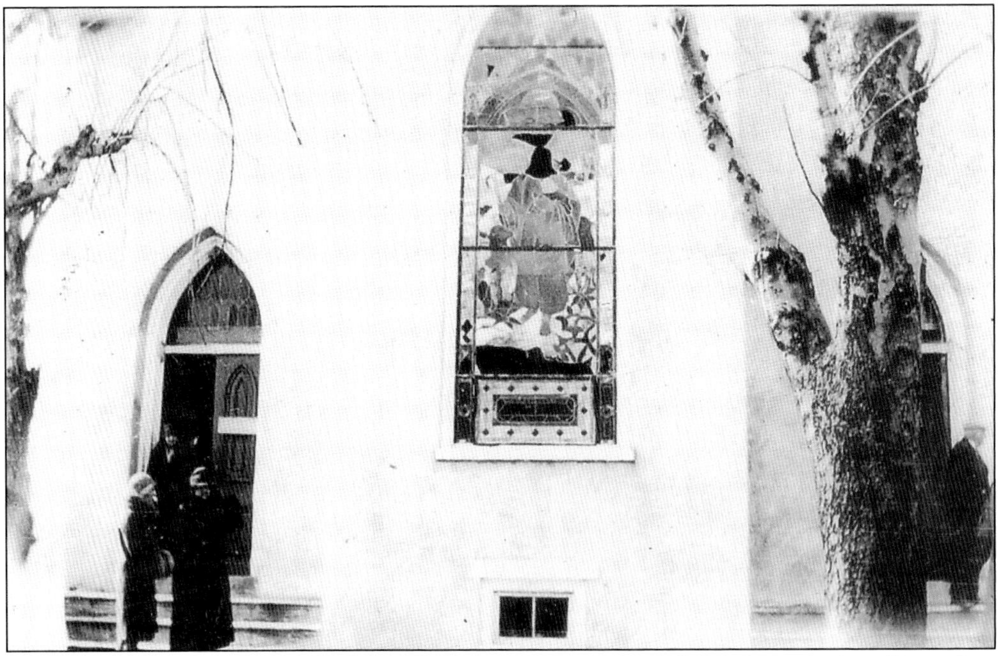

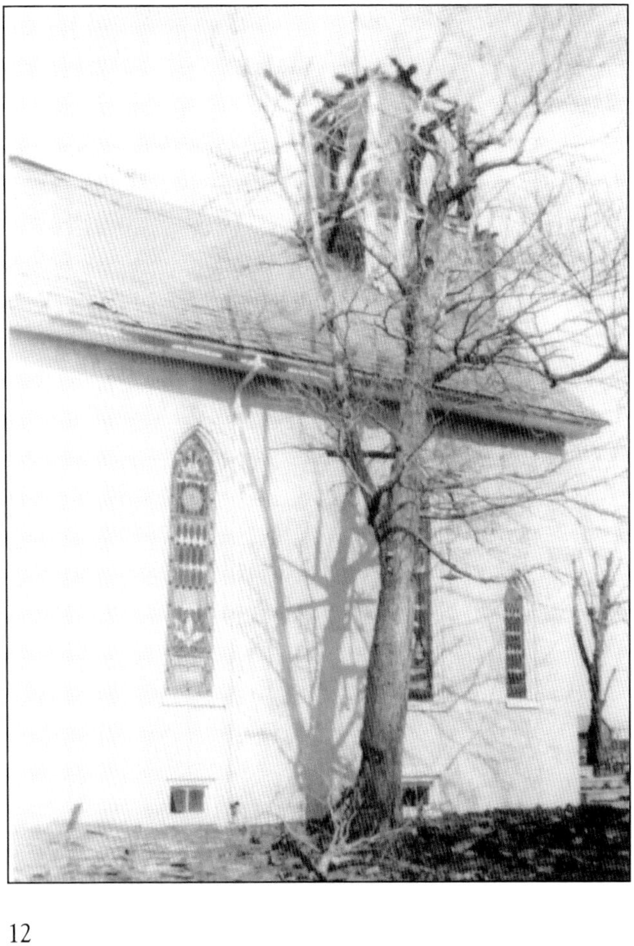

These photographs of Jerusalem Lutheran Church were taken in 1928. The major damage caused by a lightning strike that broke windows and destroyed the landmark steeple is pictured. The church underwent a nine-month reconstruction that included a new steeple, an updated pulpit, cement walkways, new Sunday school rooms on each side of the church, and lightning rods on the top of the steeple to prevent another strike. (Courtesy of Jerusalem Church.)

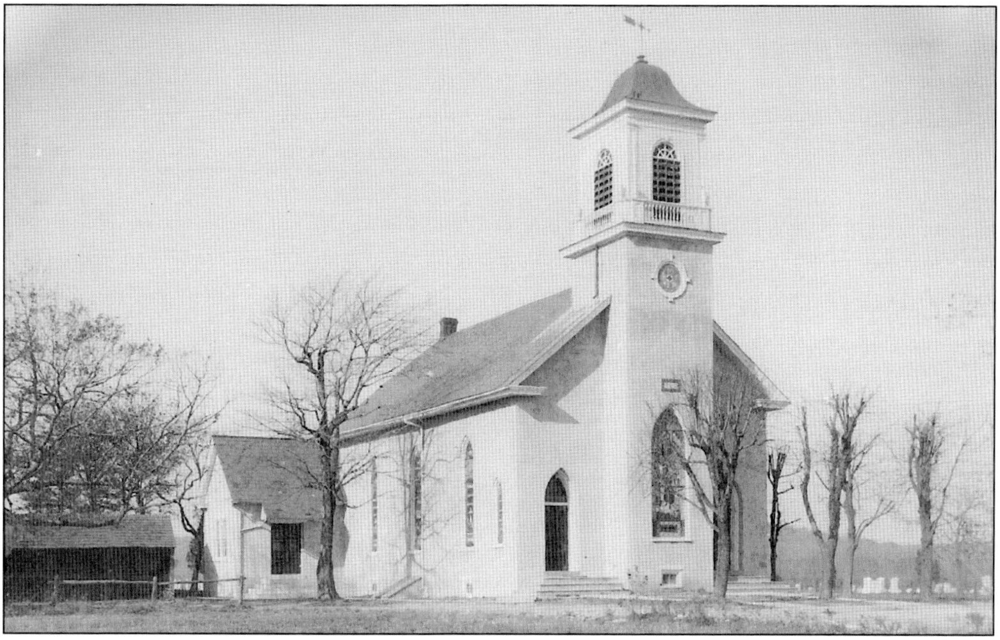

This photograph of Jerusalem Lutheran church was taken around 1940, after its reconstruction. The building remains much the same today and will be celebrating 185 years of service to the community in 2011. (Courtesy of Timothy H. Hufnagel.)

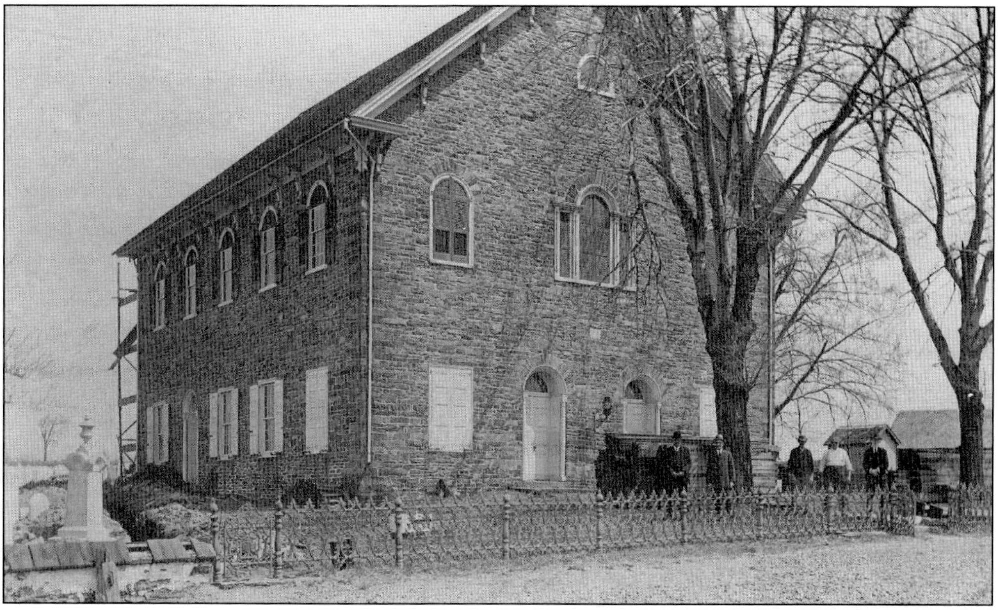

Peace Tochickon Reform Church and Peace Tochickon Lutheran Church were established in 1743 in Weisel. The two congregations shared a building that was known as the Tochickon Union Church. The stone church in the photograph was built in 1838 and is pictured being renovated (1917–1918). Over the years, the congregations grew, and after 215 years the bonds of unity were split. The Reformed Church kept the original structure, and the Lutherans built their own. Today, it is known as St. Peter's Tochickon United Church of Christ. It overlooks Lake Nockamixon. (Courtesy of Tochickon Union Church.)

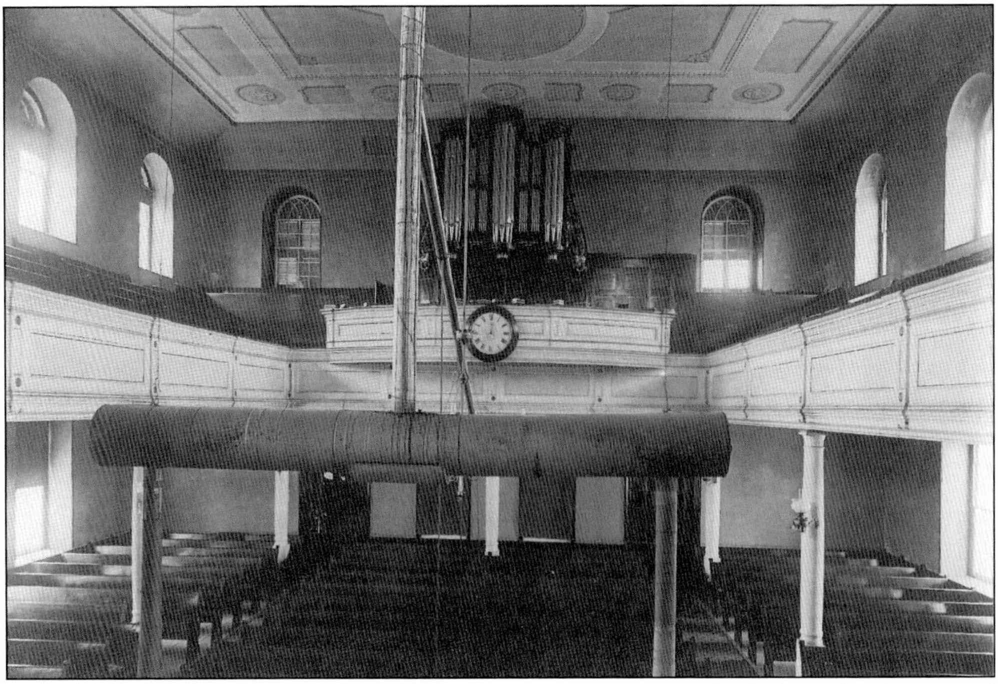

Tochickon Union Church is pictured around 1838. This pulpit view looks from the altar toward the Krauss organ. Music was the heart of the religious services. Note the elaborate frescoed ceiling. (Courtesy of Tohickon Union Church.)

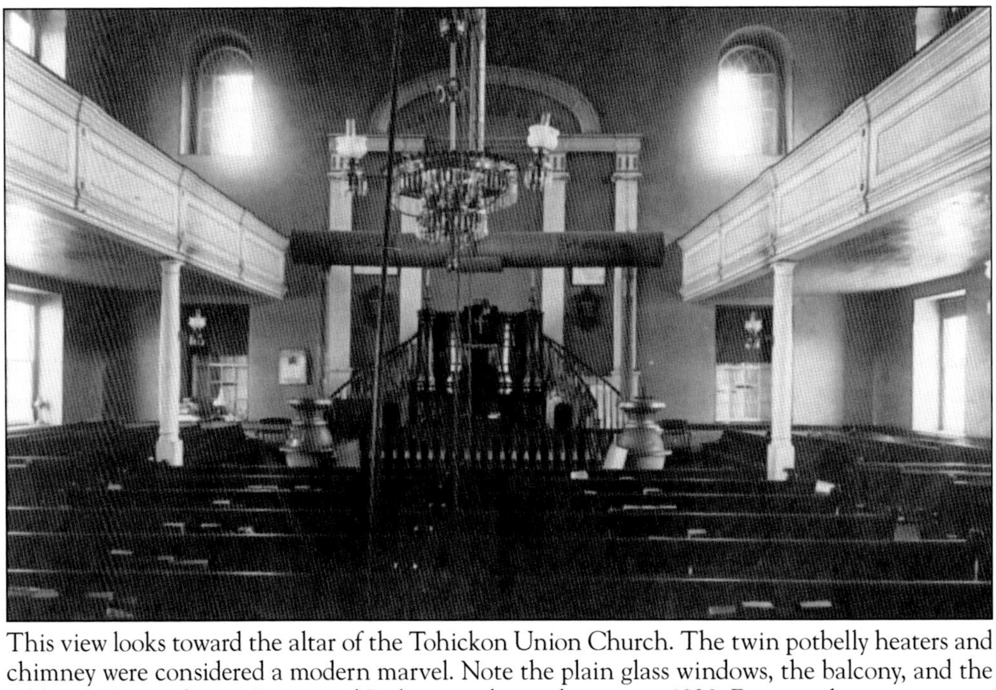

This view looks toward the altar of the Tohickon Union Church. The twin potbelly heaters and chimney were considered a modern marvel. Note the plain glass windows, the balcony, and the oil lamps. Pennsylvania Power and Light moved into the area in 1930. During a later renovation many changes were made and beautiful stained glass widows were added, which can be seen today. (Courtesy of Tohickon Church.)

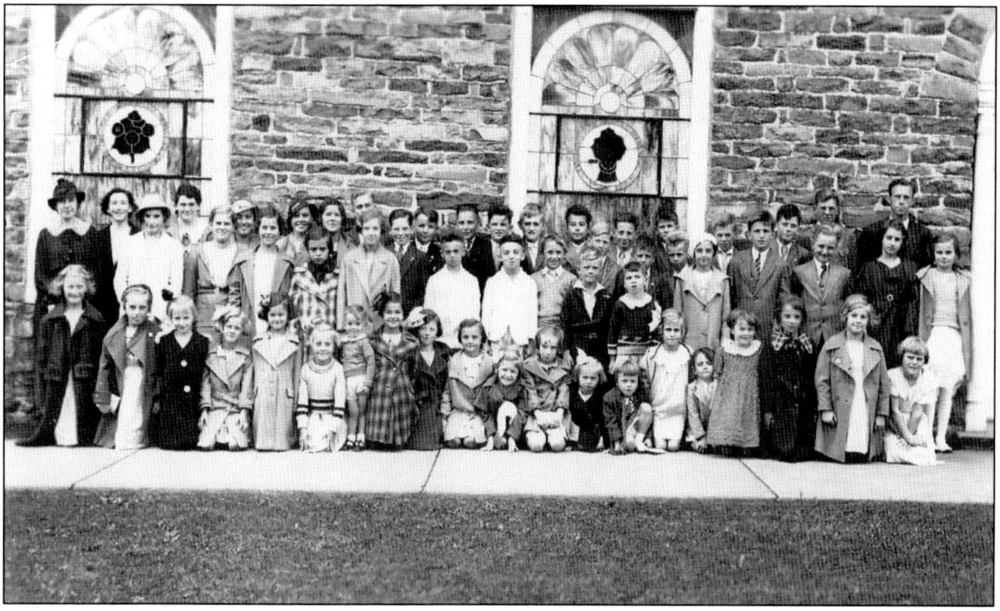

Tohickon youth gather outside the church for this photograph. Adults and children met separately on Sunday mornings. (Courtesy of Tohickon Union Church.)

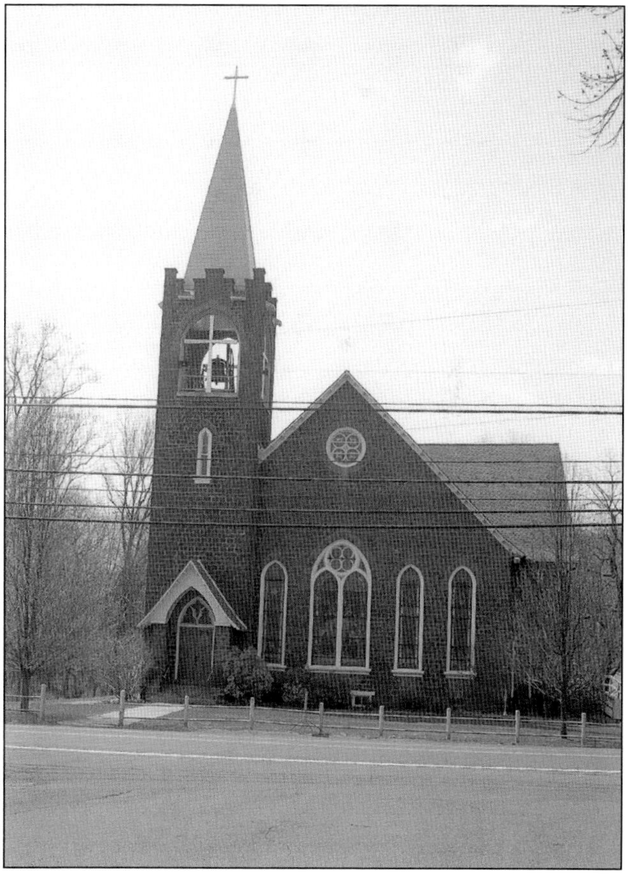

St. John's Lutheran Church is located in Ridge Valley on Allentown Road. In 1889, the Lutheran congregation voted to build their own church across the street from the St. James United Church of Christ Church. M.H. Bean of Lansdale, a prominent architect, was commissioned to design the church at a cost of $25. The church was to be fashioned of native gray stone at a cost not to exceed $8,000. The cornerstone was laid on June 10, 1899, and a year later the new church was consecrated. The congregation has existed since 1792. This church is also known as one of the twin churches, because the Reformed Church is directly across the street. (Courtesy of St. John's Lutheran Church.)

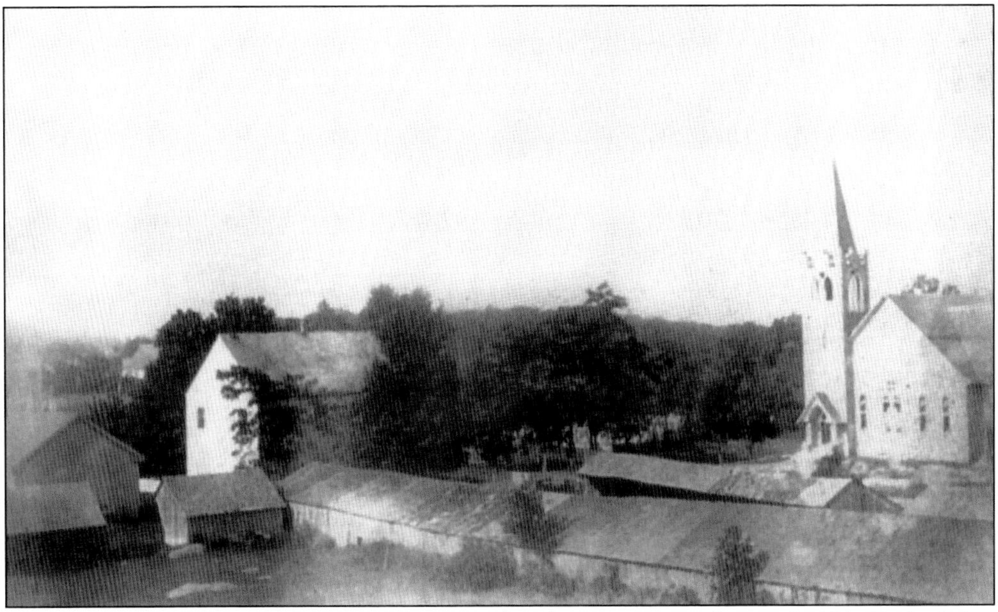

The Ridge Valley churches, known as the twin churches, are pictured around 1900. To the left is the Reformed church prior to the addition of its steeple. St. John's Lutheran Church is on the right. In the foreground are sheds for churchgoers' horses and buggies. (Courtesy of Rhoda Clark.)

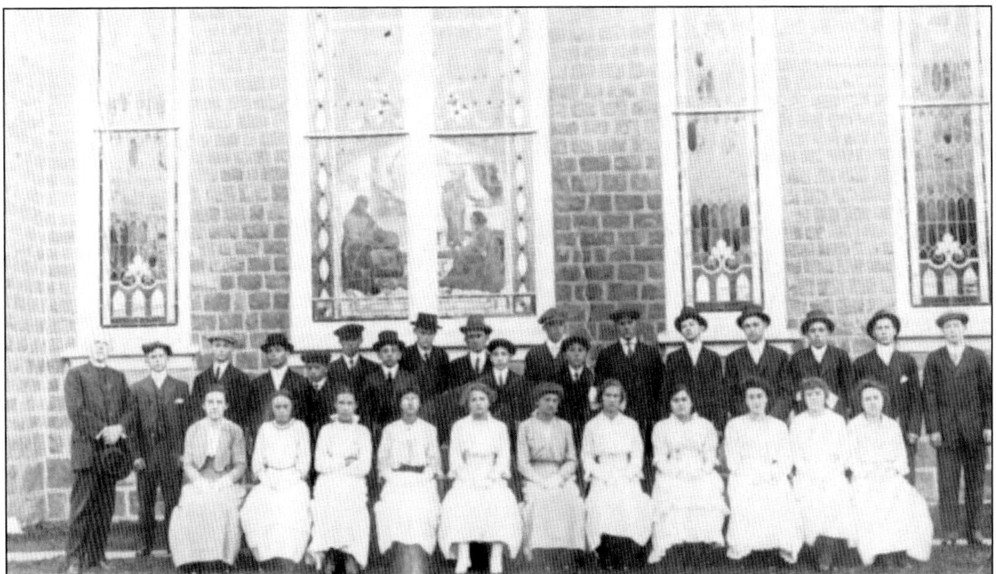

The Ridge Valley Lutheran Church confirmation class of 1915 is pictured. Included in this image are, from left to right, (first row) Anna H. Hartzel, Lydia L. Lee Croissette, Ellanone Sharp, Ida S. Roberts, Ada R. Barndt, Pear, G. Heimbach, Elsie N. Leister, Bertha B. Sheetz, Ernest Aug. Guenst, Milton N. Thomas, Marie A. Haas, Verna R. Cassel, Maggie K. Boyer, Alberta K. Boyer, Horace P. Bergey, Herman Fago, and Marcus H. White; (second row) Horace H., Thomas, John Fago, William G. Sterner, Charles H. Roberts, Jacob N. Kline, Howard R. Van Laudt, Victor E. Schukraft, William F. Schukraft, Edward Hagard, William S. Seachrist, Eugene S. Seachrist, and Walter K. Deetz. (Courtesy of Charles Guenst.)

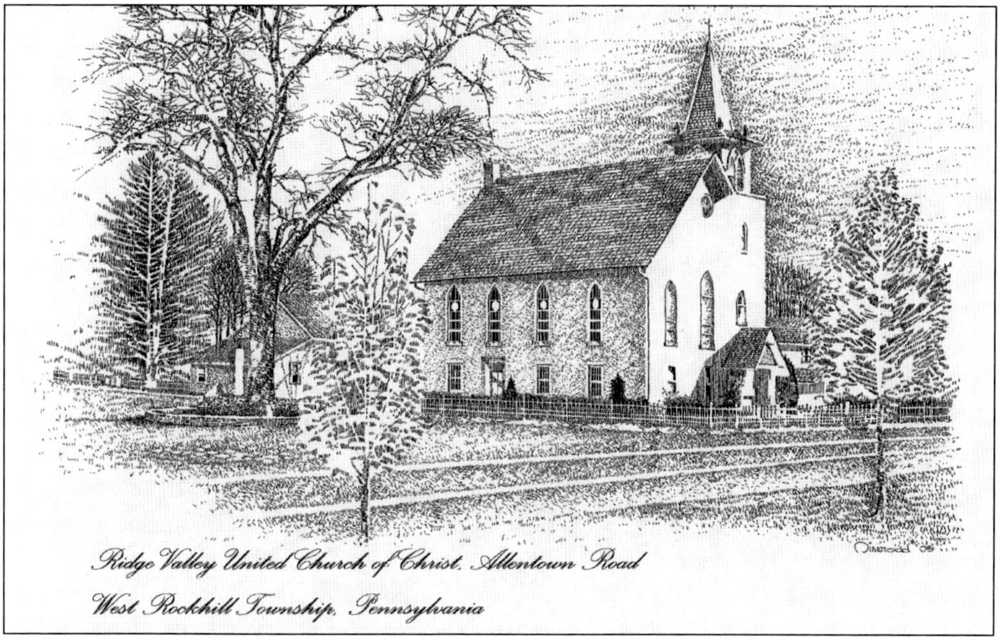

On December 12, 1792, a tract was conveyed to the Lutheran and Reformed Calvinist societies. The area became known as Ridge Valley, a tiny village located at the intersection of Allentown Road and Ridge Valley Road. A log schoolhouse served as the place of worship. By the 19th century, the following three congregations used the building: Lutheran, Reform, and Mennonite. In need of more room, a larger church was erected. Its cornerstone was laid on Ascension Day, May 25, 1854. Over the years, the Mennonites and Lutherans built their own churches. Today, this is the location of St. James United Church of Christ. (Courtesy of Fred Diseroad.)

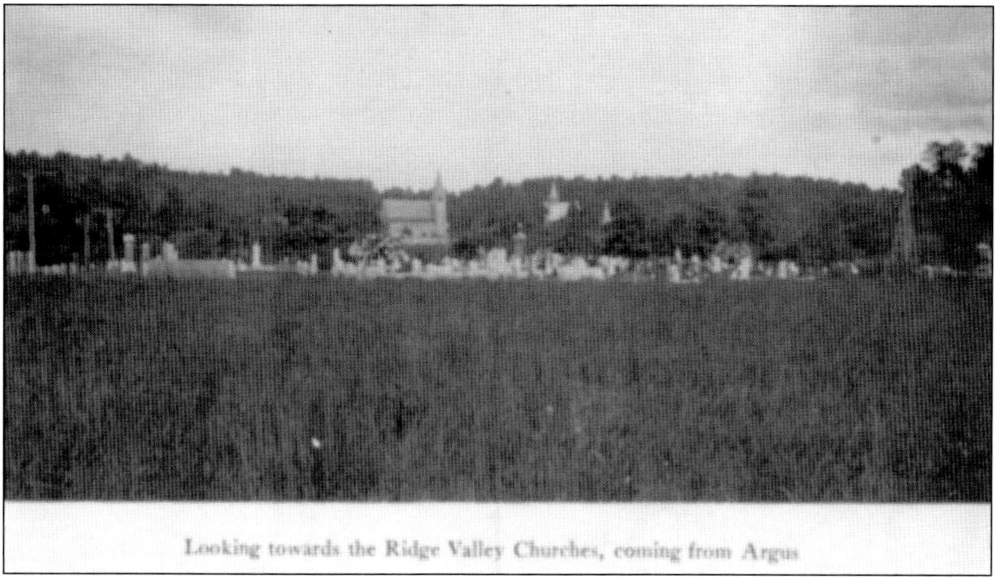

This photograph was taken by Daniel F. Zeigler, a photographer from Souderton who was hired by Charles Berkemeyer, a commercial printer from Sellersville. Berkemeyer printed 300 postcards of different scenes from East and West Rockhill and the surrounding area. This is one of the images of Ridge Valley in West Rockhill. (Courtesy of Charles Guenst.)

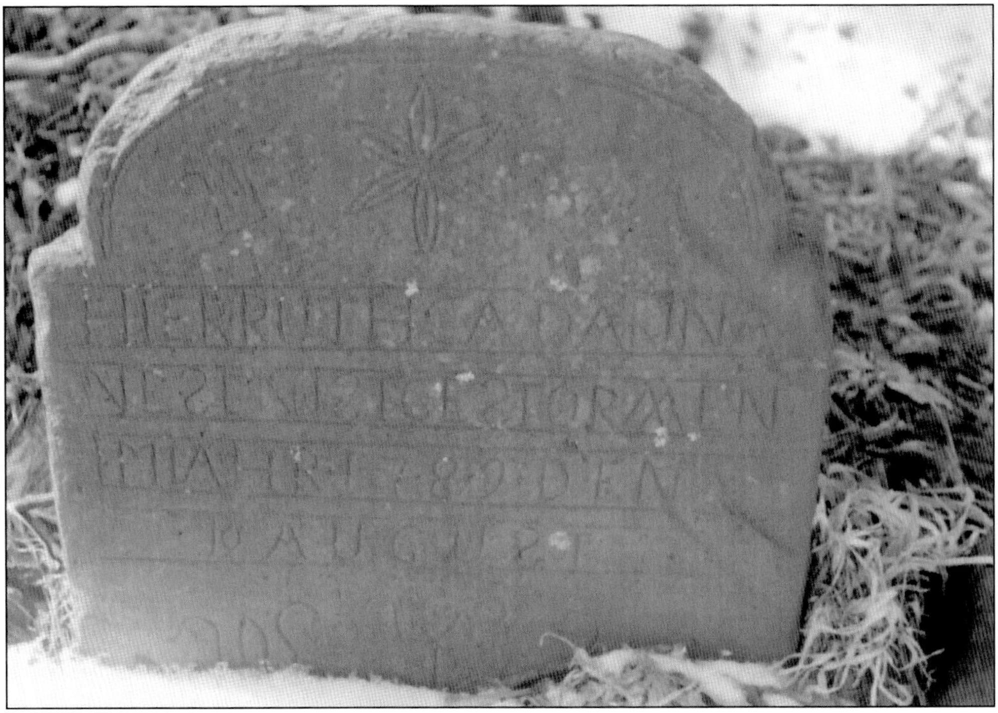

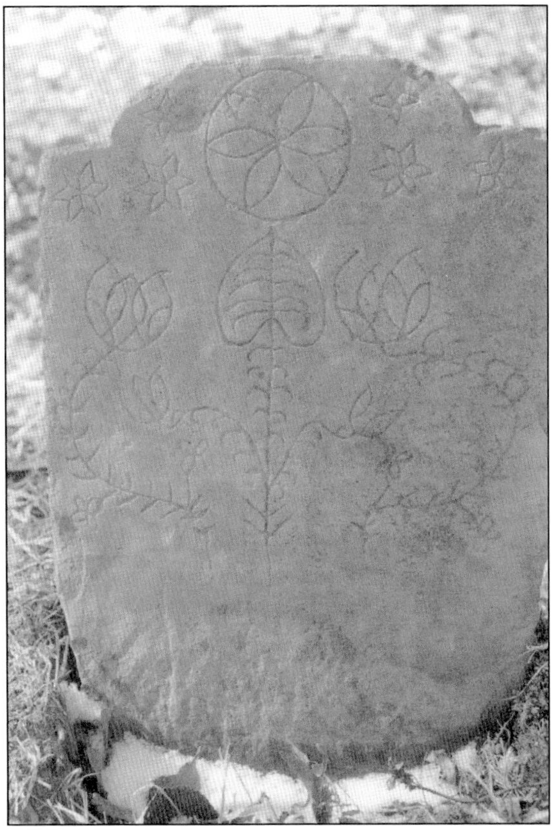

These two photographs were taken recently at Jerusalem Evangelic Church in Almont. Pictured are two tombstones made of fieldstone. The image above, dating to 1789, is not the oldest in the cemetery, as there are headstones dating to 1764. The second stone has no date, only intricate designs. There are several headstones that are of Native American origin. (Both, author's collection.)

Two

EDUCATION

During the early history of the townships, residents were not concerned with getting an education. Their primary concern was survival—building shelters and eking out a living. Penn's original 1682 charter declared that children should know how to read by the age of 12. The Colonial churches felt that education was important and that all members of the congregation should be able to read the Bible. As soon as Rockhill township was established in 1740, churches began creating schools. Students usually only attended for two years, learning the basics of "reading, writing, and 'rithmetic."

The Tochickon Reformed Church built the first school in 1740. It was a log schoolhouse on the Rockhill side of the Tochickon Creek. The Tochickon Lutherans built their school in 1754. Hexenkoft School was built in 1767 on Hexenkoft Road, located between Hagersville and Ridge Road. Hexenkoft was unique because it was built and maintained by local residents before the tax support system was legislated. A Pennsylvania law in 1834 required first to eighth grade tax-supported schools.

The early part of the 20th century saw the decline of the one-room schoolhouse. Experts believed they were inferior to urban schools and not economical for growing communities. The urbanization of farmland brought changes to the township. As manufacturing was introduced, the need for bigger and better schools became apparent. Consolidation brought the opportunity for broader curricula, newer facilities, and more jobs.

East and West Rockhill are fortunate to have so many one-room schoolhouses still standing. Schoolhouses in East Rockhill are as follows: Lessig, 1854; Fillman, 1854; Millers, 1859; Steeley, 1875; Sterner, 1889; Three Mile Run, 1894; Church Hill (former name of the village of Weisel), changed to Sunnyside in 1898; and Rockhill, 1925. Those in West Rockhill are Almont School, 1800; Benner School, 1843; Branch Valley or Sallie Rogers School; Argus School, 1870; Ridge Valley School, 1883; Rockhill Mennonite Meeting House, mid-1700s–1777; and Rock Wild School, 1850.

In 1931, West Rockhill Elementary was constructed. This beautiful Art Deco building was unique as the only multi-room building with graded classrooms in the eight school district area. The other areas did not consolidate their one-room schools until 1950, including the nearby Pennridge area. This West Rockhill school is still educating local youth.

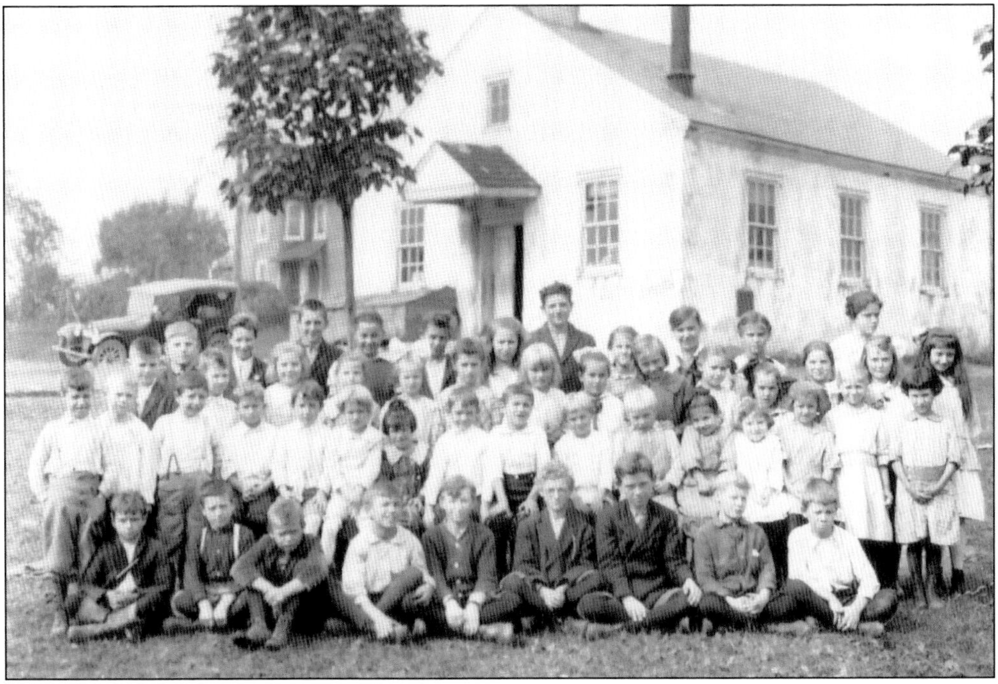

In 1782, at the intersection of Park Avenue and Ridge Road, a log school was erected. In 1854, another building was erected on this spot. It was called Lessig's School. Pictured with her students in 1920 is teacher Blanche Weisel. (Courtesy WRHS.)

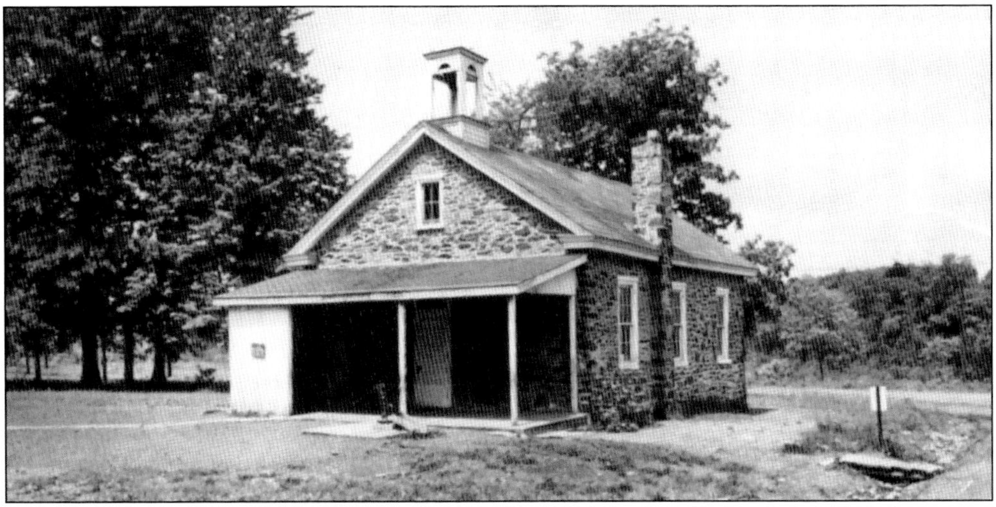

Bedminister/Keelersville School, located on Old Bethlehem Road, was operated under a joint agreement by both Rockhill and Bedminister Townships. The land was donated by Ruben Delp, and Reuben Lewis was awarded the contract to build in 1876. The total cost for the project, which included the school, outhouse, and coal cellar, was $797. Sunnyside School is across the road, and the grades were divided between the two schools. Bedminister School housed the first, second, and third grades. After the public-school consolidation in 1931, several members of the St. Peter's Tochickon UCC congregation bought the property and presented it to the church. Today, the building has been completely refurbished with desks and other items that would have been used when the school was operating prior to 1931. (Courtesy of WRHS.)

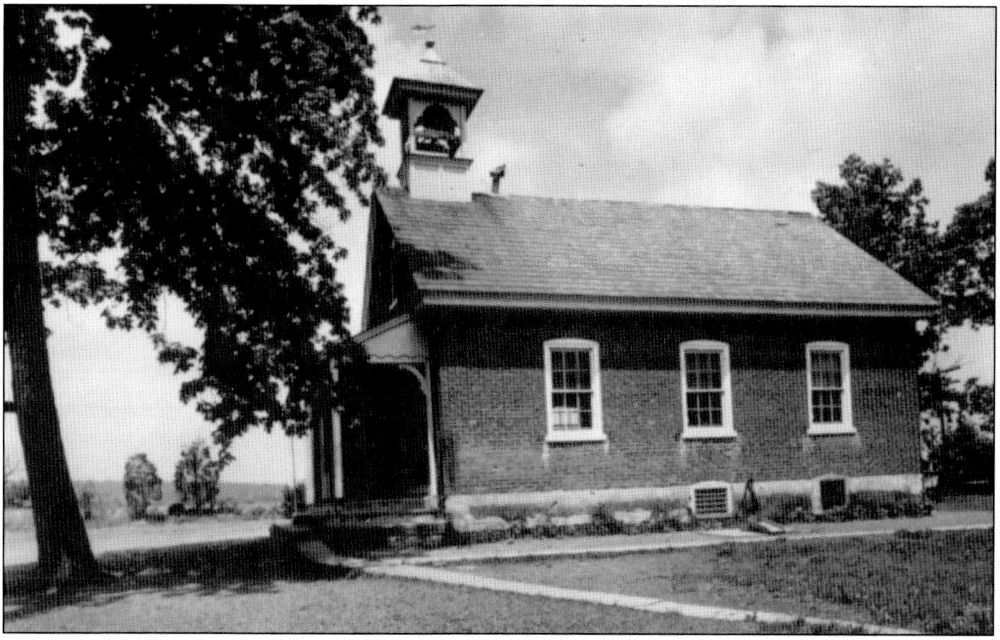

Sunnyside School, built in 1898, is across the road from the Bedminister School. St. Peter's Tochickon Church bought the property, and it is used as the church office. The Upper Bucks Lioness Club, a service organization, uses the building for their meetings. (Courtesy of WRHS.)

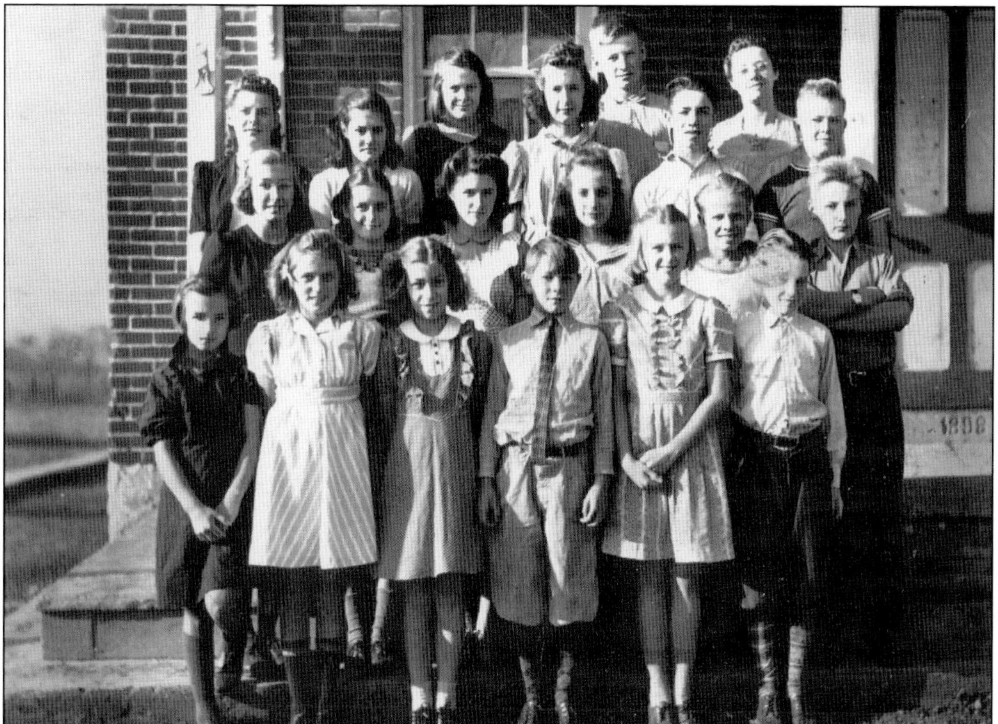

Sunnyside students are pictured around 1943. They range from fourth grade to eighth grade. Their teacher was the beloved Mrs. Butler. (Courtesy of WRHS.)

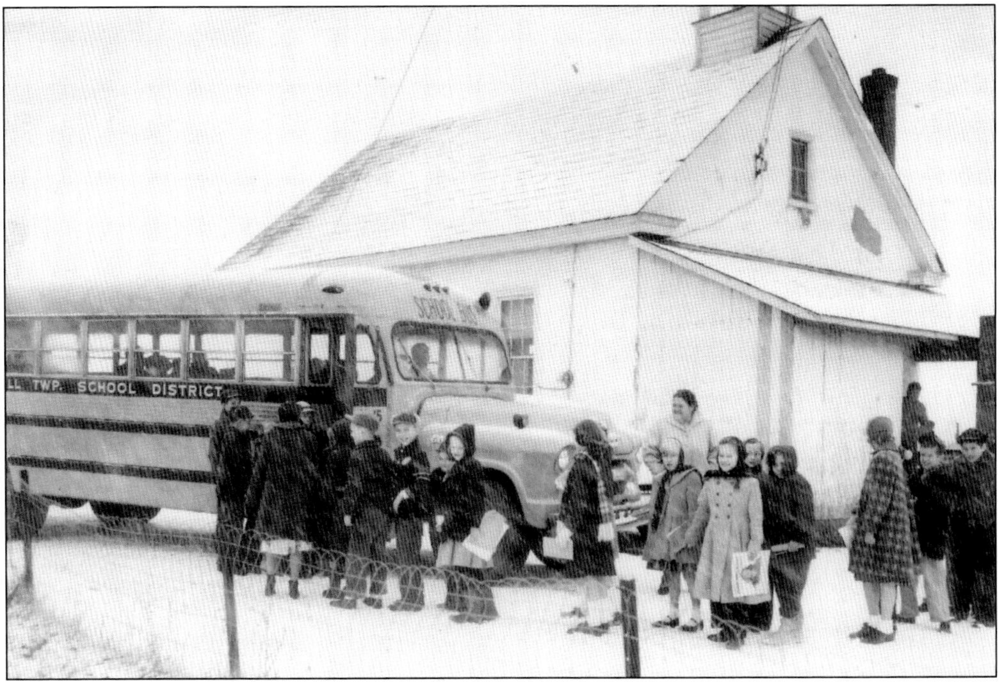

Steely School was built in 1875. It is pictured here in 1975, prior to the opening of the new East Rockhill Elementary School. Posing with the students is supervising principal Margaret M. Seylar. (Courtesy of WRHS; R.B. Deidler Elementary School Collection.)

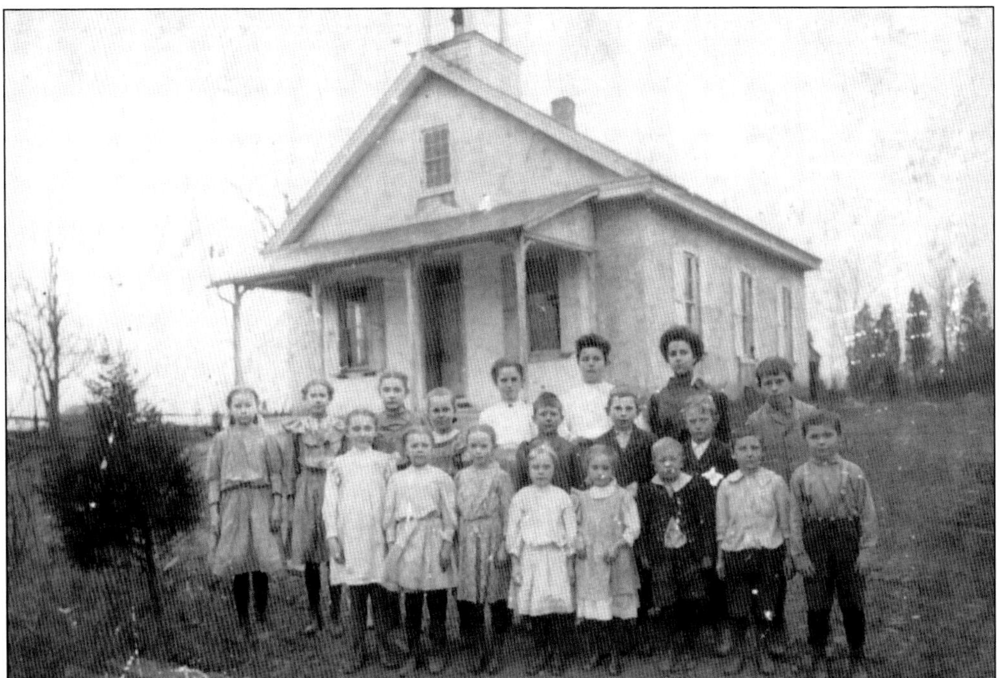

Believed to have been built in 1870 and located on Lower Rocky Dale Road, this school was known as the Barndt School. (Courtesy of WRHS.)

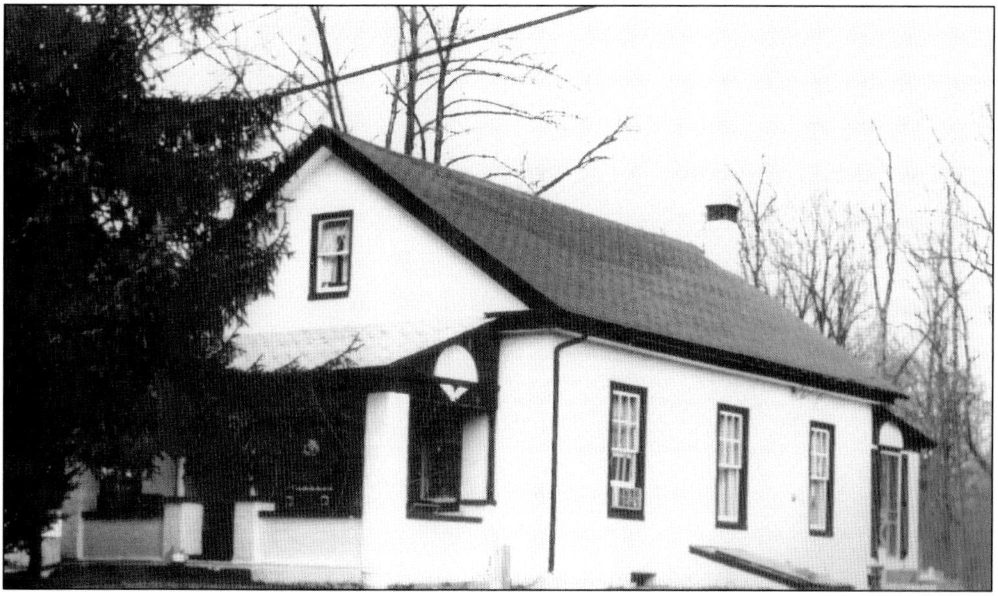

The Argus schoolhouse is pictured in this undated photograph. (Courtesy of WRHS.)

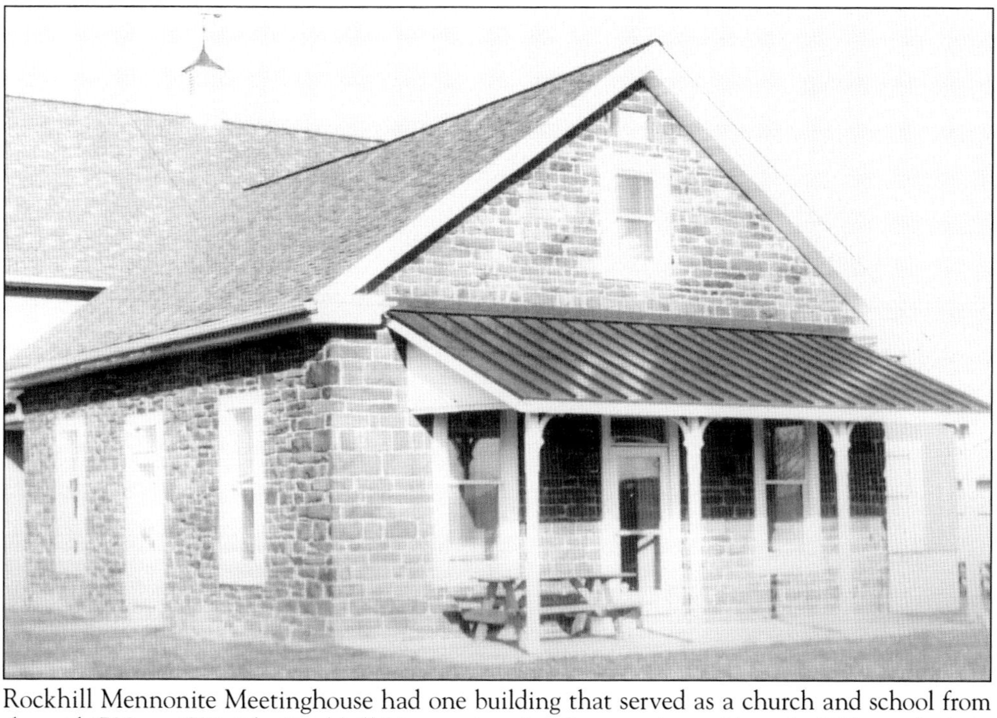

Rockhill Mennonite Meetinghouse had one building that served as a church and school from the mid-1700s to 1773. The Rockhill Mennonite schoolhouse, pictured here in 1991, was built in 1868. (Courtesy of WRHS.)

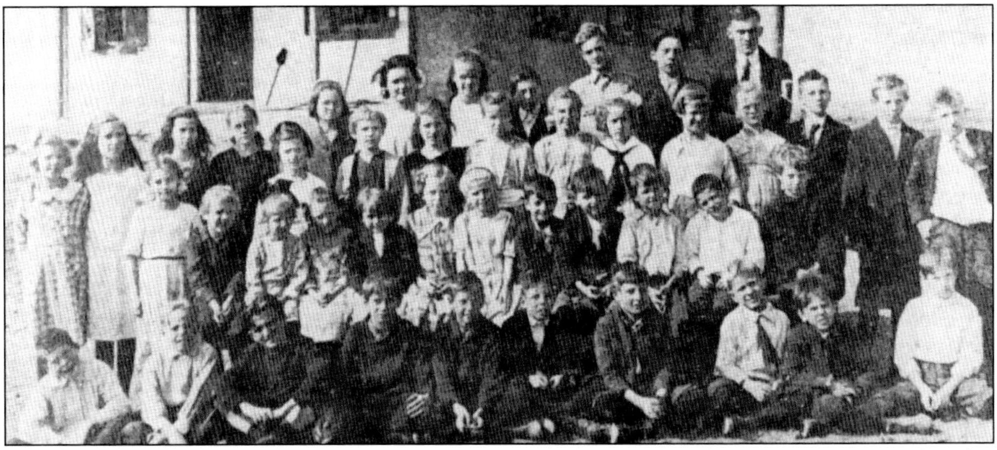

This is a photograph of the 1921 class at Benner's School, located on Gold Mine and Ridge Roads. The photographer was Ernest Bardsley. Gathered for this photograph are, from left to right, (first row) Clarence Purdy, Waldemar Klinger, William Nelson, Ernest Bardsley, Howard Bardsley, Albert Fenner, Albert Brown, George Nelson, Edward Lahacz, and Quintuo Schock; (second row) Madeline Hafler, Elinor Nelson, unidentified, Ruth Manning, Elsie Klinger, Stella Nyce, Agnes Distel, Bill Schoellkopf, Paul Schoellkopf, William Klementisz, Johnny Purdy, and Edward Nyce; (third row) Helen Schoellkopf, Helen Lahacz, Emily Esinski, Lydia Klinger, Gertrude Distel, Margaret Herzer, Grace Nelson, Florence Seider, John Herzer, Arthur Nyce, and Edmund Osinski; (fourth row) Ethel Schoellkopi. Lillian Nelson, Elinor Klementisz, Florence Piefle, Wilma Soltes, Elizabeth Eisbrenner, Adophina Klinger, William Purdy, Karl Graver, Harlan Smith, and teacher Leroy Strunk. (Courtesy of WRHS.)

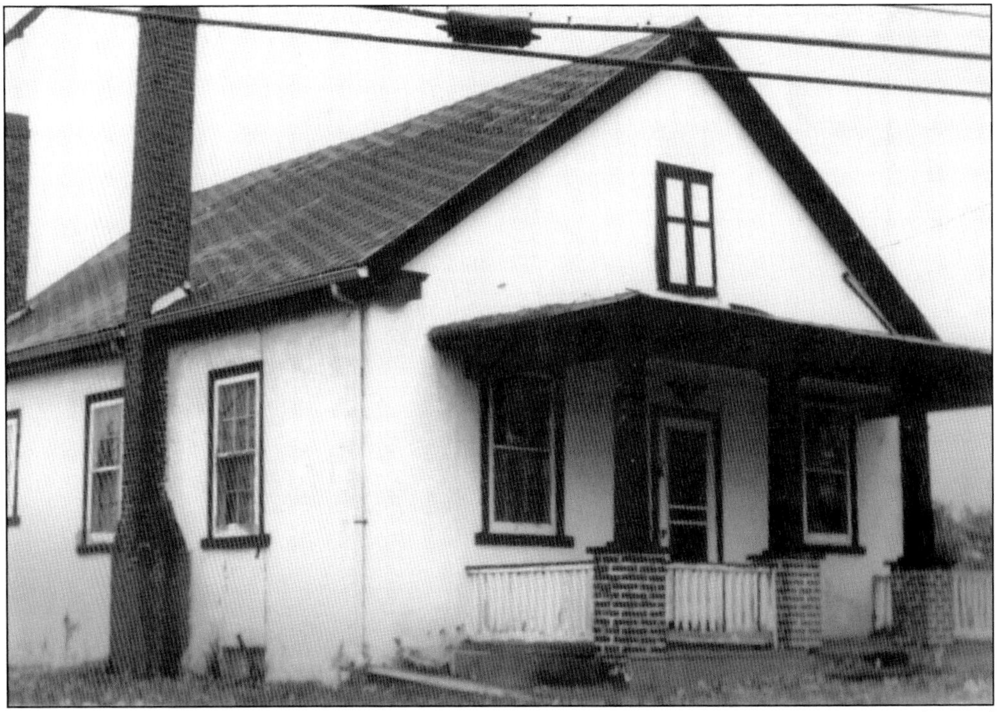

The Benner schoolhouse was built in 1846 and was used in that capacity until the 1930s. It is located on Ridge Road and is currently a private residence owned by the author. (Courtesy of WRHS.)

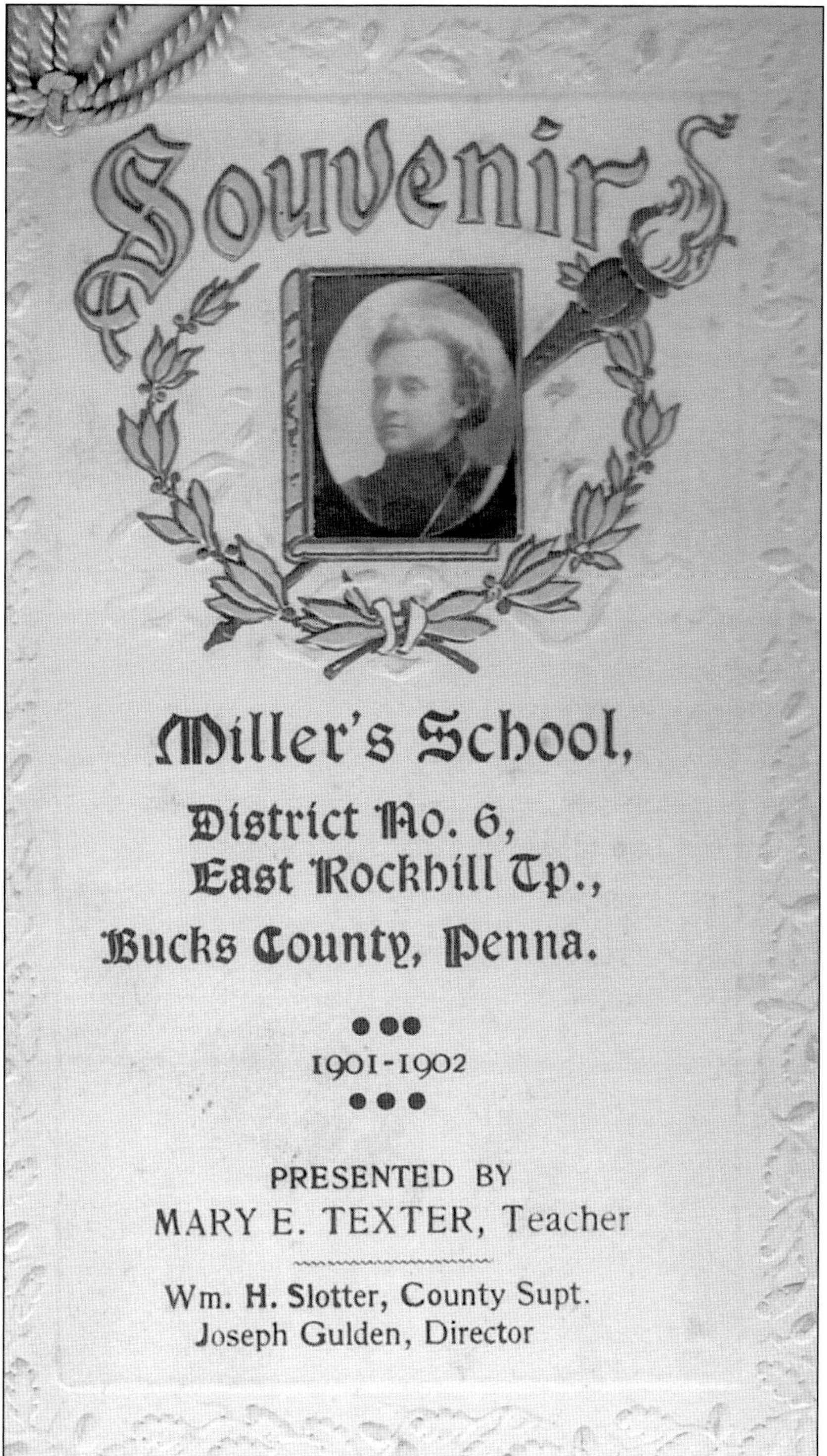

This 1901–1902 class commemoration program is from Miller's School, located in East Rockhill Township. The Miller schoolhouse was built in 1859. (Courtesy of Timothy H. Hufnagel.)

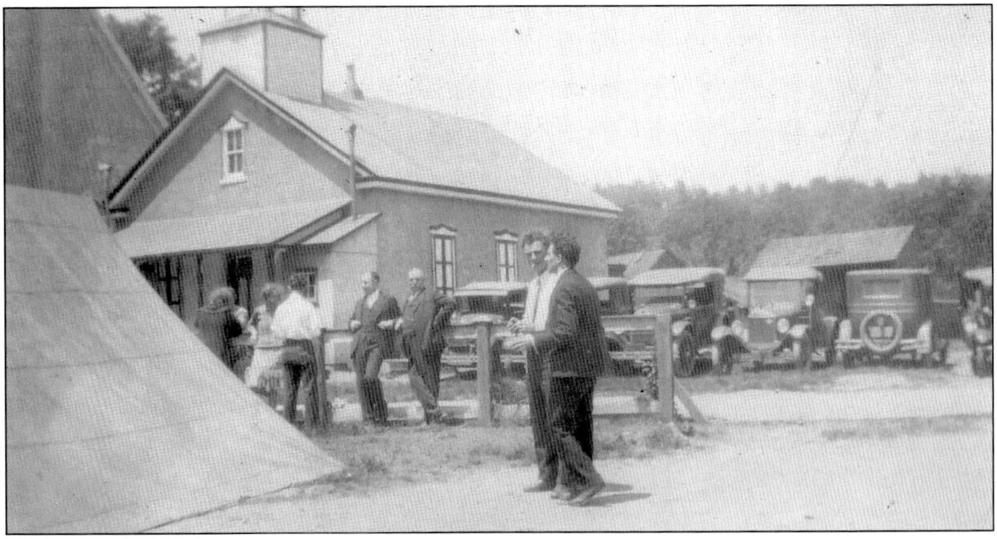

Ridge Valley School is pictured around 1900. The school was located on Allentown Road, behind the twin churches. This photograph shows the Guenst family and a guest gathered to celebrate Charles and Wilhimena Guenst's 50th wedding anniversary. (Courtesy of Charles Guenst.)

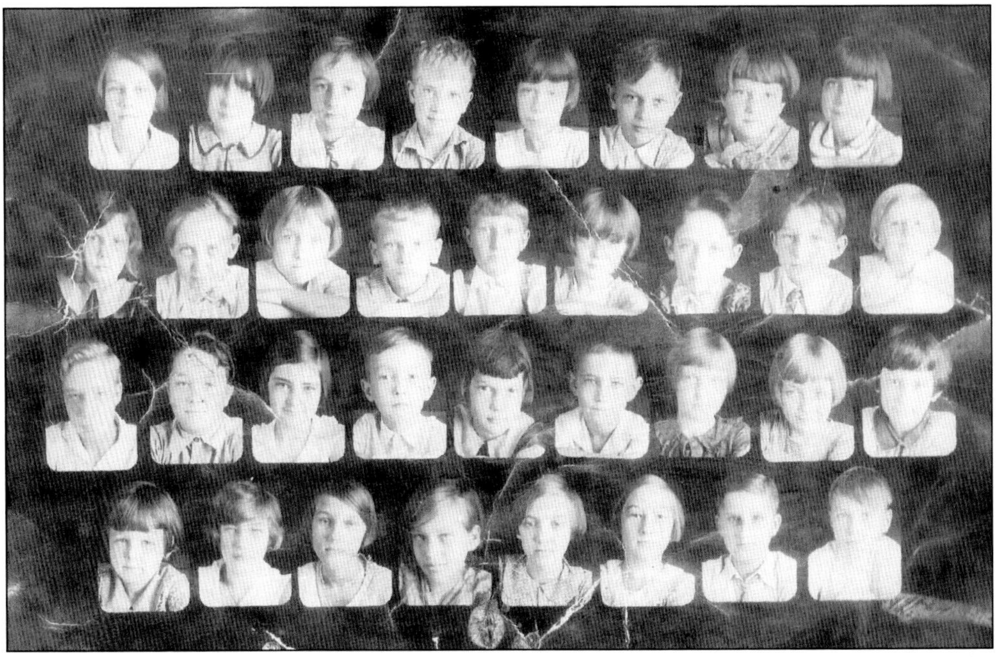

The Ridge Valley first- through eighth-grade classes of 1930 pose for their photographs. The students are, from left to right, (first row) Dorothy Long, Emma Rohl, Angeline Zacirka, Pauline Tamiski, Edna Leister, Irene Godshall, Alfred Hetrick, and Joseph Zacirka; (second row) Ralph Godshall, Howard Thomas, Priscilla Birmingham, Robert Underkoffler, Eleanor Smith, Irwin Heffendrager, Cora Leister, Helen Liester, and Dorothy Deitz; (third row) Josephine Smith, Frank Leister, Pauline Underkoffler, Albert Hangey, John Guenst, Luella Heffengrager, Harold Seachrist, Milton Long, and Mildred Hetrick; (fourth row) Jennie Zacirka, Pearl Heffengrager, Buelah Long, Francis Sonnie, Delma Godshall, John Zacirka, Stella Les, and Dorothy Seachrist. (Courtesy of Charles Guenst.)

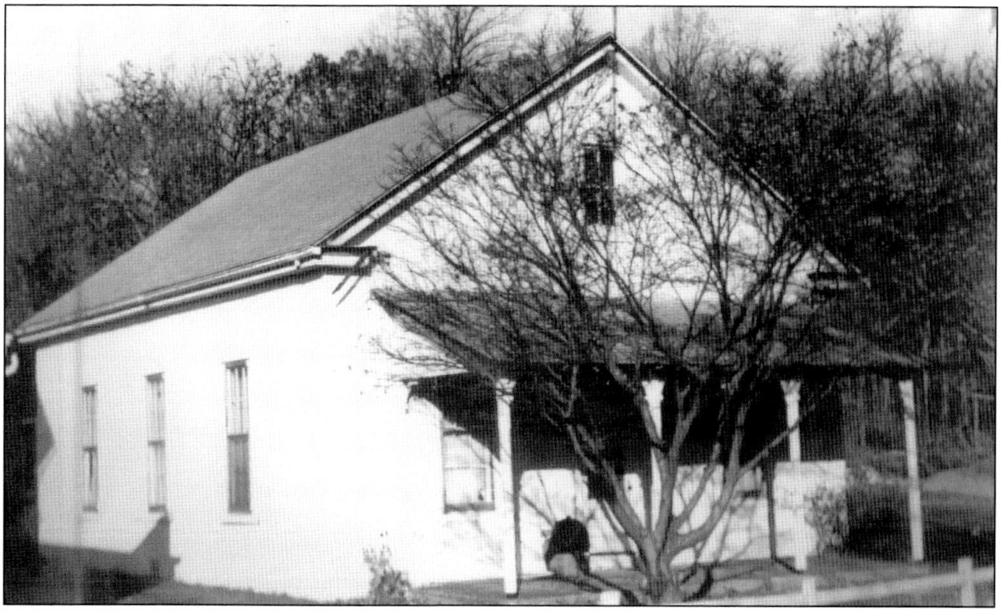

Ridge Valley School was built in 1883 and utilized as a school until 1931. The schoolhouse is located behind one of the twin churches in the historical village of Ridge Valley in West Rockhill. (Courtesy of WRHS.)

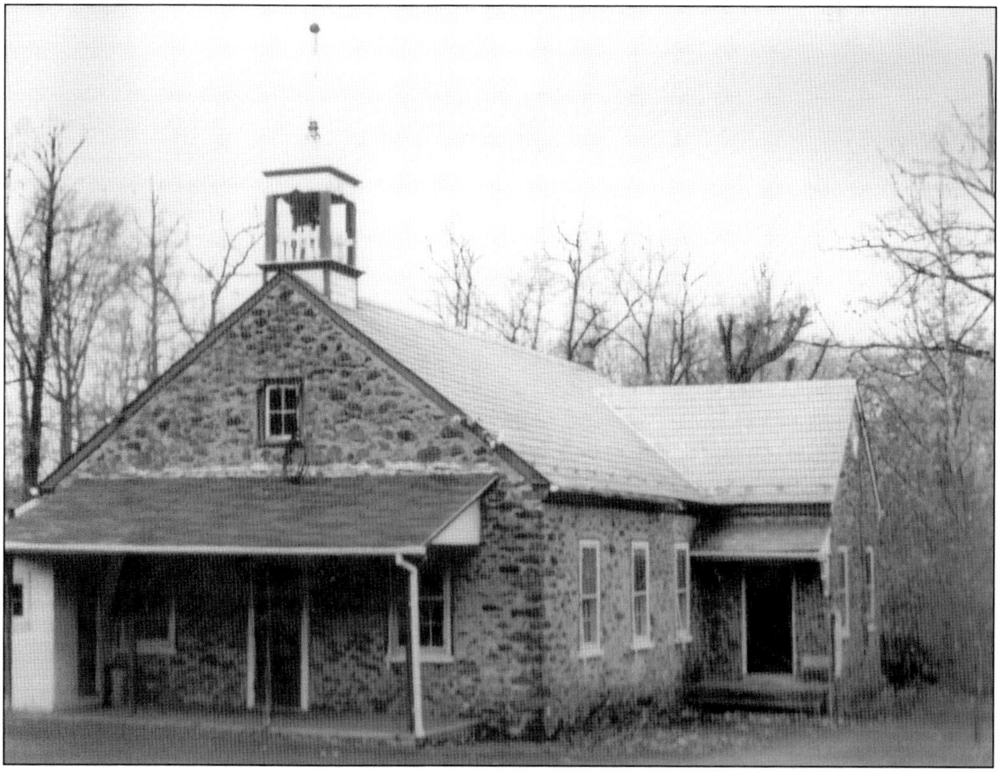

Rockwild School was located in West Rockhill township. It was built in 1830 next to the Rock Wild Store on Old Bethlehem Pike. (Courtesy of WRHS.)

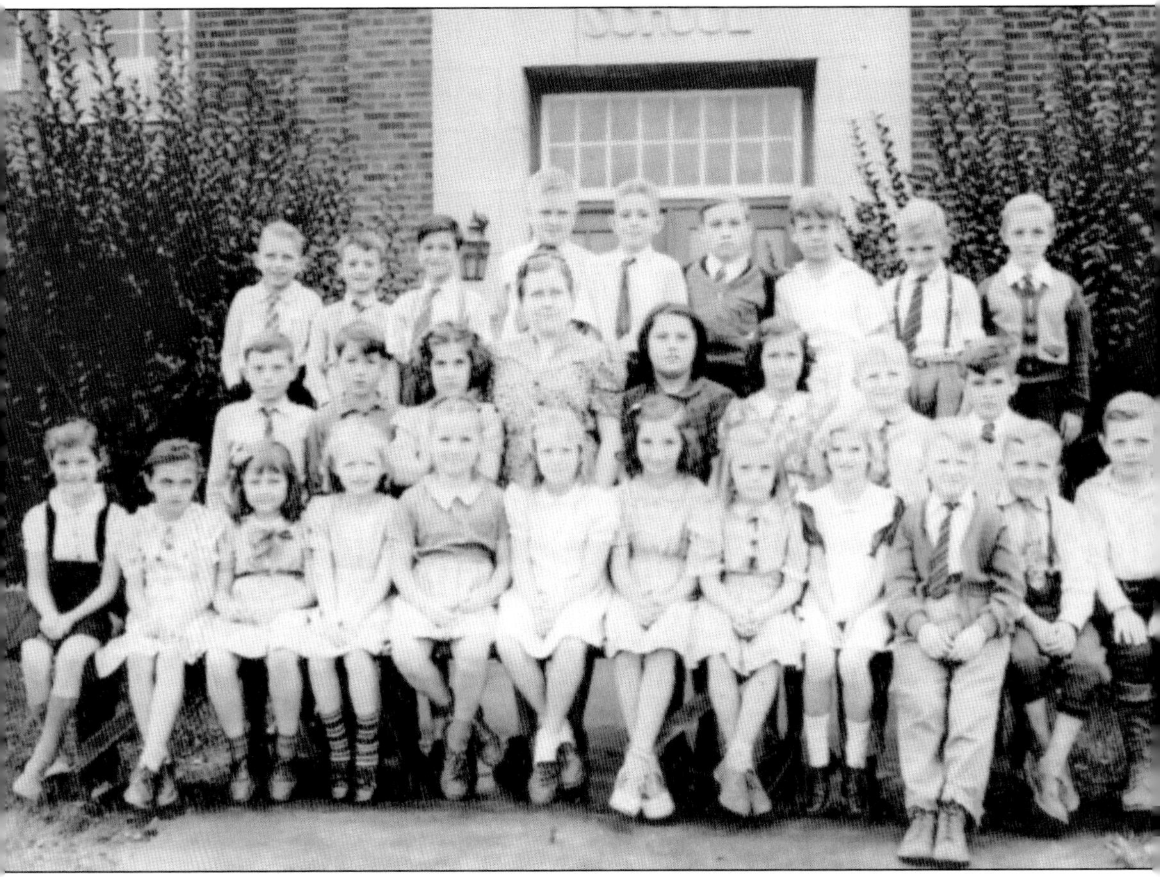

The third grade class of the consolidated school on Ridge Road in West Rockhill gathers in front of the building for a group photograph. With the creation of this first consolidated school, the era of one-room schoolhouses would soon come to an end. (Courtesy of WRHS.)

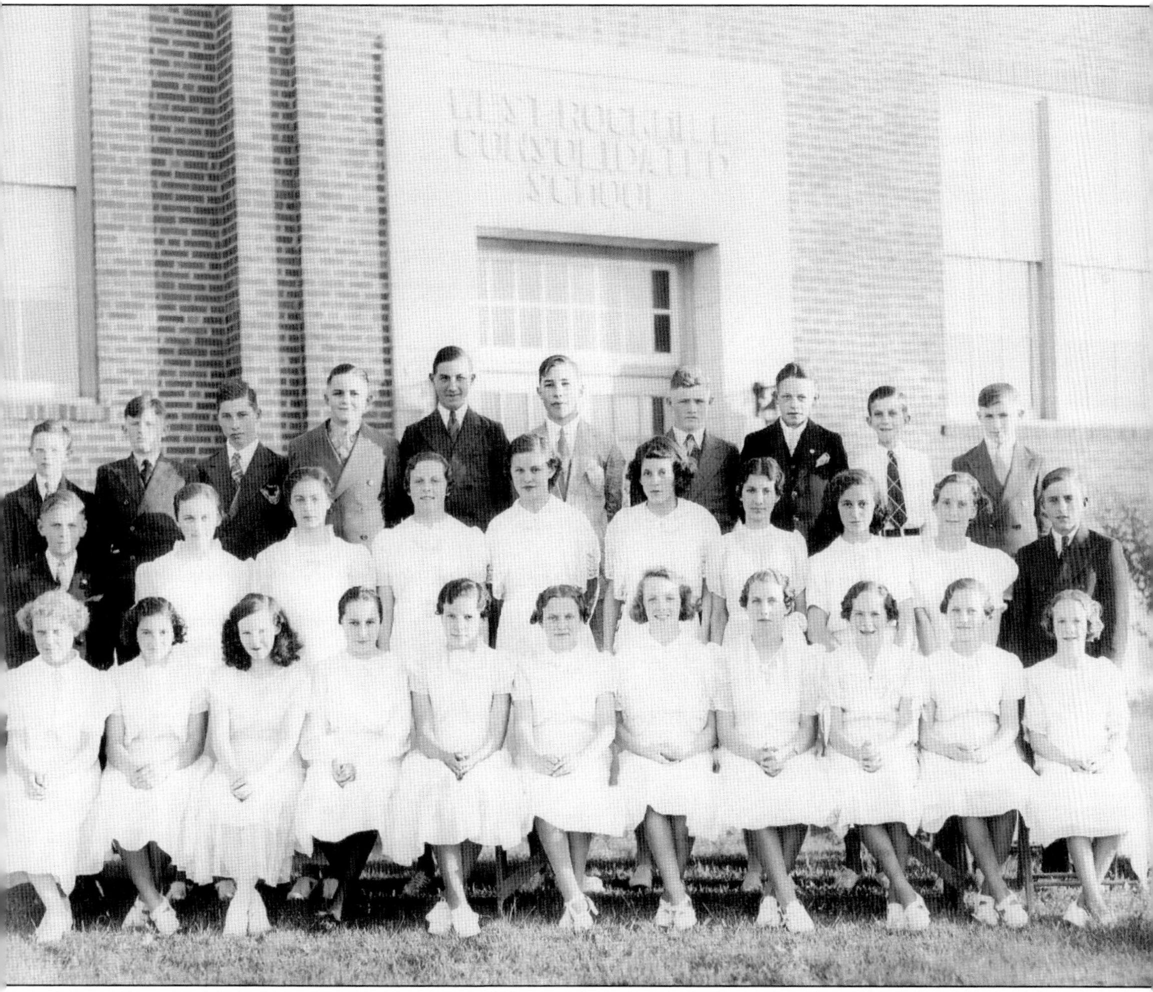

This photograph, taken May 31, 1938, is of the graduating eighth-grade class of the consolidated school. Pictured are, from left to right, (first row) Rurh Kraemer, Florance Konyk, Alma Camburn, Syella Les, Betty McKeever, Rita Ervin, Doris Becker, Martine Richard, Pauline Underkoffler, and Ruth Richter; (second row) Russel Alderfer, Edna Landis, Evelyn Landis, Helen Siek, Sadie Musselman, Helen Daniels, Alverda Wenhold, Mildred Knowles, and Otto Wied; (third row) Ralph Hafler, Raymond Hinkle, John Brozenske, Donald Derstine, Edward Russells, Charles Brozenske, J. Paul Hinkle, Alfred Klinger, Richard Sturzebecker, and Harold Benner. Eighth-grade commencement was an important event in the rural communities in the early part of the 20th century, simply because not many students continued their education past this point. (Courtesy of WRHS.)

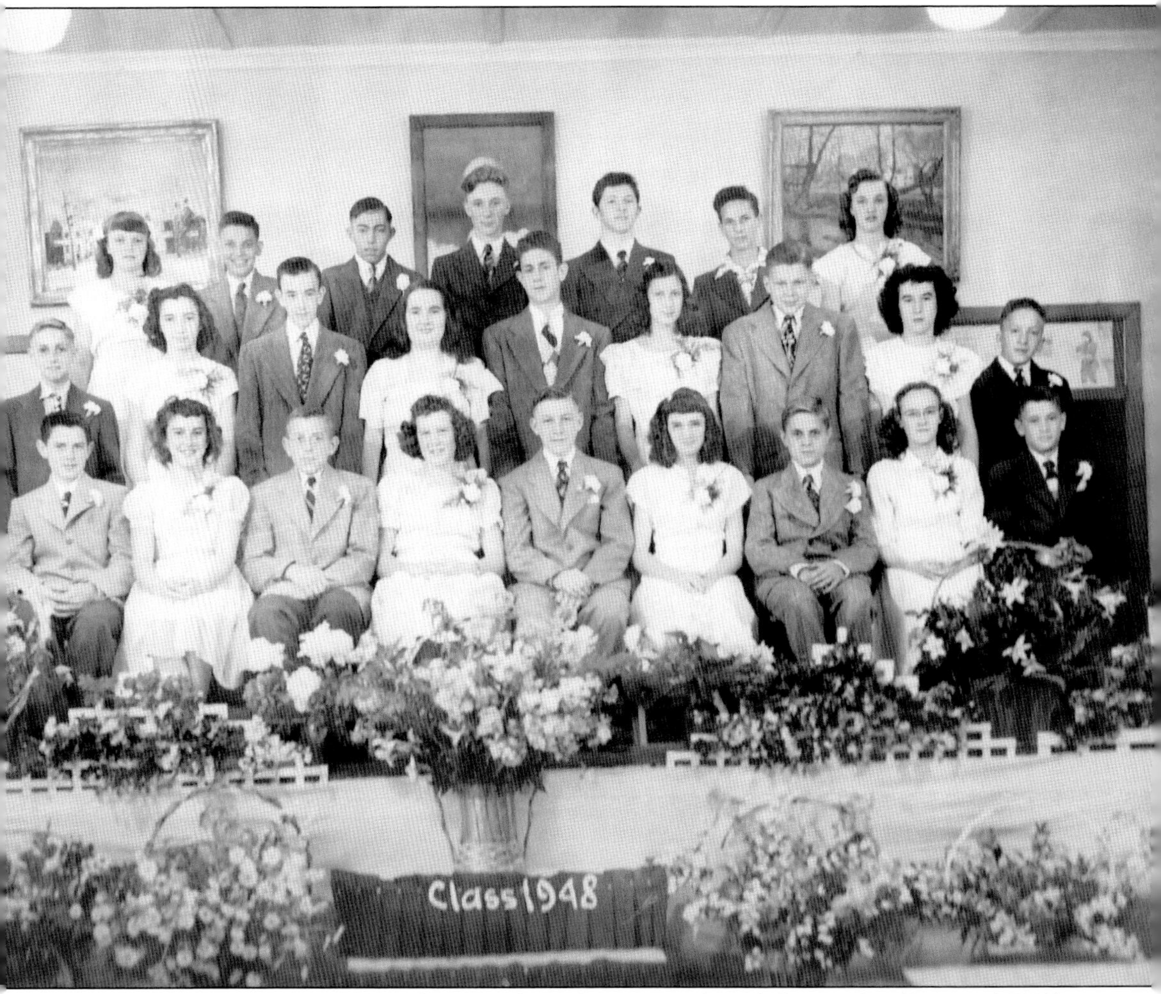

The consolidated school graduating class of 1948 are, from left to right, (first row) William Mayberry, Joyse Bucion, Stewart Blank, June Moore, Dennis Schaffer, Miriam Groft, Paul Weller, unidentified, and William Hill; (second row) William Berley, Ruth Benner, David Otto, Shirley Kaughman, Charles Guenst, Gloria Musselman, Roanald Cressman, Mary Knitter, and Louis Sitko; (third row) Shirley Wisinbaum, Richard Trumbaur, John Markley, Marvin Wissenbaum, Merit Bardnt, Charles Pizza, and Virginia Seachrist. (Courtesy of Charles Guenst.)

Three

COMMUNITY

Most of the East and West Rockhill region had small, self-sustaining villages, such as Almont, Ridge Valley, Argus, and Hagersville. These villages usually had a hotel that not only served as a resting and eating stop for travelers but also as the stagecoach stop to and from Philadelphia and Allentown. The villages usually contained a small general store that carried products from local farmers and other items essential to the community. Villages were generally comprised of a post office, a wheelwright, and a blacksmith, and they were usually in close proximity to a church and schoolhouse. A village was the hub of a small community, serving as a place to socialize and do business. They have become treasures from the past.

The majority of people living in East and West Rockhill either farmed livestock or dairy for a living or ran small farms to help sustain the needs of the family. Chicken farming was essential, and many families raised fowl for consumption and in order to sell the eggs.

Resident Rhoda Clark has many stories of the area, including one passed down to her by her father. As a young boy, he filled his bicycle's basket with eggs to sell and rode to the Inter County Bridge. Before he could cross, he slipped on the gravel and fell, but he did not break a single egg and took them to town to sell. As indicated by this story, it was important to get the eggs to market since even a small amount of money helped each family. Not only did the men work the farms, but all family members had a job to complete. Most farming was done by manual labor, common sense, and ingenuity. Rhoda Clark was a very industrious resident, raising vegetables for sale at the local summer campgrounds that dotted the landscape. She also recalls the residents of Ridge Valley lining up at the nearby waterhole to take their weekly baths. Of course, first they had to wait until the cows had quenched their thirst.

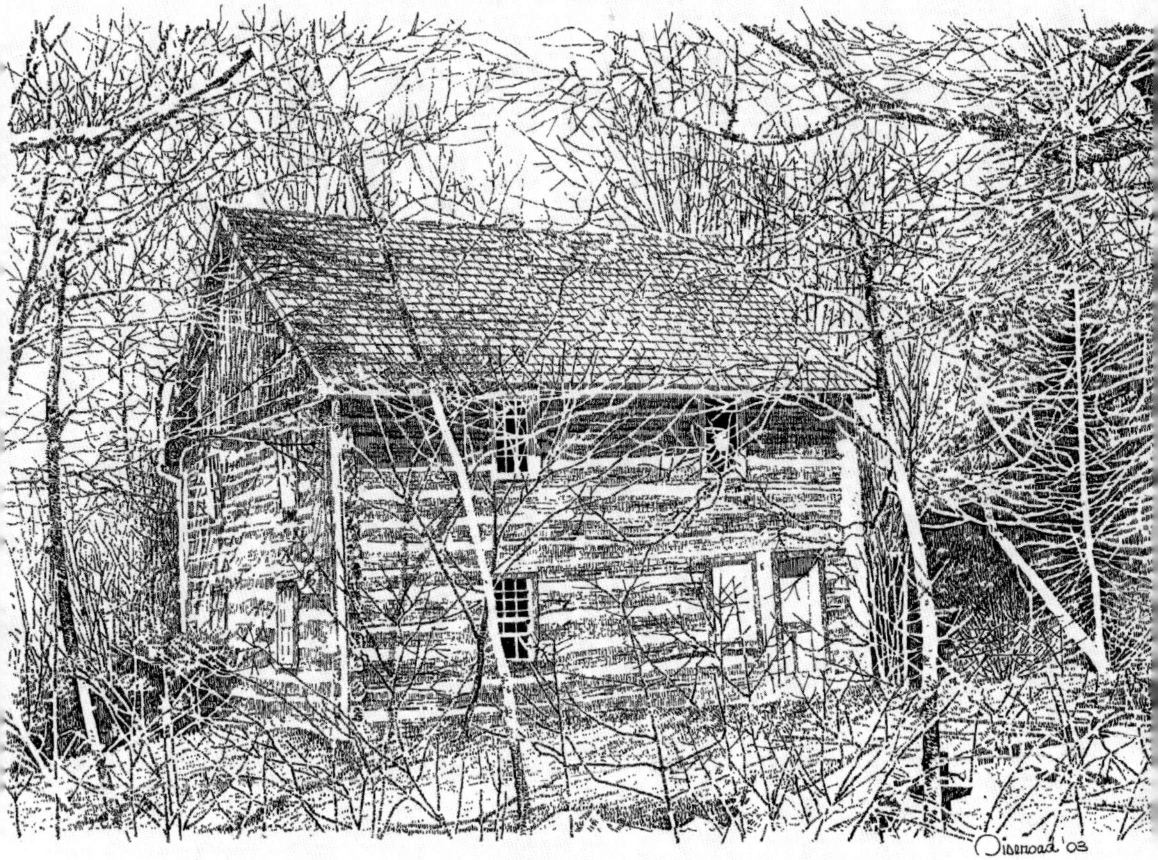

Residents in the area refer to what was one of the oldest dwellings in the township as "the log cabin." This dwelling was built by William Watts, a cabinetmaker, on a small farm above the Sellersville catch basin. William was married to Katherine Nase, who became one of the oldest residents on record in West Rockhill township. Katherine was special not only because of her longevity, but also because of her health. She was seldom sick, and she was active until the day she died. Born in 1791, she lived in two distinct centuries, dying in 1896. Unfortunately, this structure was lost when it was consumed by fire in the early part of the 21st century. (Courtesy of Fred Diseroad.)

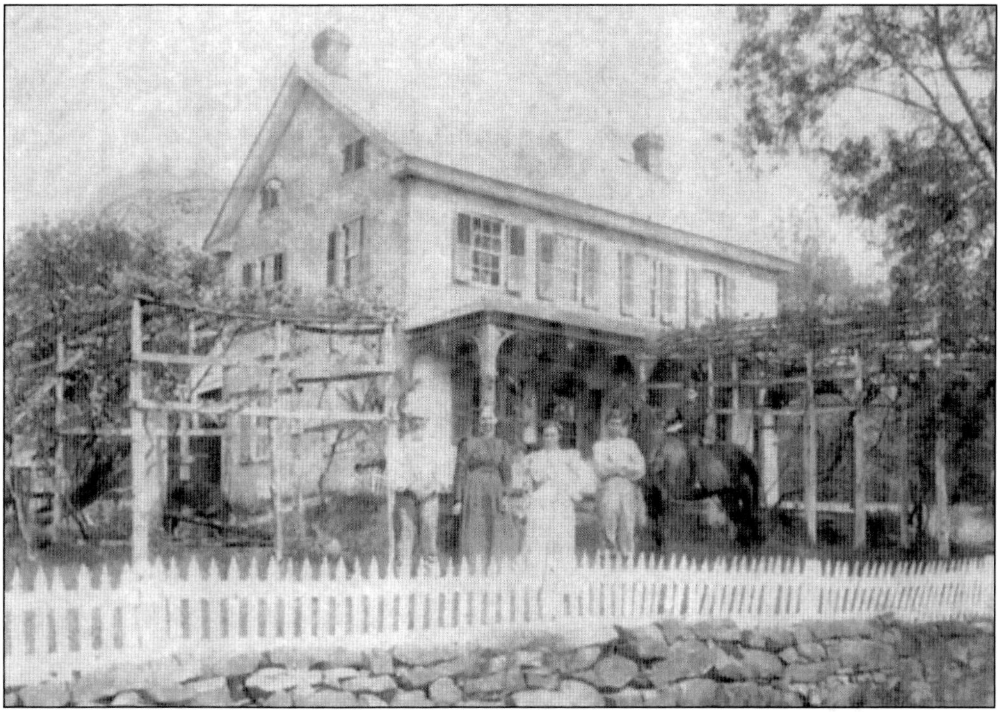

This c. 1880 photograph is of the Barndt family gathered in front of their farm, located on Allentown Road next to Rocky Dale Road in West Rockhill Township. The farm was also owned by Roland Becker. (Courtesy of Charles Guenst.)

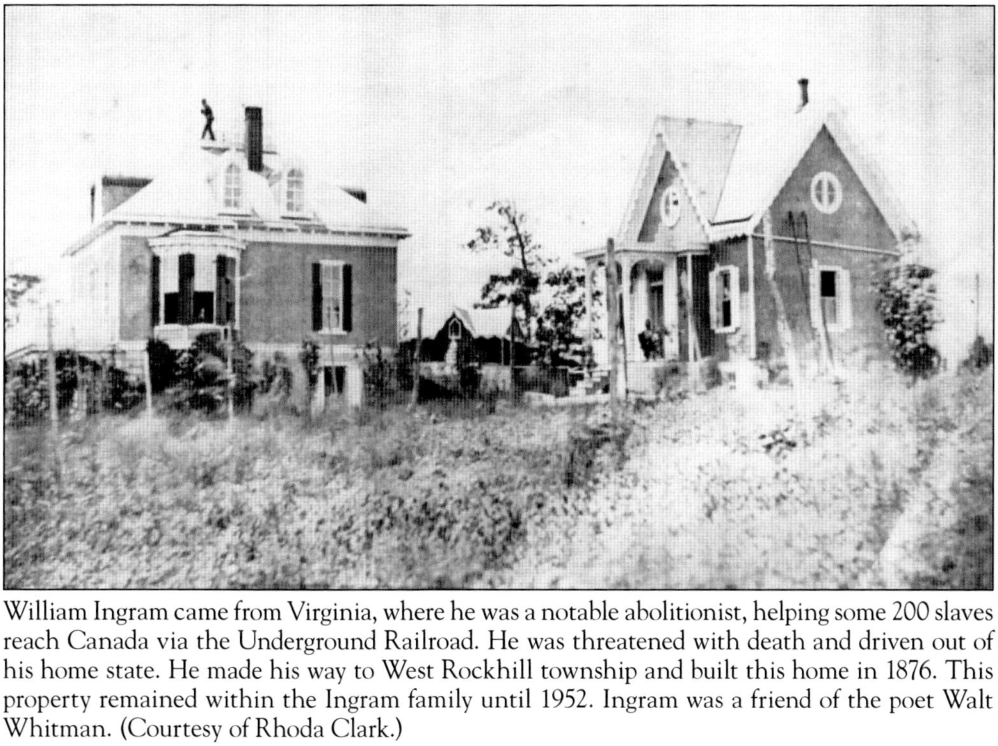

William Ingram came from Virginia, where he was a notable abolitionist, helping some 200 slaves reach Canada via the Underground Railroad. He was threatened with death and driven out of his home state. He made his way to West Rockhill township and built this home in 1876. This property remained within the Ingram family until 1952. Ingram was a friend of the poet Walt Whitman. (Courtesy of Rhoda Clark.)

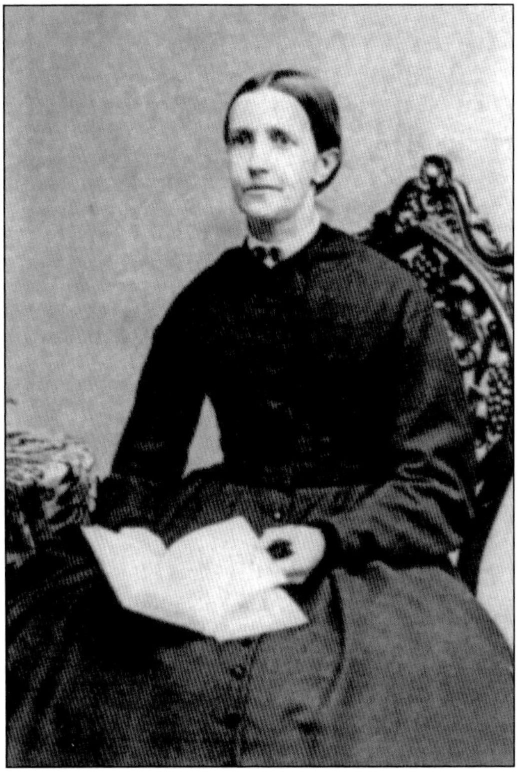

This photograph of Dr. Emily Ingram, one of the first women to earn a medical degree, was taken in 1880. She received her degree from Penn Medical University. Because women were not well accepted in the medical profession, she went into social work along with her father, and they both worked with the Prison Society. (Courtesy of Rhoda Clark.)

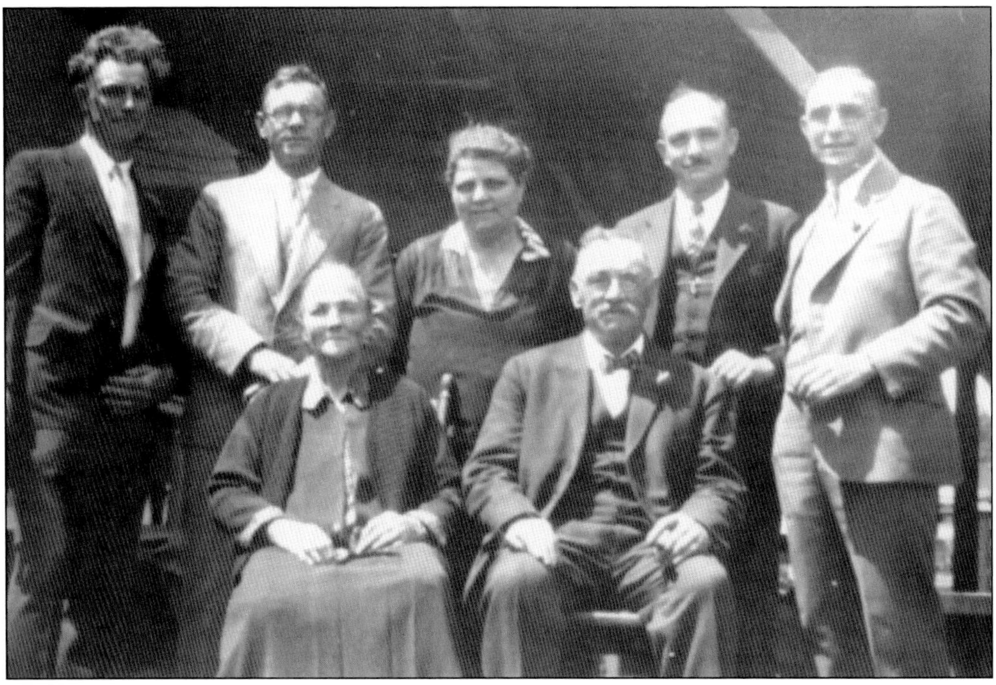

In this 1929 photograph of the Guenst family are, from left to right, (first row) Wilhemia (born in 1860) and her husband Charles (born in 1858); (second row) children Ernest, Henry, Minnie, William, and Charles. (Courtesy of Charles Guenst.)

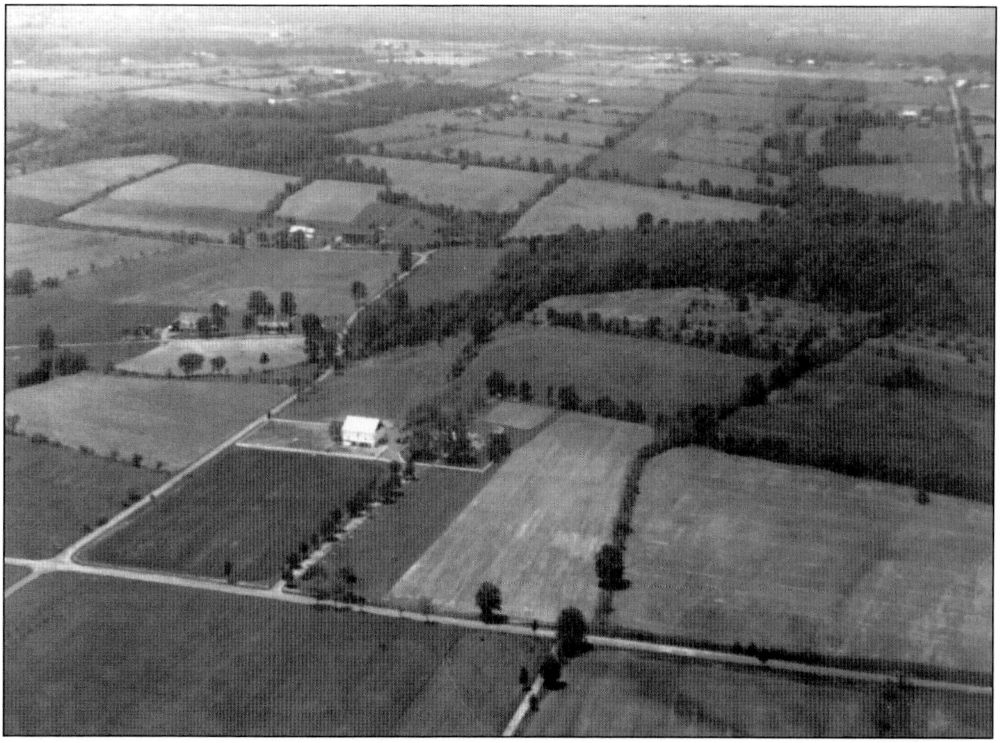

The Palomino Farm on Cathill Road in West Rockhill township is pictured in this aerial view from the mid-1930s. This photograph illustrates how rural the area was at that time. (Courtesy of WRHS.)

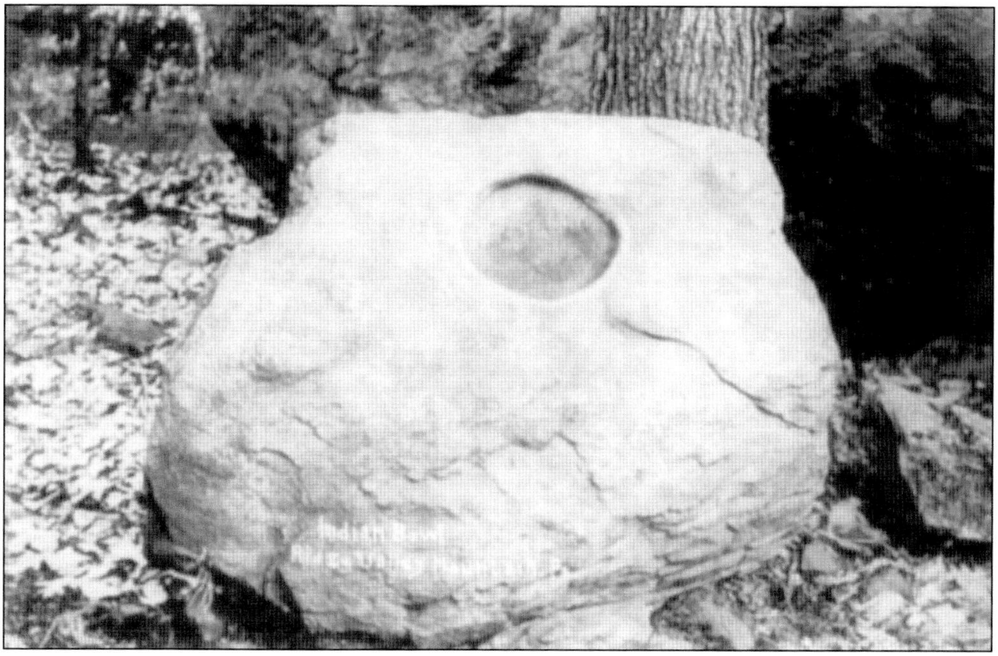

An "Indian bowl" is pictured in this early-20th-century image. An Indian bowl is a circular spot worn away by grinding meal with pestles made of handheld rocks on a large boulder. There are many such rocks in and around East and West Rockhill Townships. (Courtesy of Rhoda Clark.)

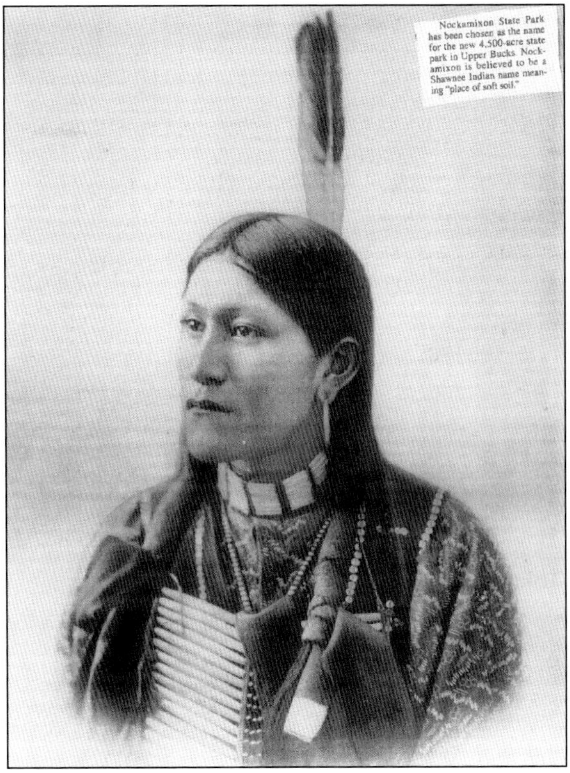

This photograph of a Native American was reportedly given to a resident of West Rockhill in exchange for some coal. The date of the photograph is unknown. (Courtesy of Rhoda Clark.)

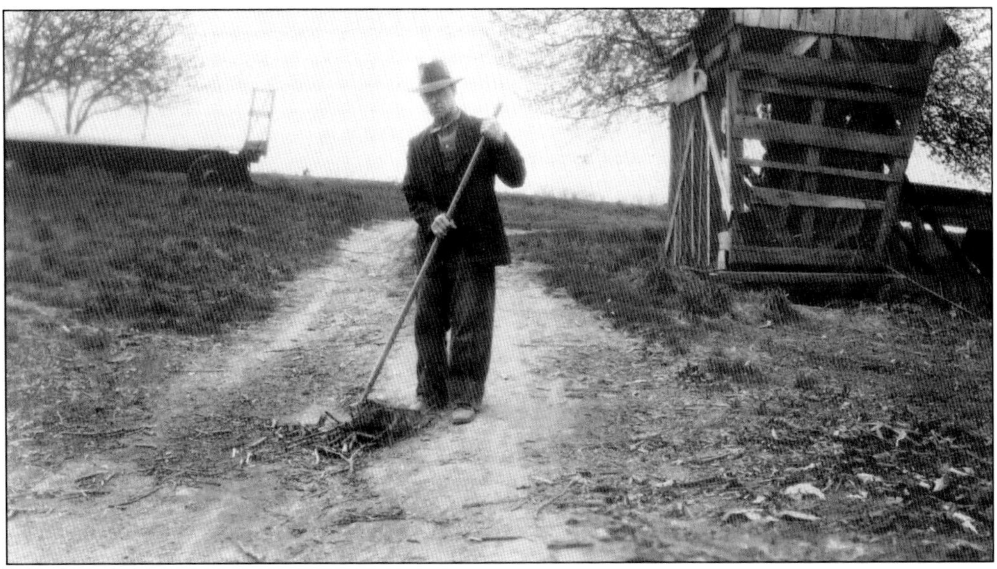

Edward V. Charles was a resident of East Rockhill Township. Typical of many of the people who live in the Rockhills, his family lineage goes back to the mid-1700s. Early in his career, he ran a concrete business, and some of his sidewalks from the early 1900s are still being used in Perkasie. He married Alice Tausic and eventually bought a farm on East Rock Road. He worked for the government during the 1940s, helping farmers receive loans. Over the years, Charles became quite active in politics, and at one point, he was township supervisor. In his 90s, he became known as "Mr. Republican." (Courtesy of Petrona Charles.)

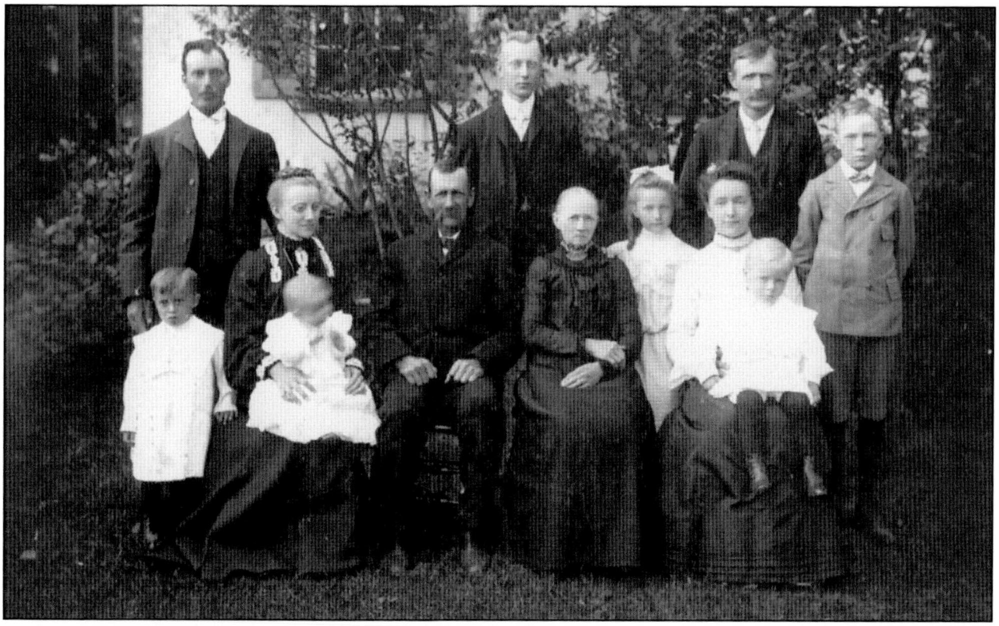

This c. 1902 photograph of the Gerhart/Mann family was taken on the side of the Mann house on Old Bethlehem Road (Minsi Trail) in Keelersville. Levi Mann is on the right in the last row. The boy standing to his left is his son, who grew up and went into business with his father at L.D. Mann & Son Marble and Granite Works. Mrs. Mann's parents, the Gerharts, owned a farm near the Tochickon Union Church. (Courtesy of Charles Mann.)

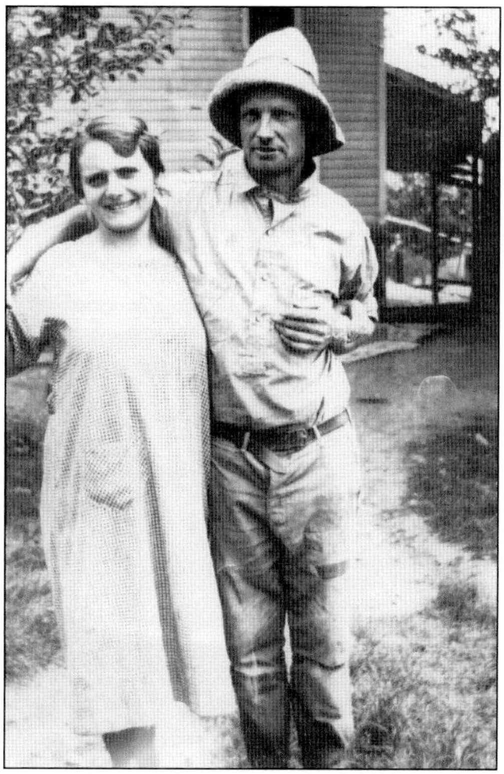

Mr. and Mrs. Edward V. Charles pose in front of their newly bought home on East Rock Road sometime around the 1920s. (Courtesy of Petrona Charles.)

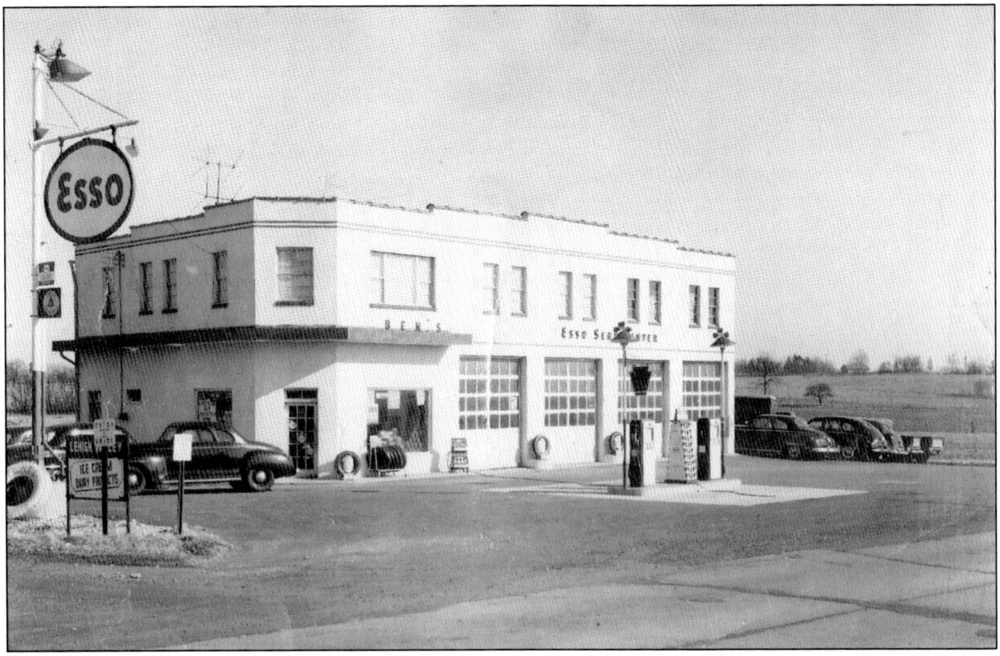

Ben Scholl and Sons was a classic garage and gas station of the late 1940s and early 1950s. Located on the corner of Fifth Street and Route 313, it is still in operation today. As one of only three gas service stations between Quakertown and Doylestown, it was an important business. (Courtesy of Petrona Charles.)

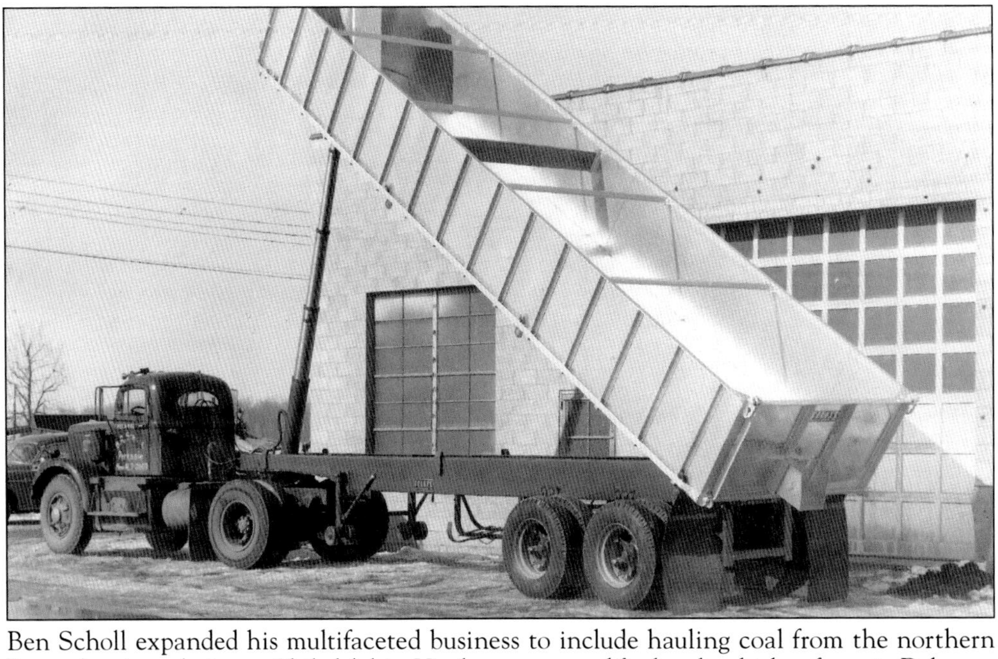

Ben Scholl expanded his multifaceted business to include hauling coal from the northern Pennsylvania coalmines to Philadelphia. He also transported feed to the chicken farms in Delaware and Maryland. His business was the first to haul bulk milk from Lehigh Dairy. Many a swimming pool was filled with water from his trucks. The business was also a GMC agency and sold trucks. For many years, Scholl plowed the roads of East Rockhill township. (Courtesy of Petrona Charles.)

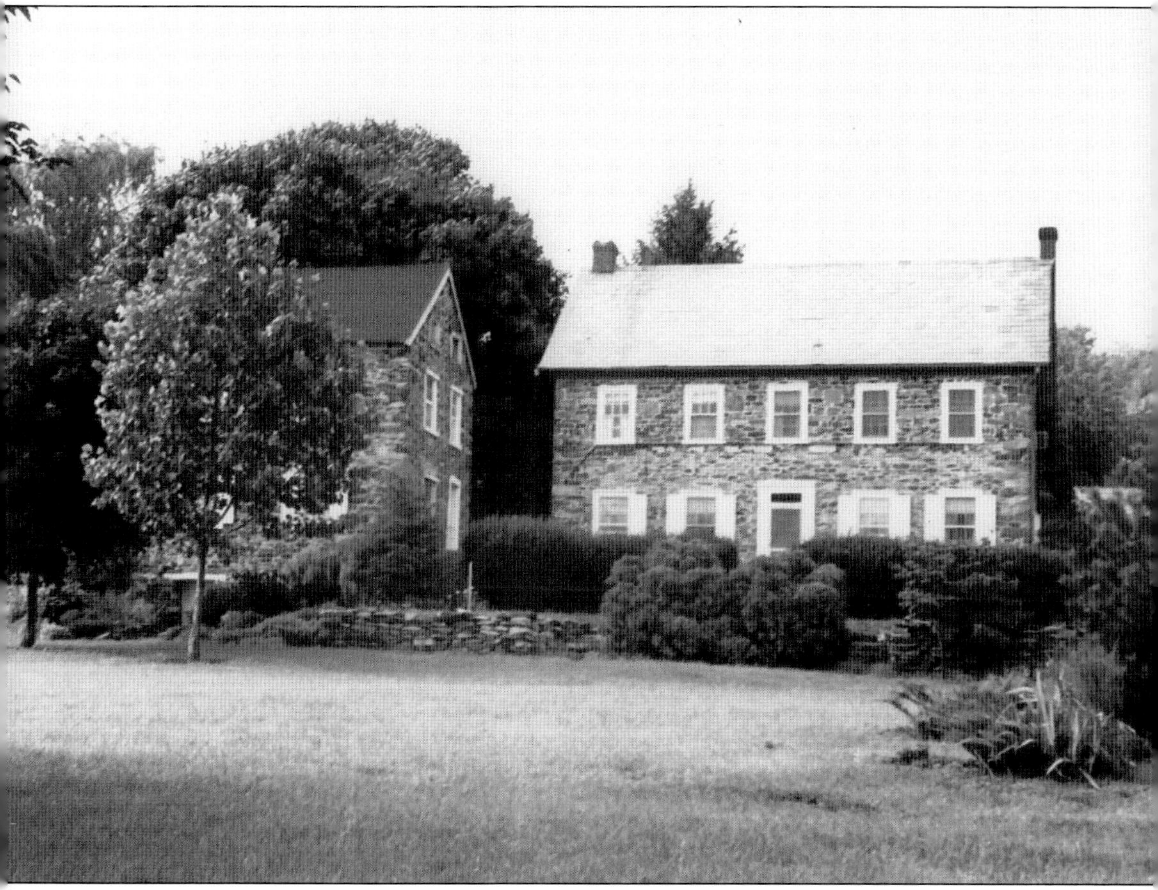

This classic vernacular Georgian house was built in 1843 by Abraham and Catherine Hartzel and is located on Barndt Road in West Rockhill township. On the west side of the house is a tenant house. The Hartzels were related to the Hartzel who lived in what is now known as the Hartzel Strassberger House on Old Bethlehem Pike. The Hartzel homes all display the same unique architectural features. This late 1940s photograph shows the rear of the home. The building in the front is the summer kitchen, believed to be older than the house. (Courtesy of Eleanora Gruber.)

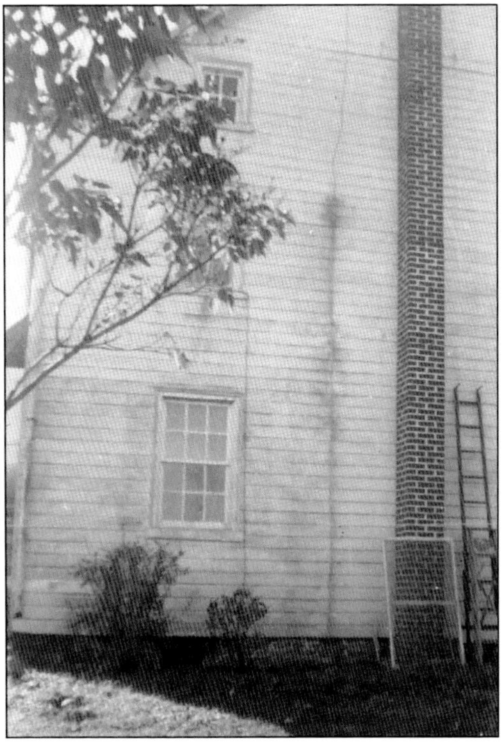

This stone house, built by Abraham and Catherine Hartzel, is sided with wood on one side to protect from the weather. This was a common practice during the 1800s. (Courtesy of Eleanora Gruber.)

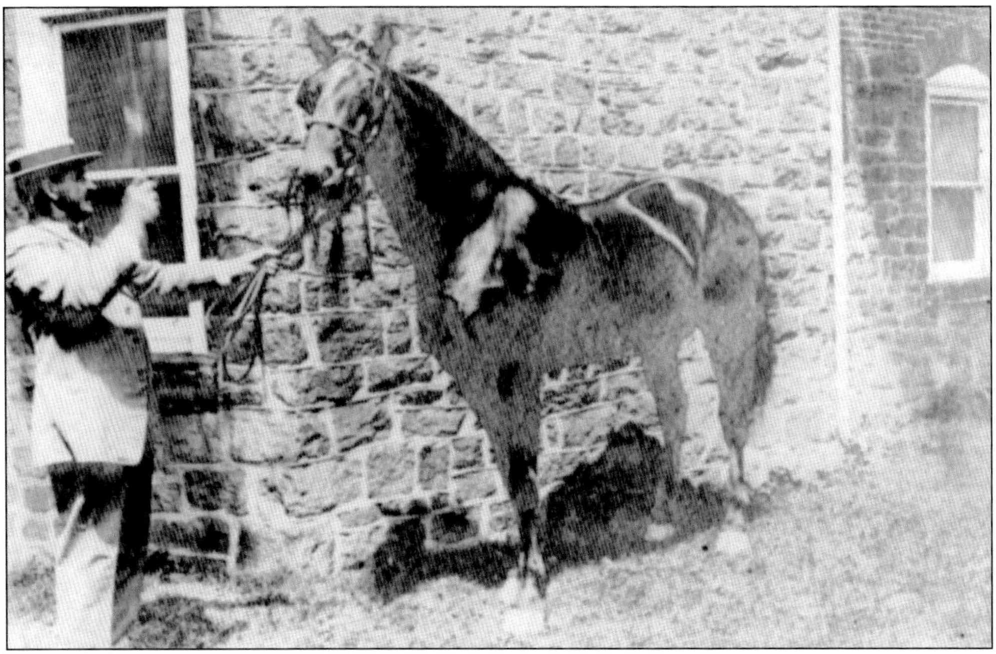

Joseph Gulden worked as a director for First National Bank in Quakertown. He was a Bucks County commissioner from 1915 to 1919. He also owned the creamery in Wesiel on Three Mile Run Road. Creameries, or factories for manufacture of dairy products, became essential businesses and were built all over Bucks County around 1880. Today, Joseph Gulden's Creamery is used by Nockamixon State Park and stands next to the Lake House in East Rockhill. (Courtesy of Charles Mann.)

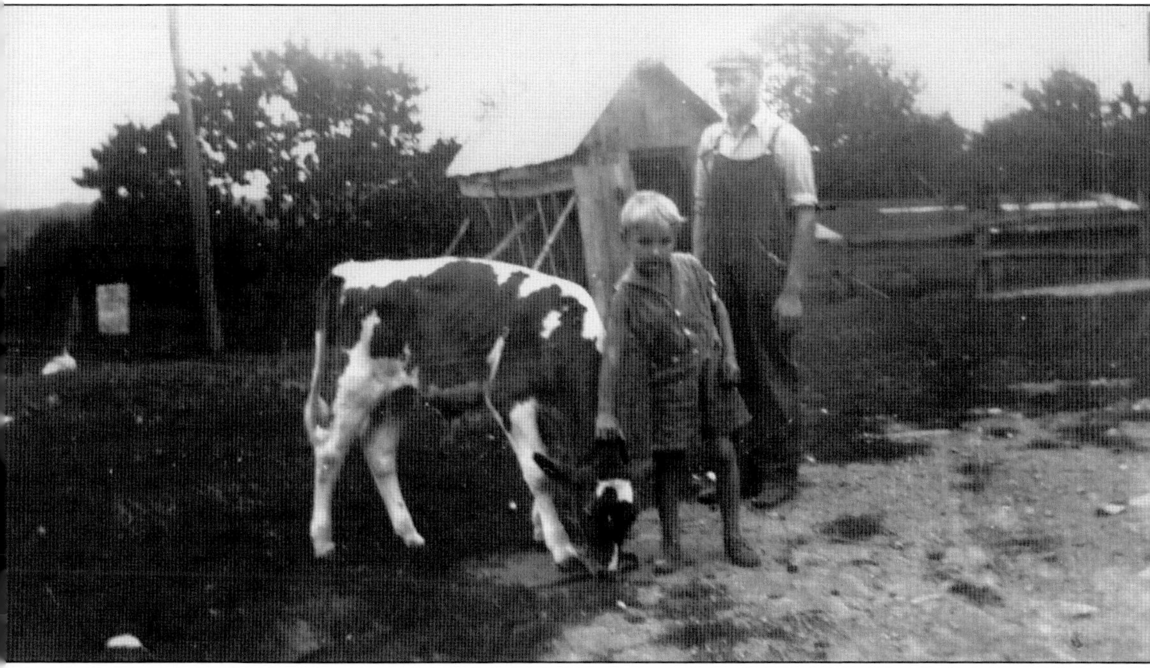

Farming was a major industry in East Rockhill Township. These kids pose with their young pet bull on East Rock Road in 1939. (Courtesy of Petrona Charles.)

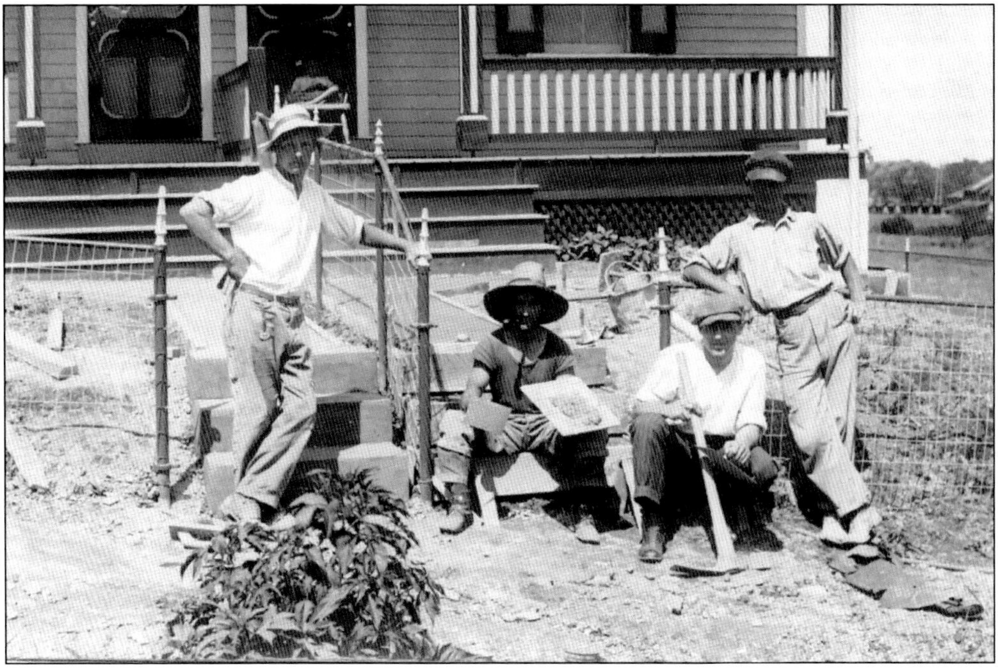

Edward Charles and his crew of concrete workers are pictured in the Perkasie area around 1919. (Courtesy of Petrona Charles.)

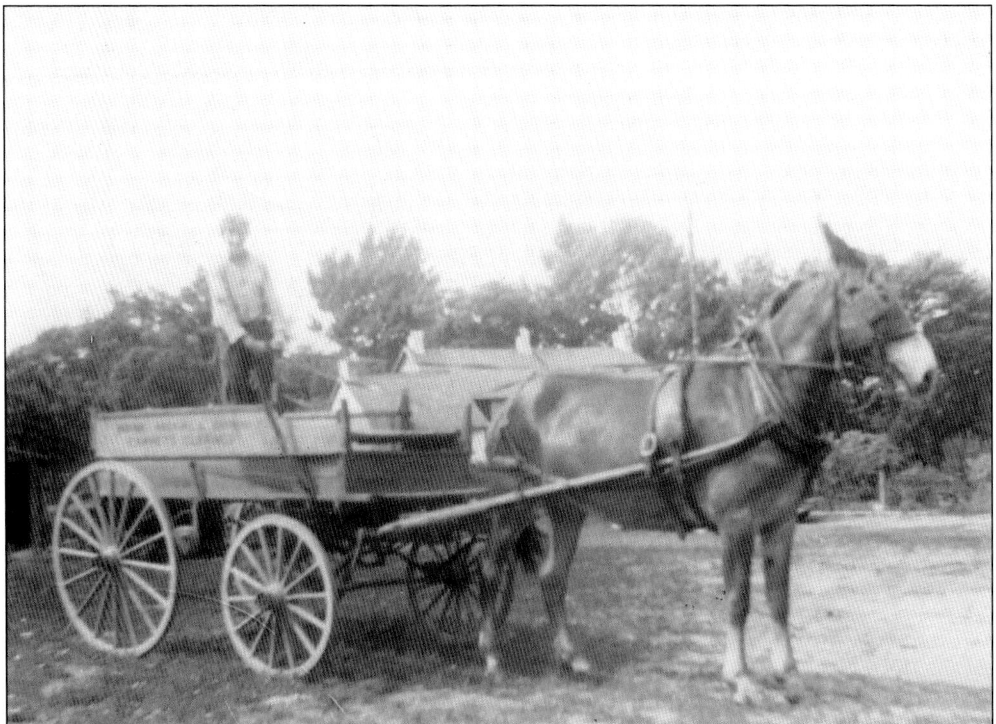

This photograph from East Rock Road captures farm life prior to the introduction of tractors and cars. (Courtesy of Petrona Charles.)

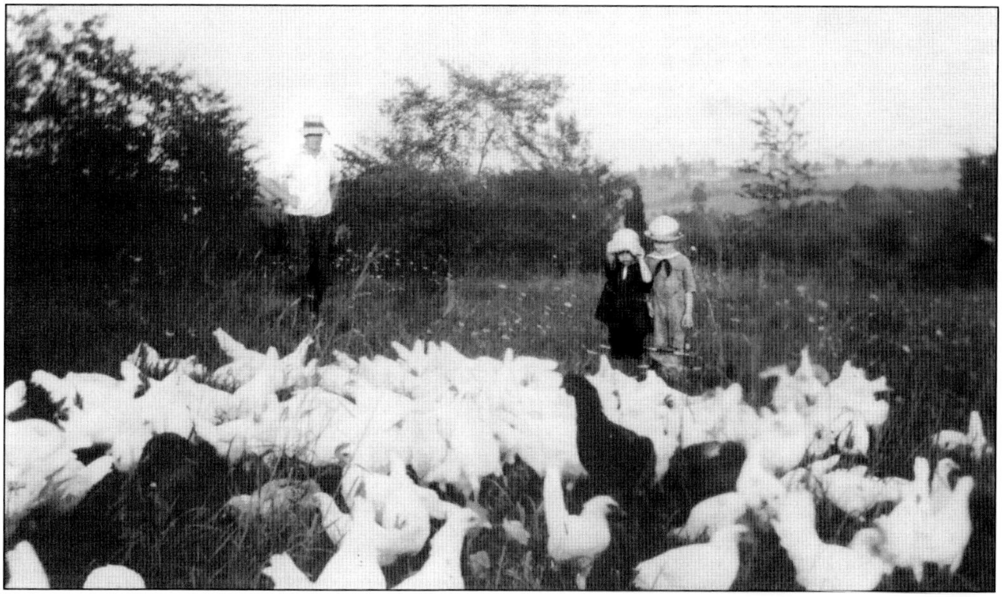

These were common scenes on most farms in both East and West Rockhill Townships. During the Great Depression, many a farmer raised chickens, both for the meat and for their eggs, and not only for consumption, but also for sale. Pictured at right is the James A. Clinger farm. (Above, courtesy of Petrona Charles; right, courtesy of WRHS.)

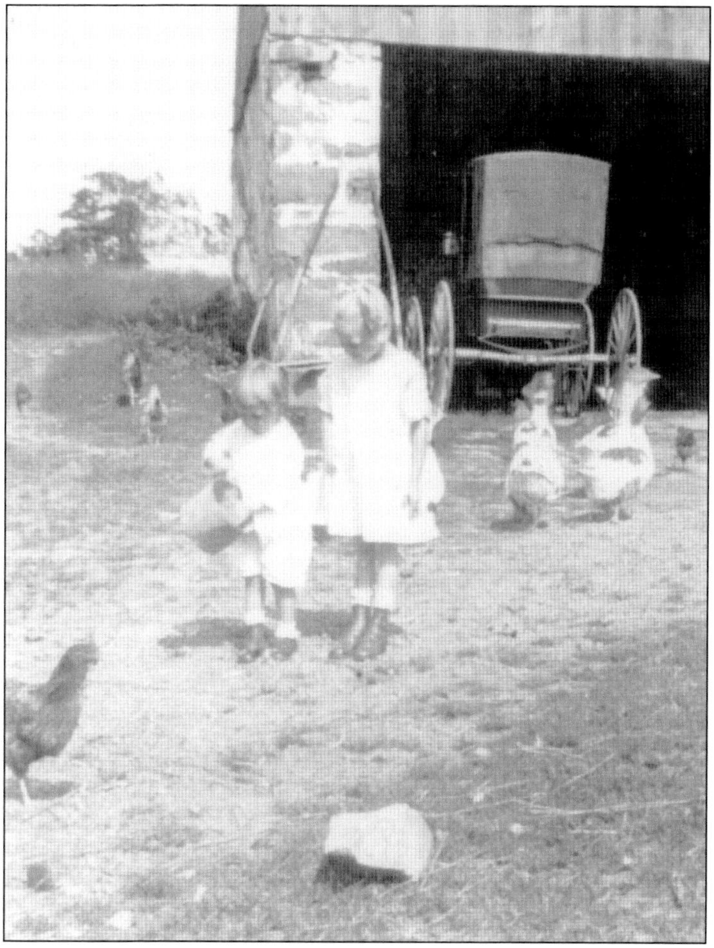

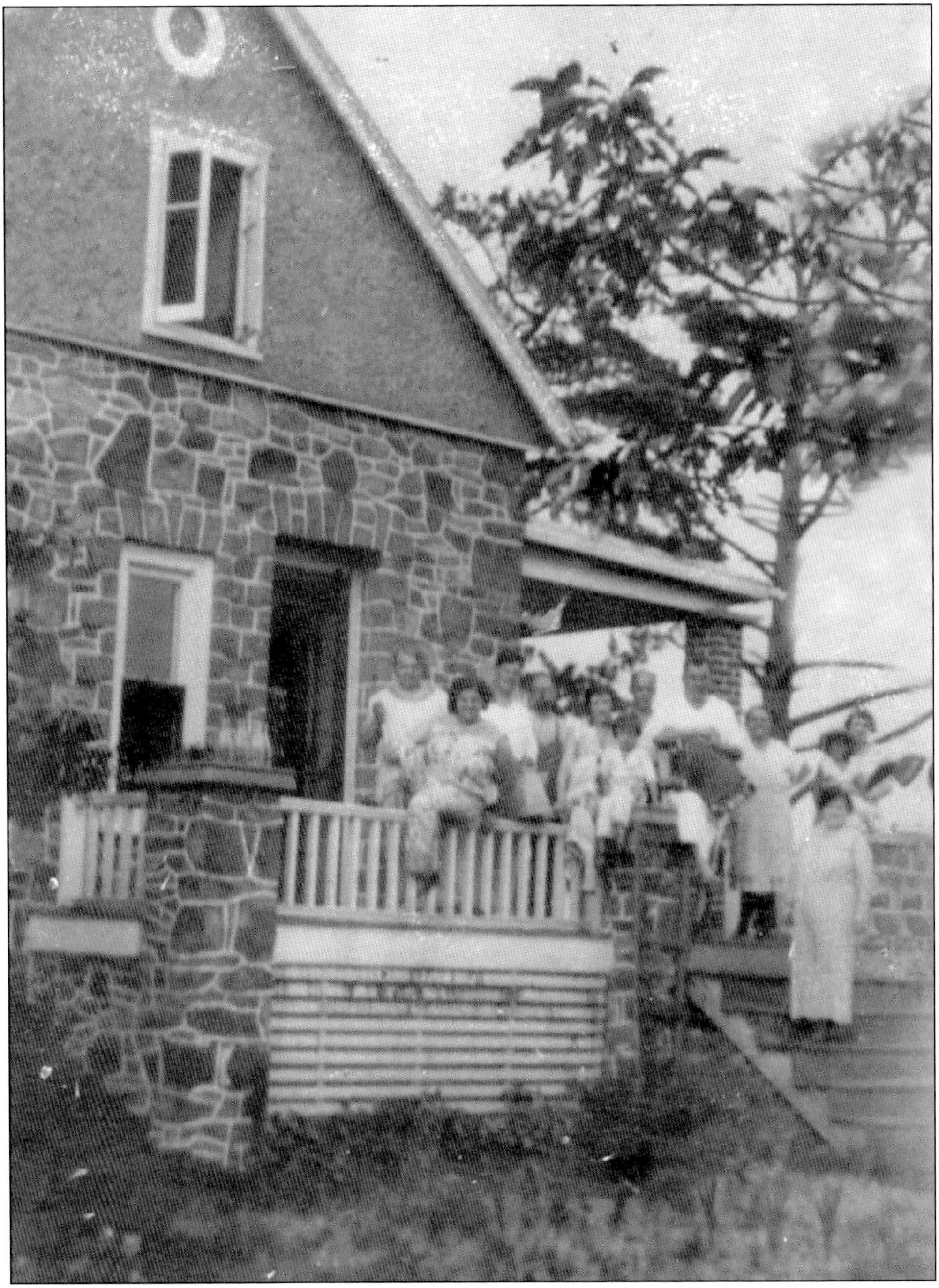

Emigrants fleeing Europe during the 19th and early 20th centuries began to trickle into East Rockhill Township. The husbands, using the train, would often work in the city while the wives and children ran the farm. Relatives who lived in Philadelphia would spend weekends enjoying country life and visiting their country cousins. This photograph captures one of those weekends at a bungalow on West Rock Road in East Rockhill Township around the 1920s. (Courtesy of Petrona Charles.)

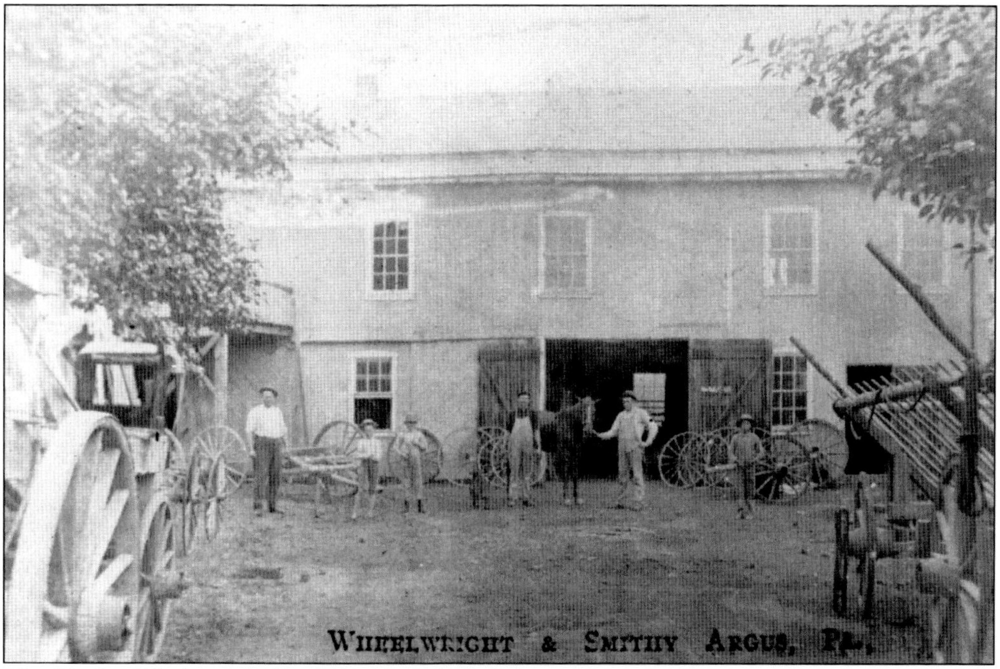

This blacksmith shop was located next to the Clark residence on Allentown Road in Argus, West Rockhill. It is pictured around 1914. (Courtesy of Rhoda Clark.)

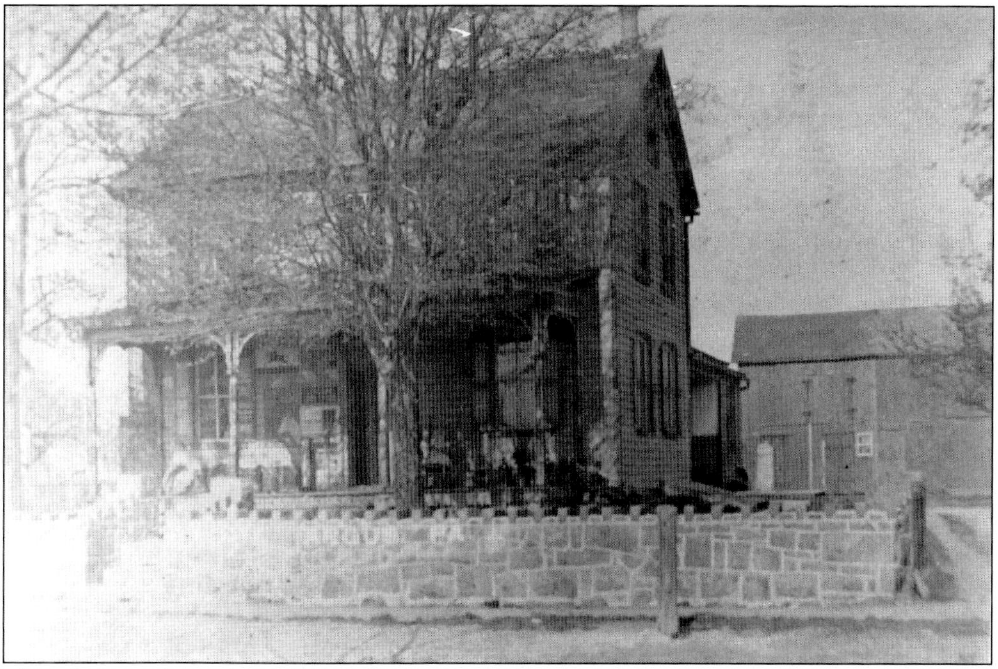

The Clark residence, located on Allentown Road, is pictured in 1920. Rhoda Clark is a fixture in West Rockhill Township; she has been a resident for over 70 years. At age 92, she has seen many changes, not just in the township but in the world. She is considered an authority of the township, and a few of her stories can be found in the beginning of chapter three. (Courtesy of Rhoda Clark.)

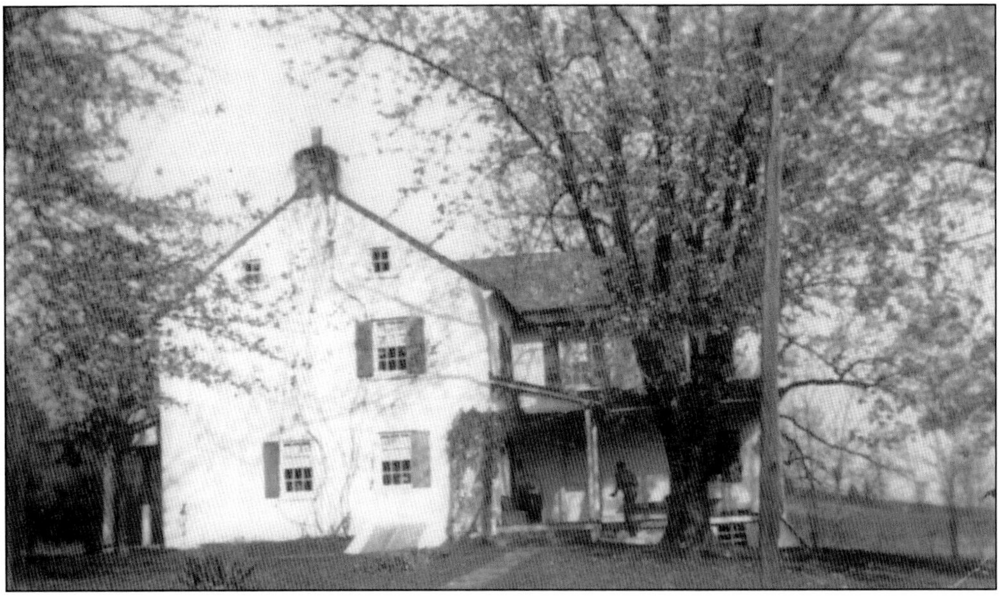

This house is located near the corner of Barndt and Simmons Roads in West Rockhill Township. It is a typical example of late-18th-century architecture. George Adam Kober, an early German settler, first owned the property. It is therefore in the Bucks County records as the Kober house. Research indicates that the house was built in 1796. (Both, courtesy of David Collingwood.)

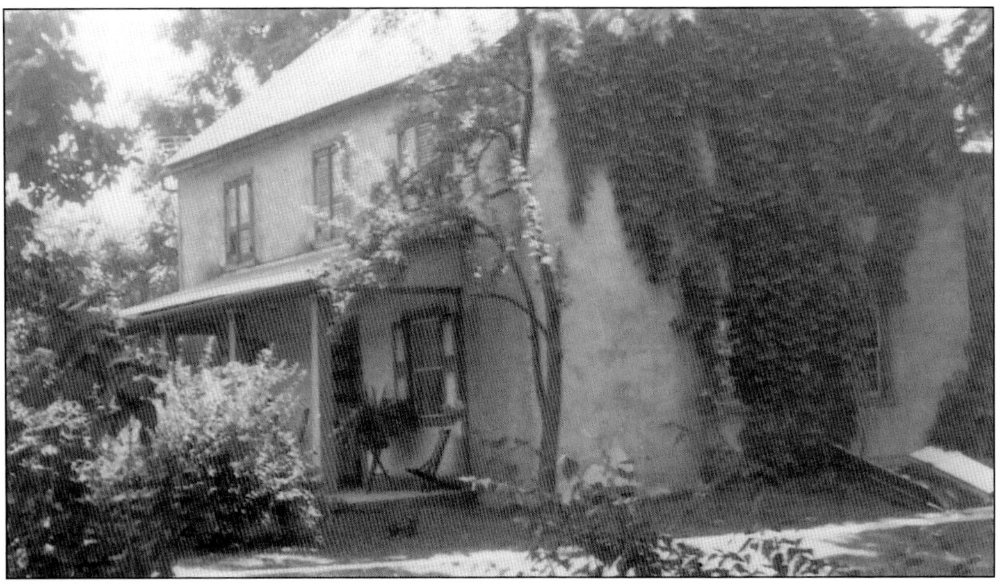

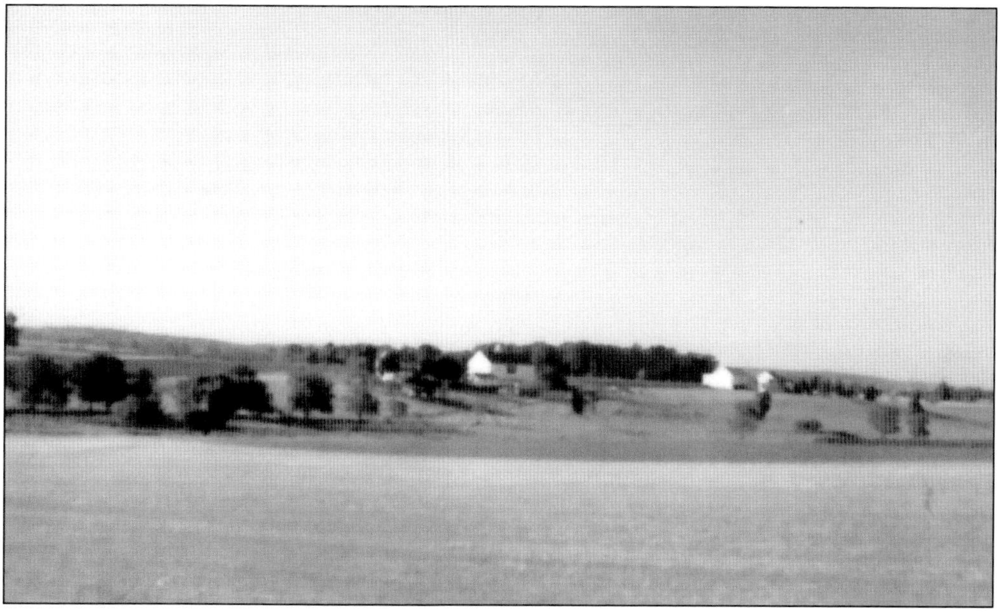

The Detweiler home on the Detweiler farm is pictured around 1960. Both farms in this photograph were owned by Jim and Merrill Detweiler. The Detweiler property encompassed 100 acres, and a dairy farm was once operated there. This photograph was taken prior to the development of Routes 309 and 152. (Courtesy of Jim Detweiler.)

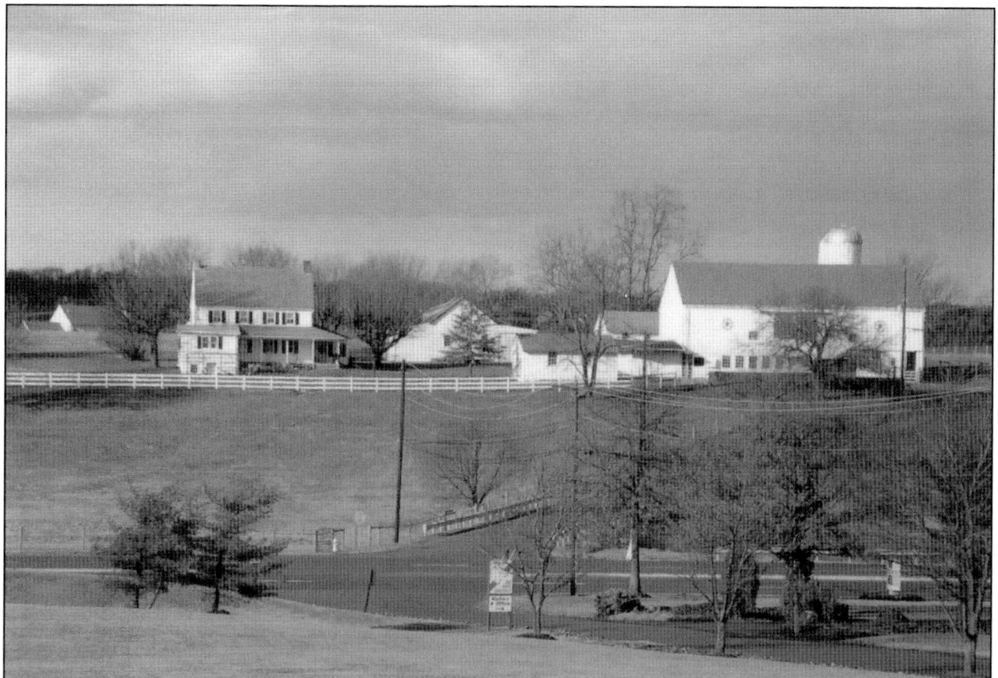

This photograph of the Detweiler farm was taken recently and shows the development of West Rockhill township. The Detweiler farm has been in the family for four generations, starting with Mahlon Detweiler. The farmhouse was built in the mid-1800s. In the foreground, Route 309 is visible. The farm now consists of 20 acres. (Courtesy of Jim Detweiler.)

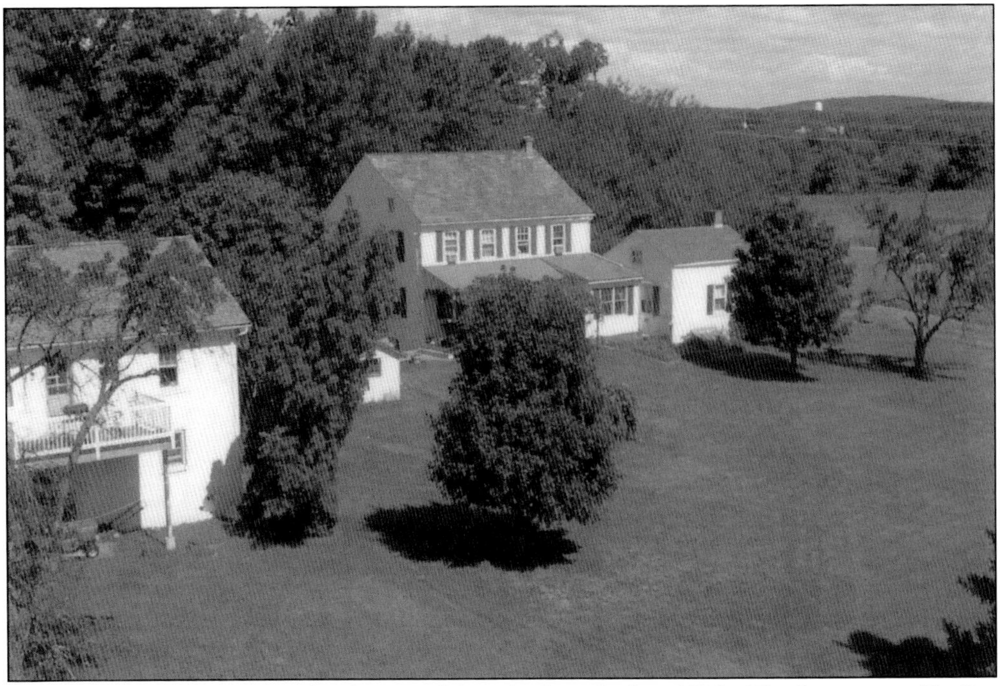

This photograph is an example of a typical farm built in the late 1800s. The farm, owned by Jim Detweiler, is located on Route 309 and sits slightly behind the original Detweiler farm. (Courtesy of Jim Detweiler.)

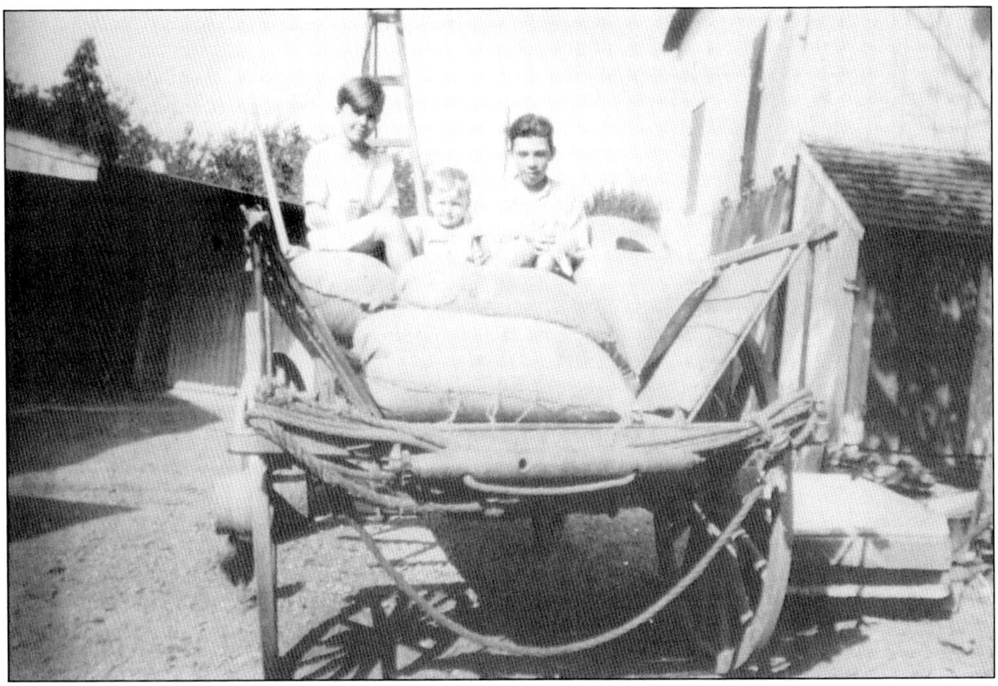

Boys play in a cart on a farm on Cathill Road around 1914. (Courtesy of WRHS.)

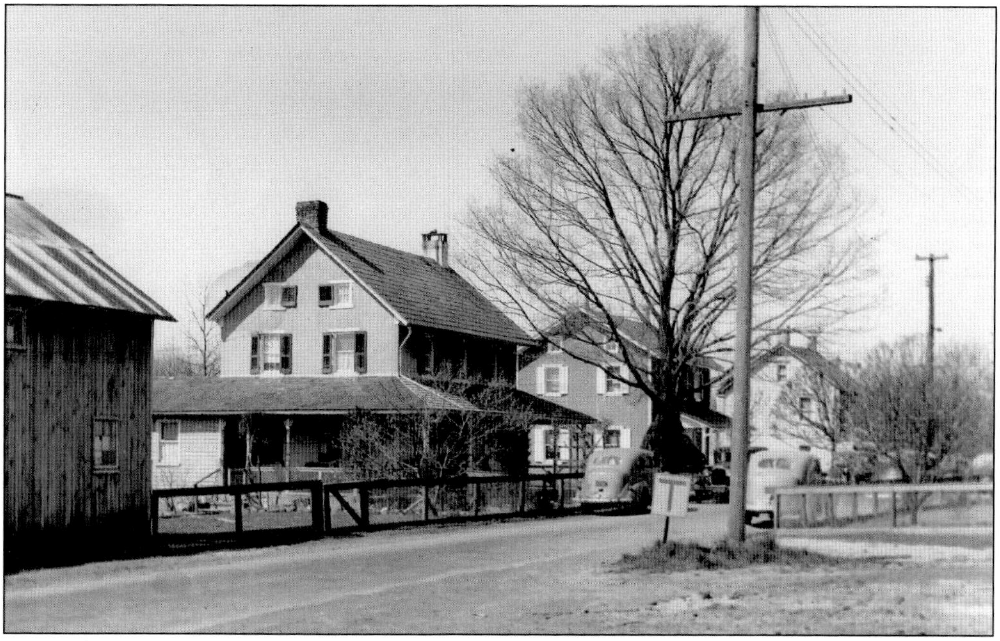

Pictured is the Guenst family farm in Ridge Valley, West Rockhill, around 1940. The Guensts settled in West Rockhill in 1898, where they ran a sawmill and raised and butchered livestock for market. (Courtesy of Charles Guenst.)

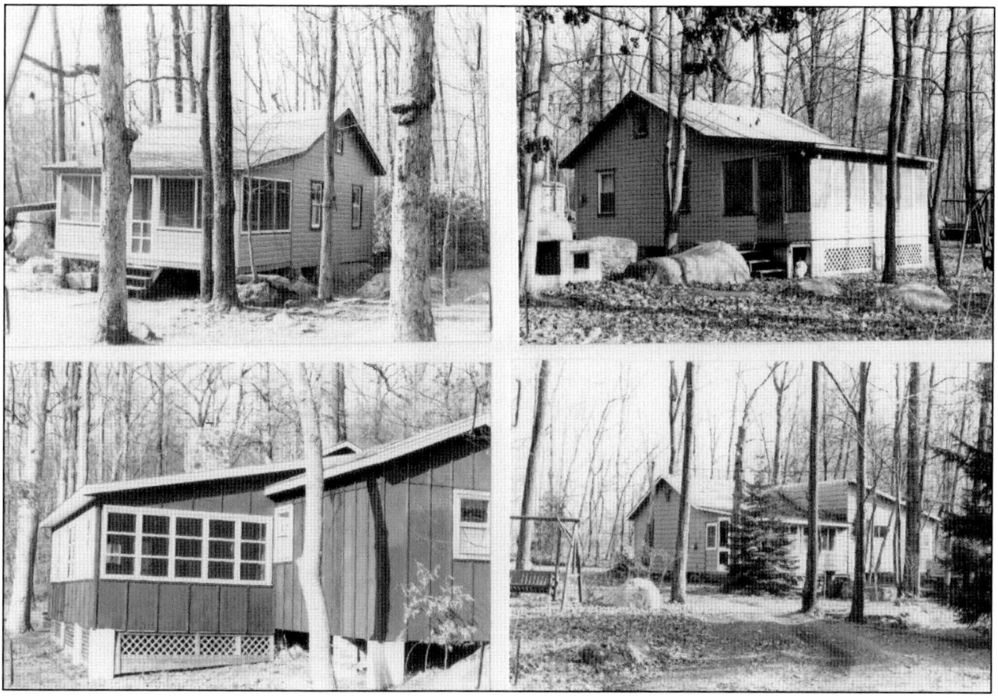

These cottages, located on Ridge Valley Road in West Rockhill, were built in the 1920s in wooded areas and along creeks as summer vacation homes. Some are still used for summer recreation, and others have become primary residences. Travelers can see these same types of cottages dotting the landscape all over East and West Rockhill Townships. (Courtesy of WRHS.)

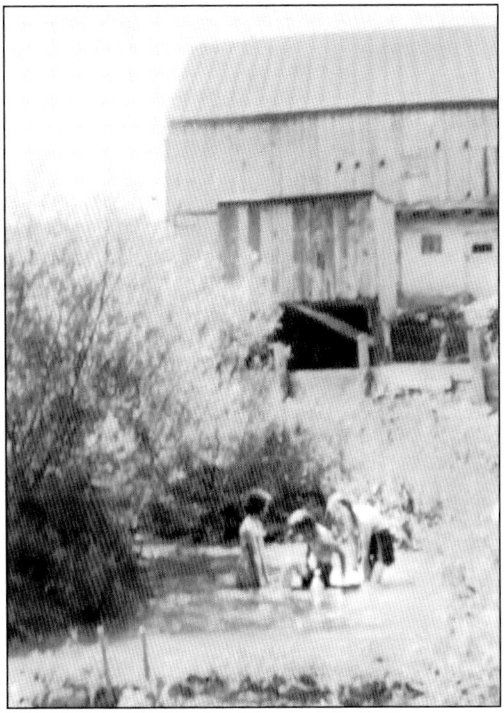

This is a 1937 photograph of a house on County Line Road in West Rockhill. It was built in 1800 on land from Abraham Gehman, pastor at Rockhill Mennonite Meetinghouse, who gave it to his daughter Mary and her husband, John Yoder. Enjoying the old swimming hole, children play at the Gehman house. This was a typical pastime for kids during the summer months in rural West Rockhill. (Courtesy of Jill Cardell.)

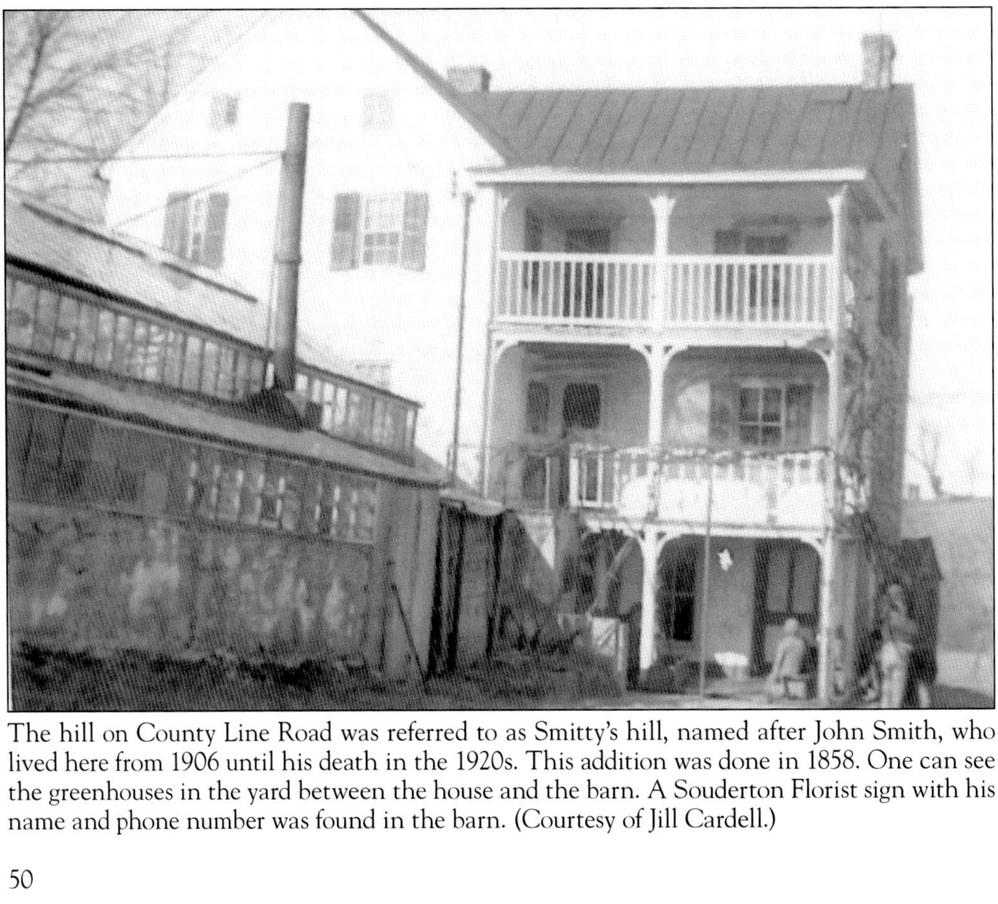

The hill on County Line Road was referred to as Smitty's hill, named after John Smith, who lived here from 1906 until his death in the 1920s. This addition was done in 1858. One can see the greenhouses in the yard between the house and the barn. A Souderton Florist sign with his name and phone number was found in the barn. (Courtesy of Jill Cardell.)

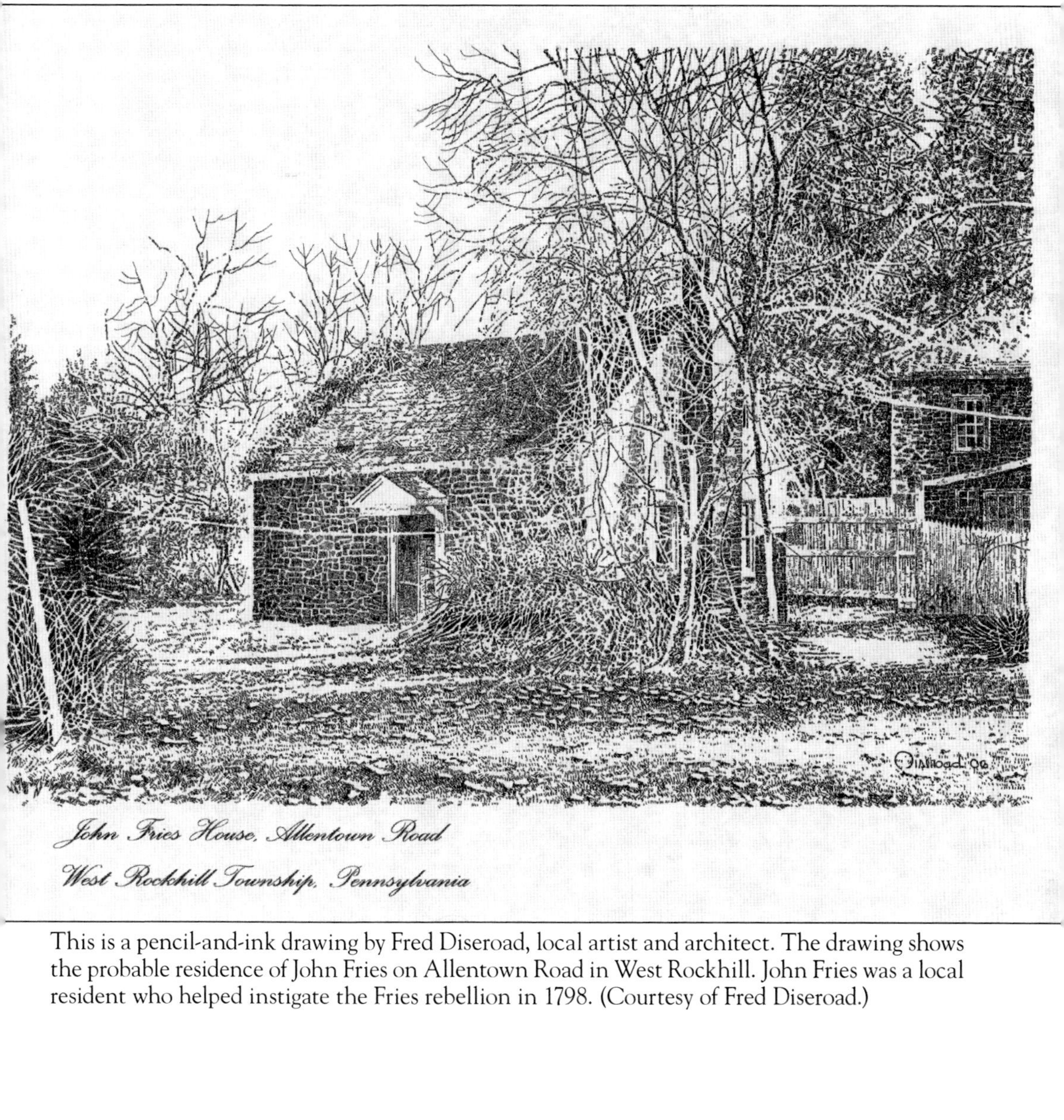

This is a pencil-and-ink drawing by Fred Diseroad, local artist and architect. The drawing shows the probable residence of John Fries on Allentown Road in West Rockhill. John Fries was a local resident who helped instigate the Fries rebellion in 1798. (Courtesy of Fred Diseroad.)

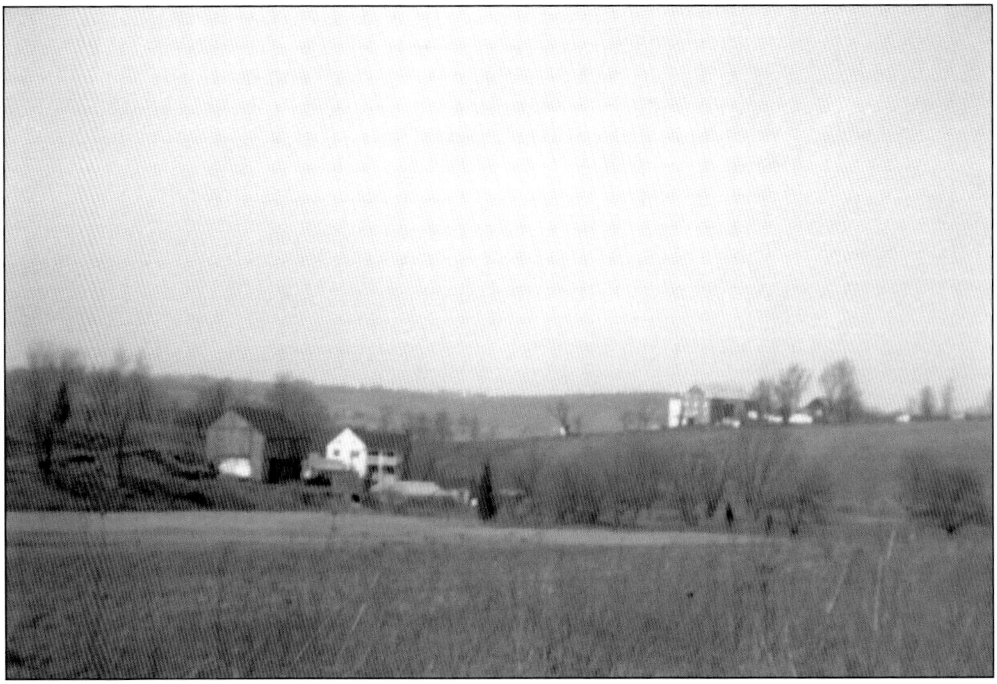

This 1937 photograph illustrates how wide open and rural West Rockhill was. The farm on the top of the hill was owned by the Wile family. The property is now owned by a local quarry and is scheduled for demolition. (Courtesy of Jill Cardell.)

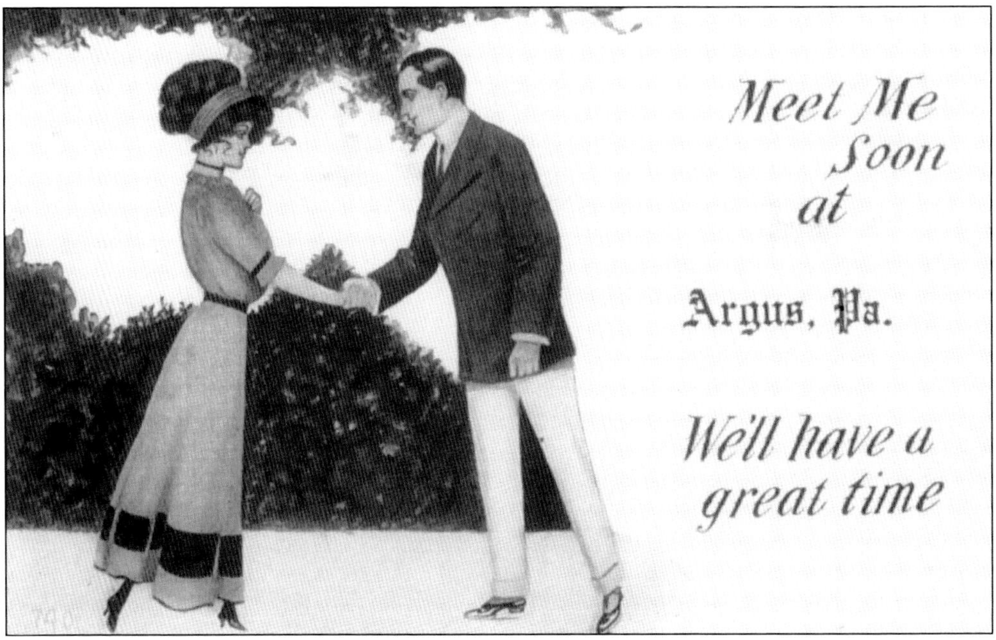

This is a local postcard from Argus, Pennsylvania, dated from 1929. (Courtesy of WRHS.)

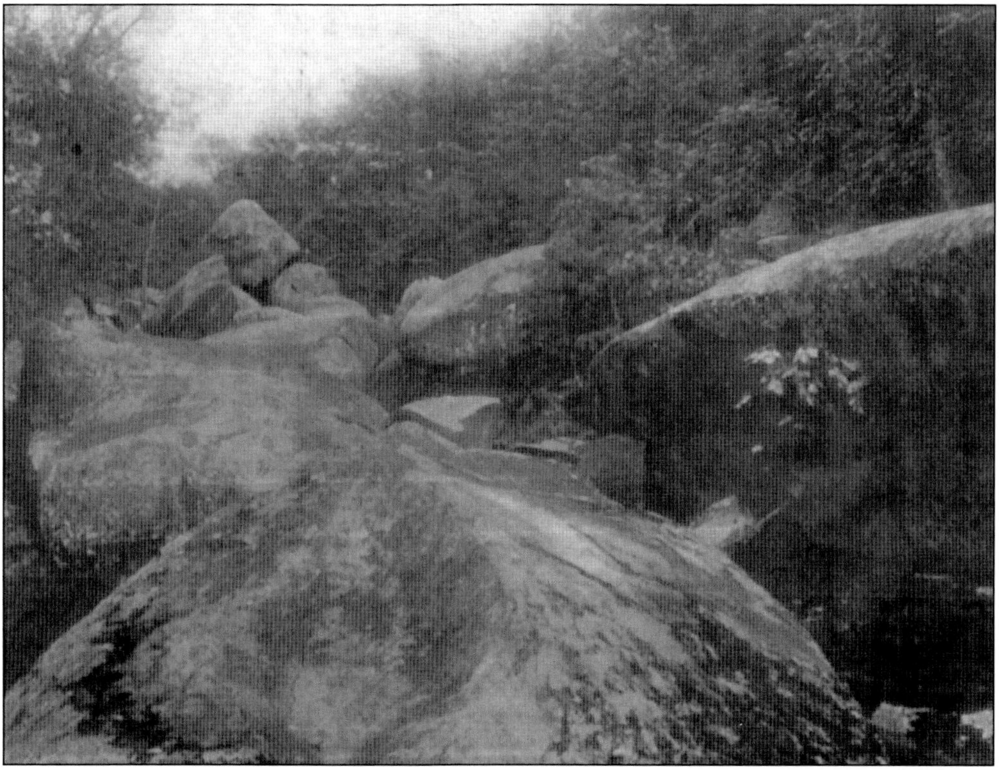

Rocky Dale Miracle Rocks was located in West Rockhill. Throughout both townships, there are many locations that are connected to Native American legends of healing powers. (Courtesy of Rhoda Clark.)

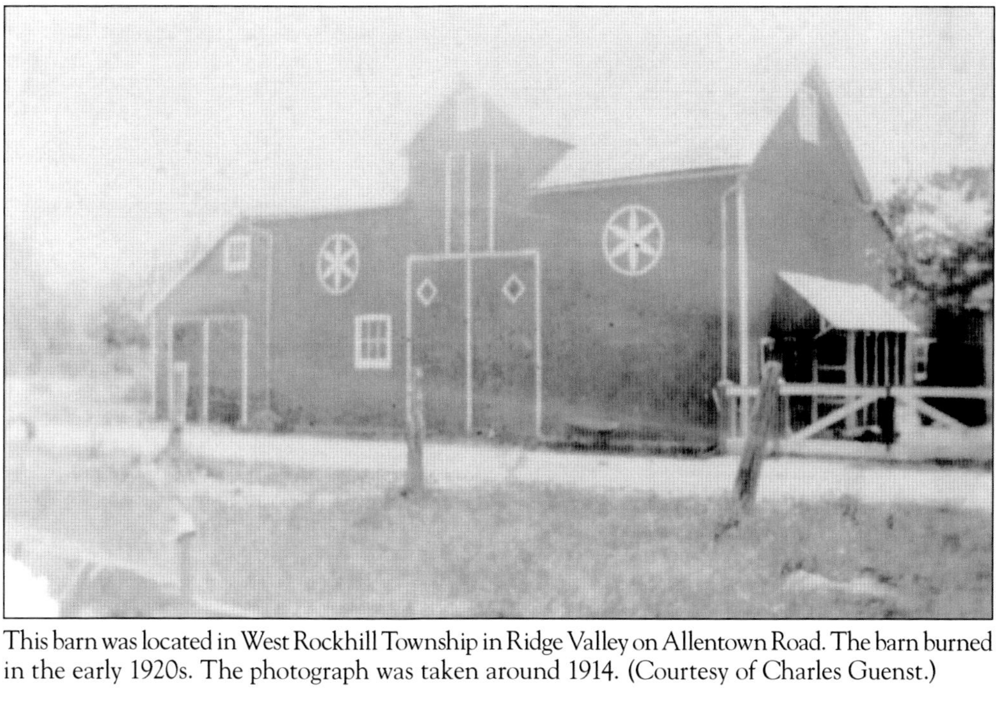

This barn was located in West Rockhill Township in Ridge Valley on Allentown Road. The barn burned in the early 1920s. The photograph was taken around 1914. (Courtesy of Charles Guenst.)

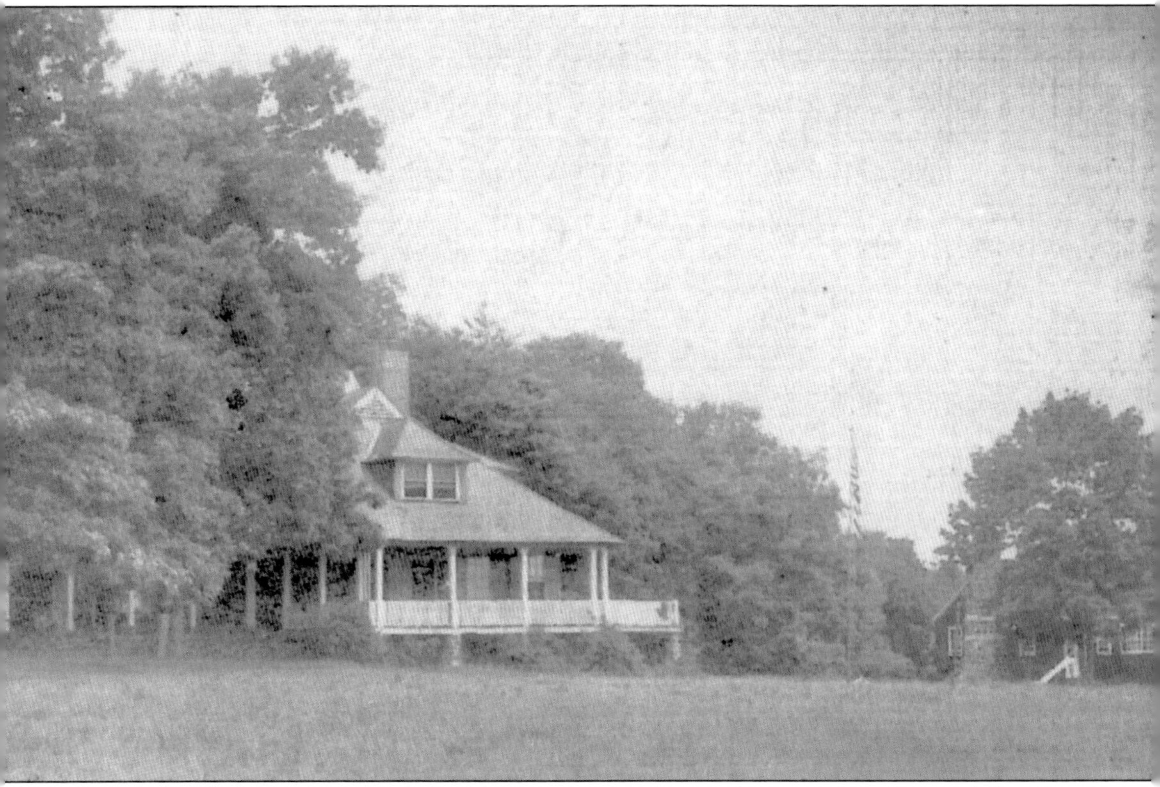

Nestled on a partially wooded 15-acre tract overlooking the Branch Valley, Holiday House was a fresh-air retreat. Each summer, it provided numerous two-week-long vacations for the Philadelphia parish's impoverished women and children. The property was sold in the late 1960s to a joint West Rockhill Township and Sellersville Borough commission authority. In 1970, an Olympic-sized public swimming pool was opened on the Washington Avenue site. (Courtesy of Timothy D. Hufnagle.)

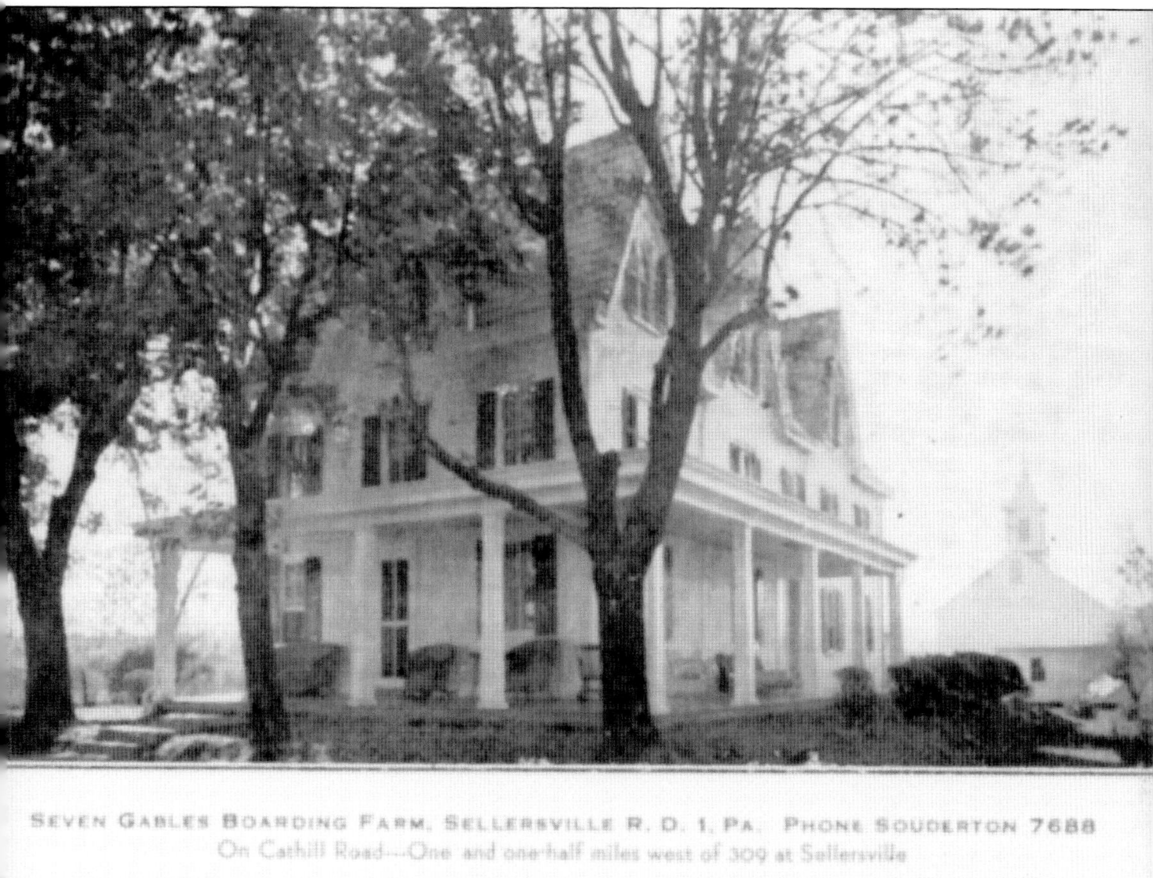

The origins and architect of West Rockhill's own House of the Seven Gables are shrouded in mystery. Located on the old bend of Cathill Road (now known as Lonely Road), this 20-room edifice had its share of interesting tenants over the years. In 1916, the farmhouse became part of a 510-acre project known as the Artman Home for Lutherans, which, in 1924, relocated its operations to Ambler. During the 1920s and 1930s, a Scranton-based engineer, William Wilhelm, owned the house and surrounding farmland, utilizing them as a summer resort. Then in 1938, the infamous pro-Nazi Deutschhorst Country Club (otherwise known as the German-American Bund) acquired the farm and used it as part of their "recreational" grounds until the group was disbanded in 1942. The house was then used as a tourist house (as seen in this postcard image). In modern times, the property has been used as an emu farm and a year-round private residence. (Courtesy of Timothy D. Hufnagle.)

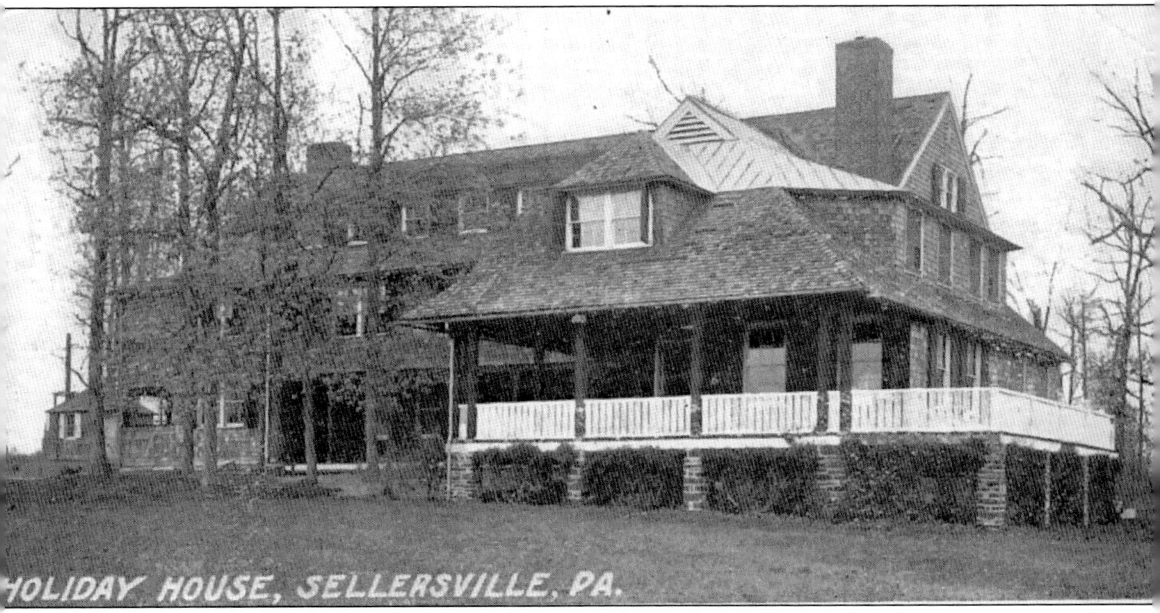

In 1895, the Episcopal Church of the Holy Trinity of Rittenhouse Square, Philadelphia, constructed this three-story manor house in West Rockhill. Appropriately named the Holiday House, the home provided accommodations for hundreds of city guests each summer for over 70 years. Sellersville photographer Joseph W. Daub captured this view in 1906. It was published as a postcard by the town's newspaper, the *Sellersville Herald*. (Courtesy of Timothy D. Hufnagle.)

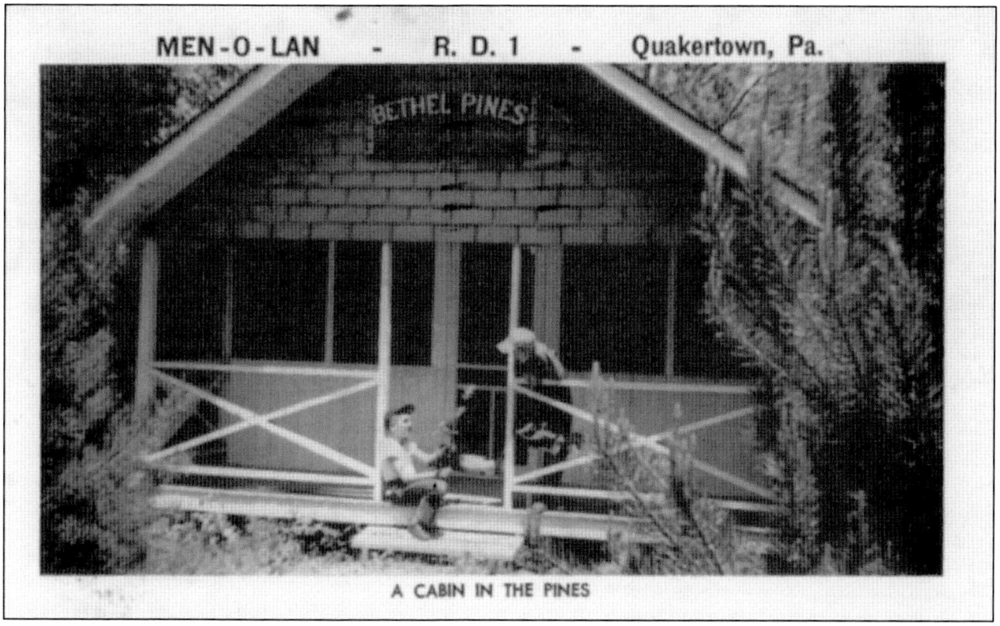

Camp Men-O-Lan, located in West Rockhill Township on Doerr Road, is the oldest continually operated Mennonite camp in North America and was established in 1941. The name derives from the denomination Mennonite and the name Landis, who was the landowner who donated 174 acres for this camp. The camp has 11 cabins and many other recreational activities. (Courtesy of Timothy D. Hufnagle.)

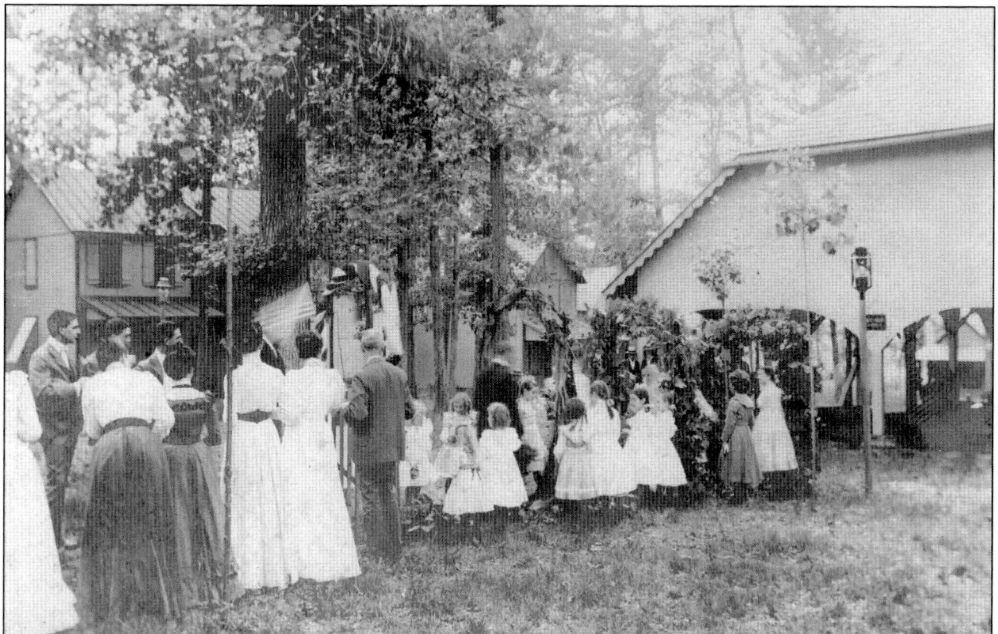

Campers gather for a celebration at Highland Park in this undated photograph. The Highland Park camp meeting is located in rural West Rockhill township at the corner of Bethlehem Pike and Highland Park Road. There are a total of 57 buildings built between 1896 and 1936 on the wooded camp meeting grounds. (Coutesy of Sellersville Museum.)

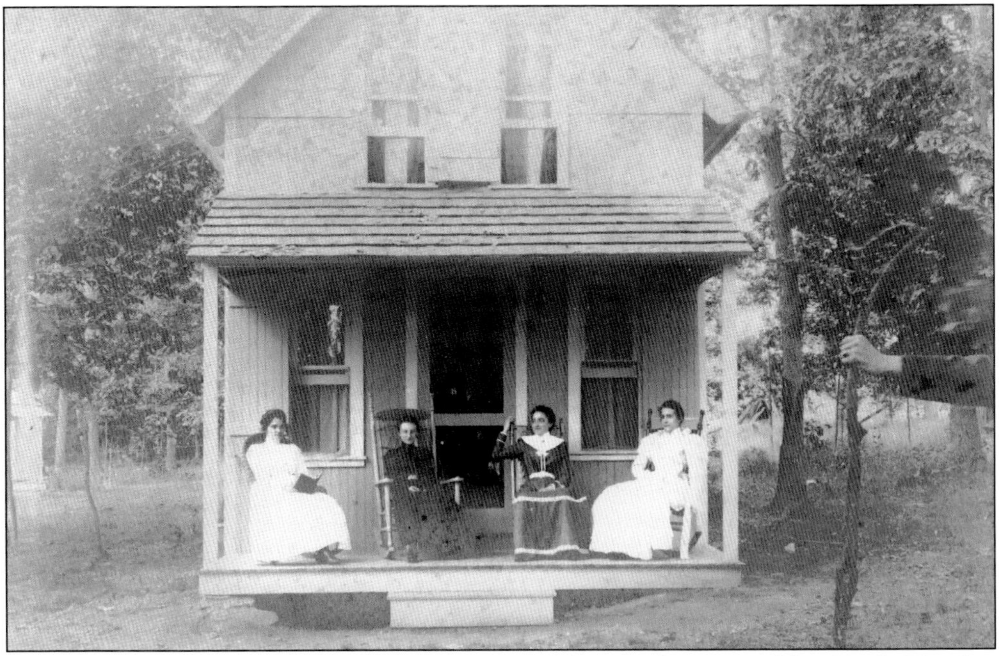

Unidentified women sit on the front porch of one of the 57 cabins at Highland Park. The first camp meetings were held in 1797. After the summer harvest was completed, families would gather to hold Christian meetings, to sing, and to socialize. This photograph was taken in the mid-1800s after small cottages were built to accommodate participants. (Courtesy of Sellersville Museum.)

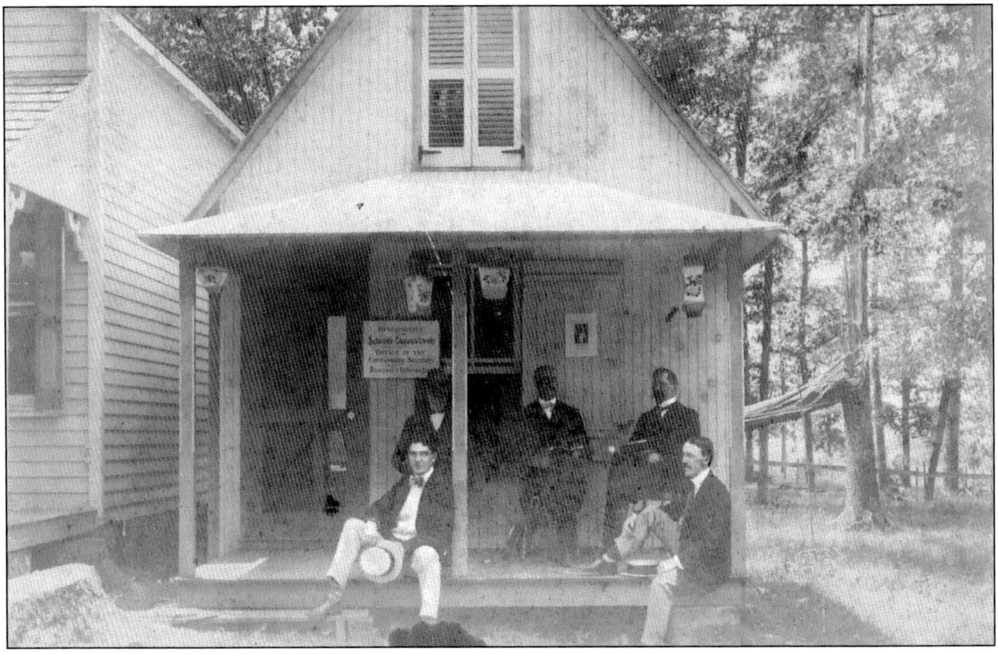

Unidentified gentlemen socialize at Highland Park around 1850. By the mid-1800s, Christian family camping became a national phenomenon and was an alternative to secular middle class resorts. Prior to the building of the cabins seen in this photograph, participants would bring their own bedding, provisions, and tents. (Courtesy of Sellersville Museum.)

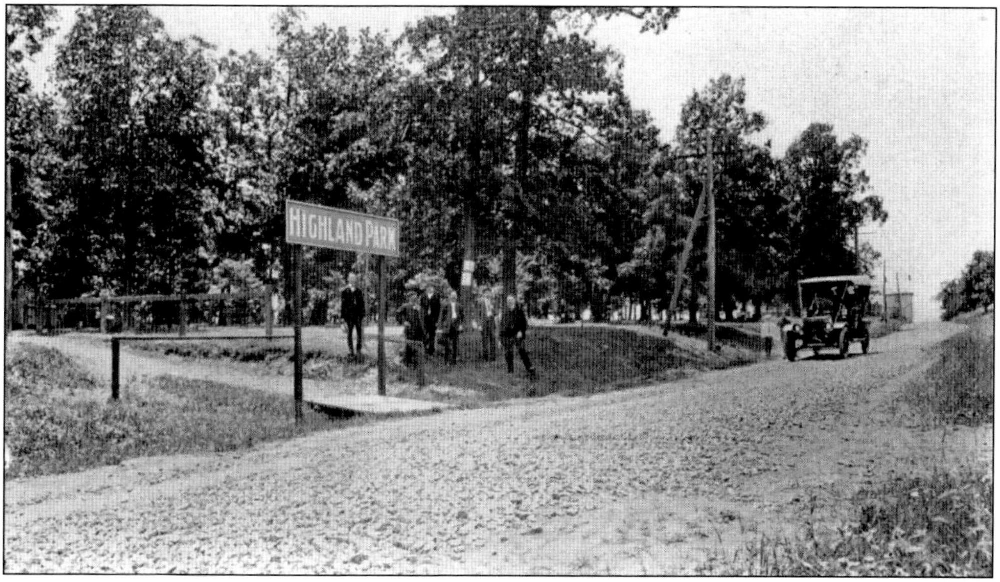

This c. 1907 Berkemeyer postcard is of Highland Park, West Rockhill, on what was than Derstine Road. (Courtesy of WRHS.)

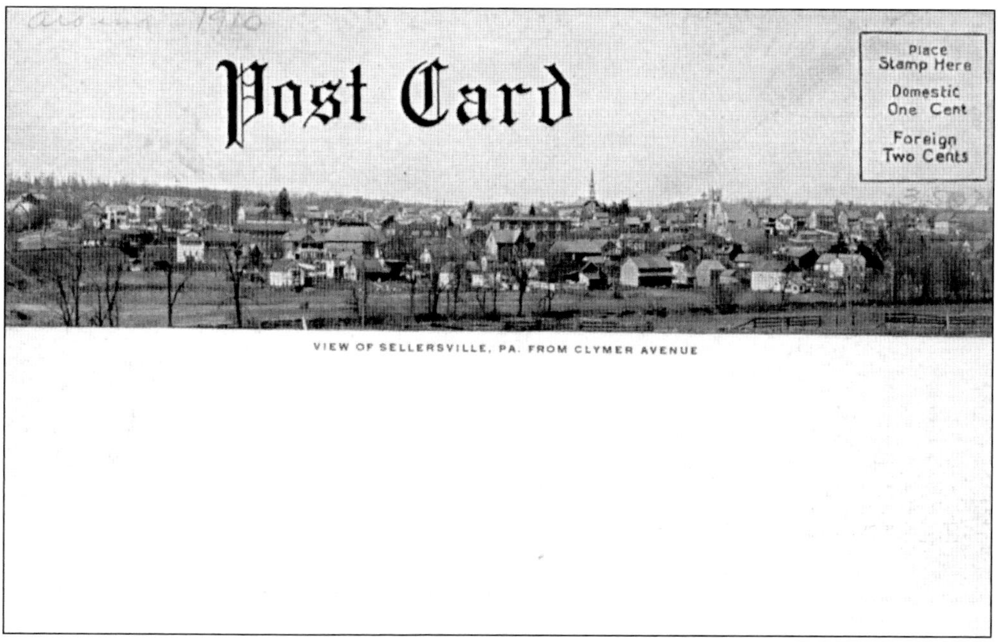

Berkemyer decorated his postcards with landscape photographs of nearby villages. This particular postcard is a photograph of Sellersville taken from Clymer Avenue. (Courtesy of WRHS.)

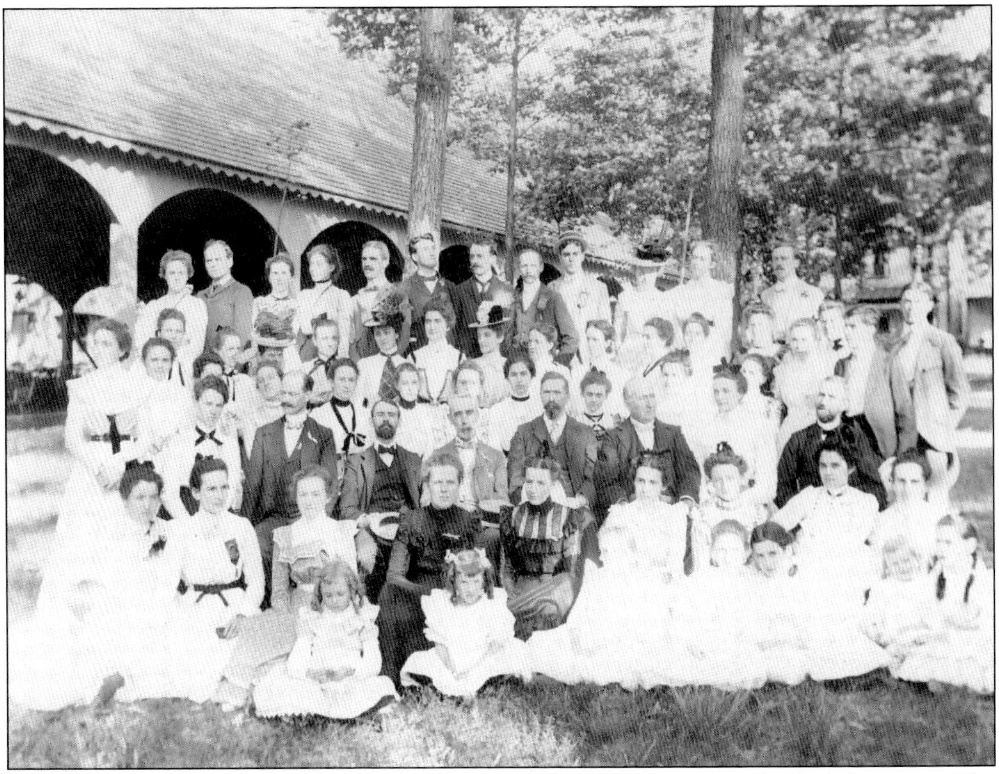

Highland Park participants gather for a group photograph in the latter half of the 1800s. The first official Highland Park camp meeting was held at Destines Grove in 1895. (Courtesy Sellersville Museum.)

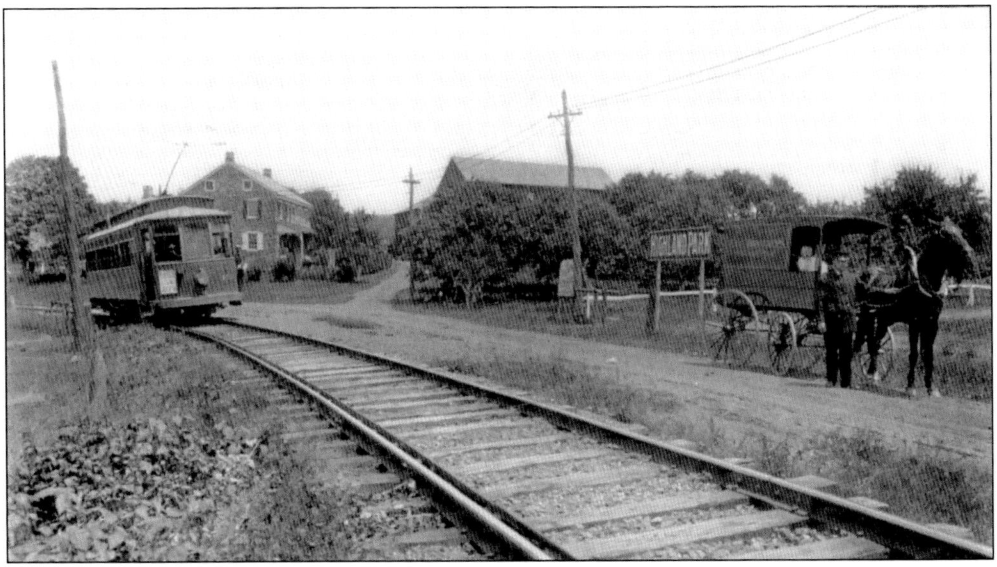

This c. 1906 Berkemeyer postcard captures the trolley coming in to pick up or drop off passengers in West Rockhill Township. A walking trail to the left of the tracks leads to Highland Park. To the right is a traveling merchant from Lit Brothers Department Store, located in Philadelphia. (Courtesy of WRHS.)

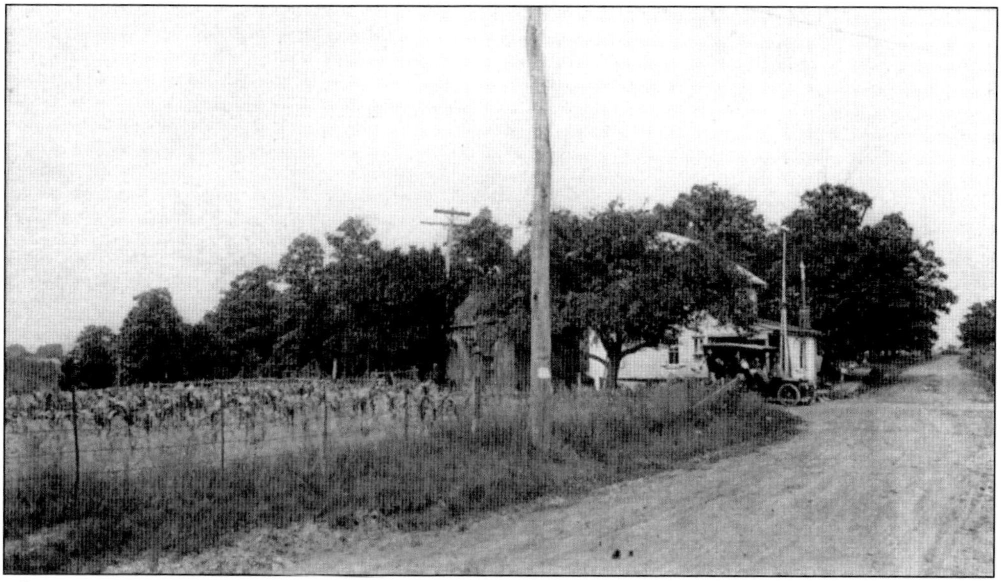

This c. 1907 Berkemeyer photograph captures a car as it is leaving the south-end tollgate on Derstine Road from Highland Park in West Rockhill Township. (Courtesy of WRHS.)

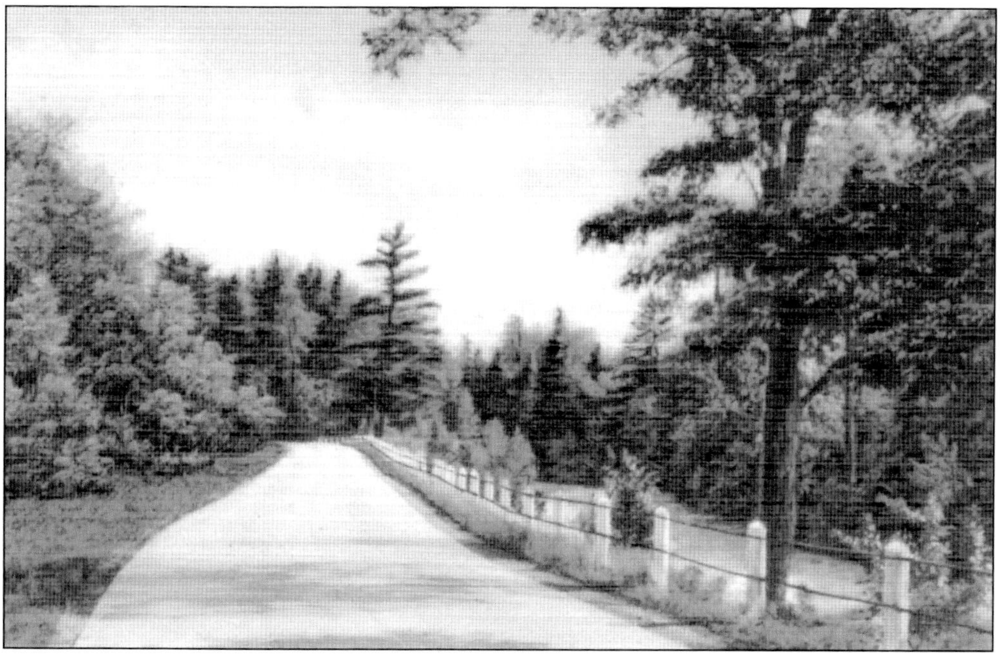

This postcard shows a picturesque view of Almont in West Rockhill Township. It was sent from the Almont Post Office. (Courtesy of WRHS.)

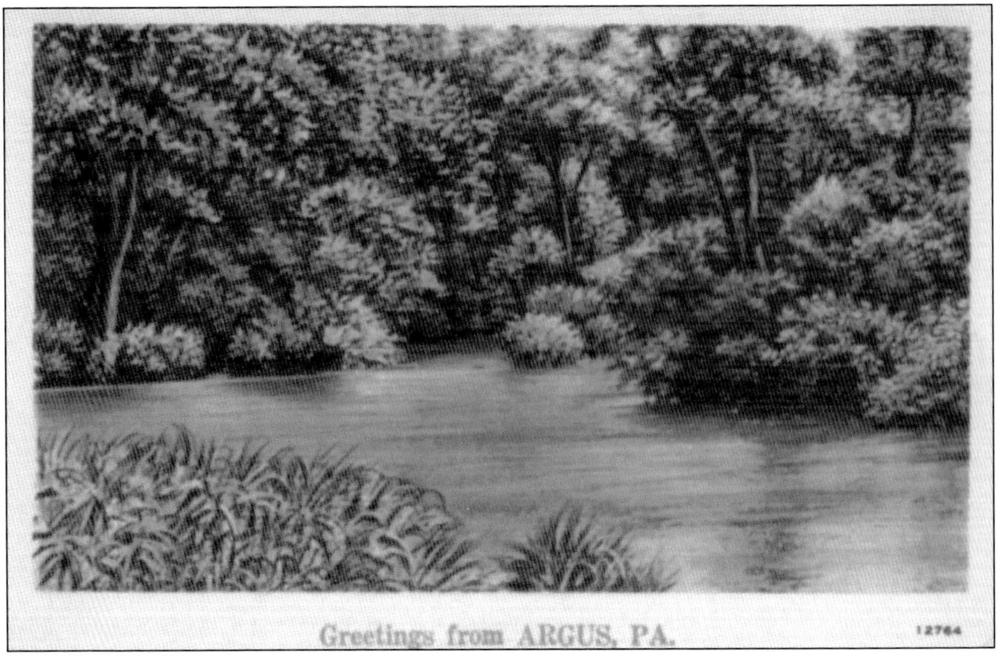

This c. 1944 postcard is an example of why people came from Philadelphia to Rockhill to vacation and get away from city life. It was sent from the Argus Post Office, which was closed in 1953 on the same day as the Almont Post Office. (Courtesy of WRHS.)

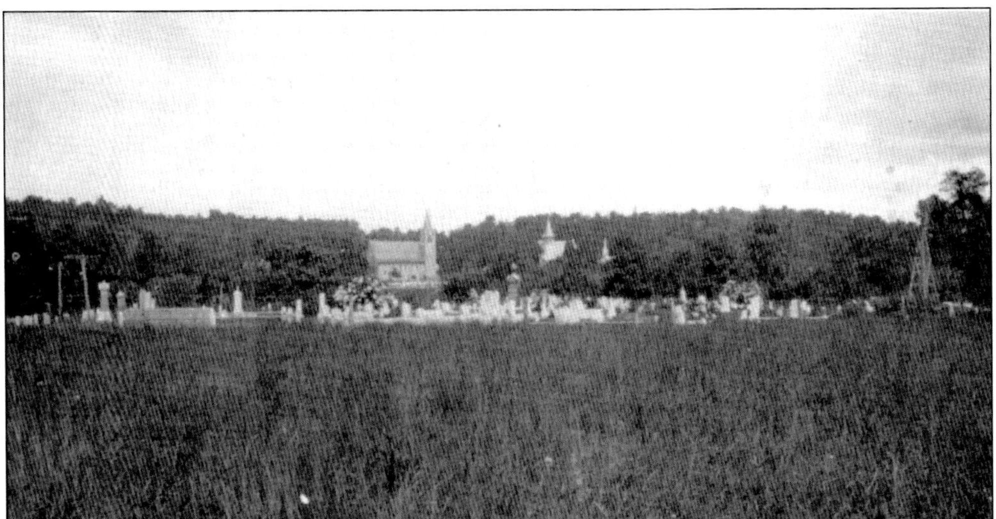

This is a c. 1920 Berkemeyer postcard of the Ridge Valley and its churches as seen from Argus, West Rockhill. (Courtesy of Charles Guenst.)

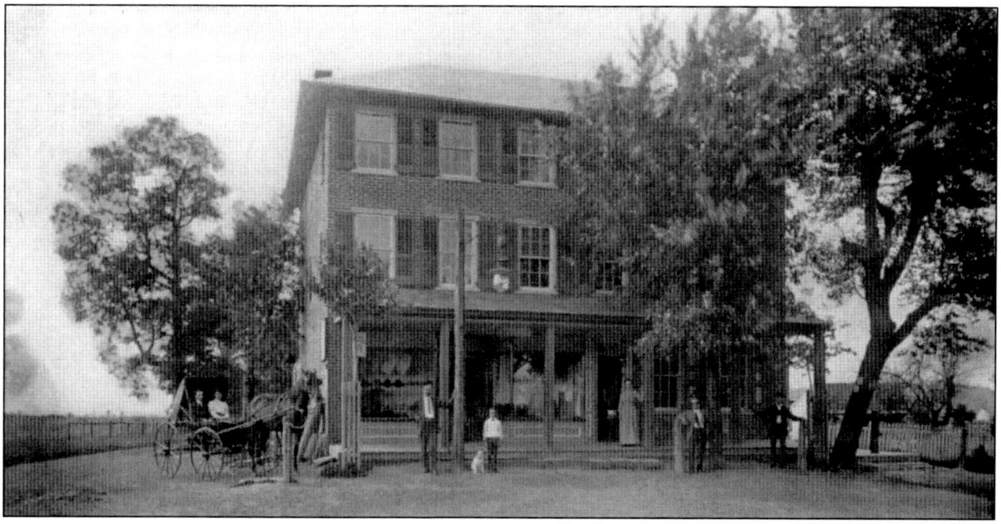

The General Store of O.M. Nase and the Almont Post Office are pictured around 1920 in this Berkemeyer postcard. Berkemyer printed 300 different views of Upper Berks, Upper Montgomery, and surrounding counties. (Courtesy of Charles Guenst.)

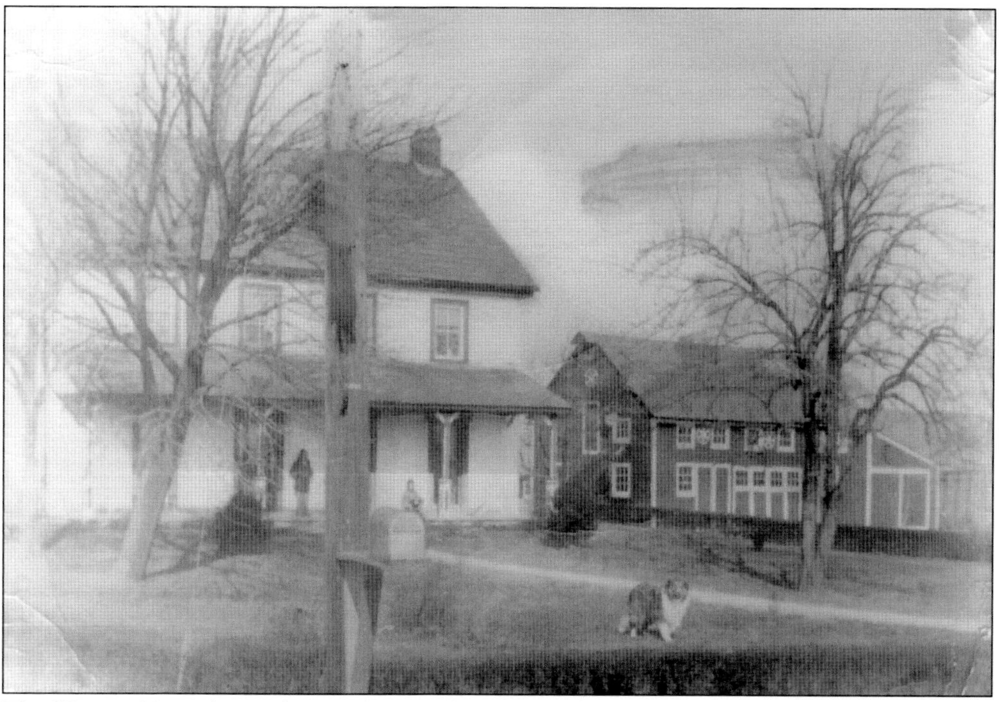

The Klinger Farm, located on Ridge Road, is pictured in 1930. The township purchased the property, and the house is now used as the regional police department. Elsie and Alfred Klinger stand on the porch watching the family pet. The barn to the left is no longer standing. (Courtesy of Emil Klinger Jr.)

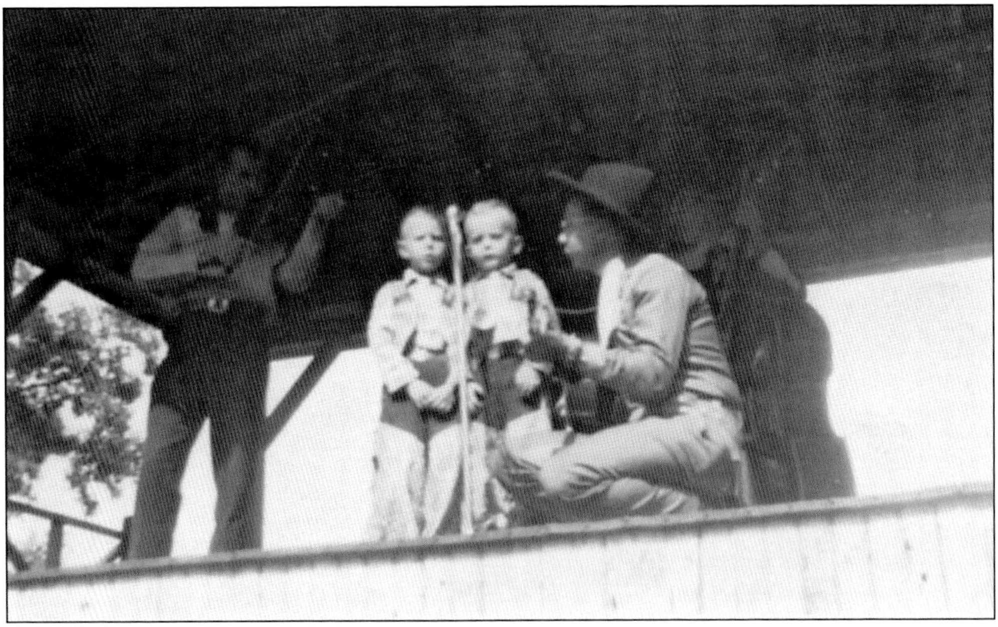

The Klinger family band are at a performance in 1949 at camp Men-O- Lan. Pictured are, from left to right, Emil Jr., Richard, and their father, Emil Klinger. The Klingers started performing in 1936 and still perform at local events, camps, and nursing homes. The band consists of Emil and Richard Klinger, Phil Grida, and Walt Colb. The Klingers have also added a member from another generation, Emil IV. (Courtesy of Emil Klinger Jr.)

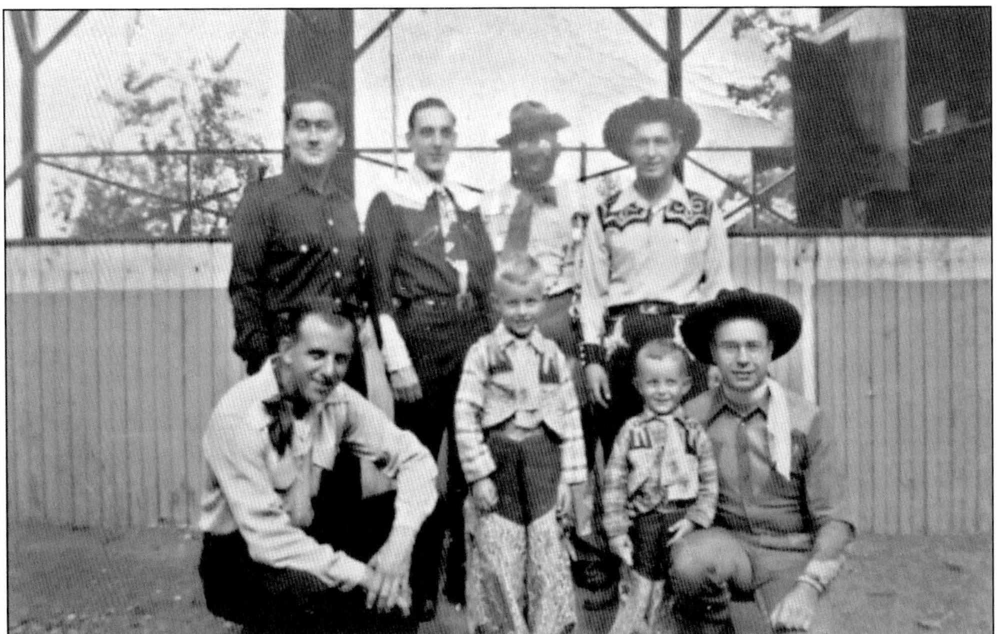

This is a group photograph of Emil Kiplinger and the Happy Rangers after a performance at Men-O-Lan Park in 1949. Pictured are, from left to right, (first row) Frank Shearer, Emil Klinger Jr., Richard Klinger, and Emil Klinger; (second row) Phil Grida, Art Trauger, Bob Sheetz, and Warren Kemmerer (Slim). (Courtesy of Emil Klinger Jr.)

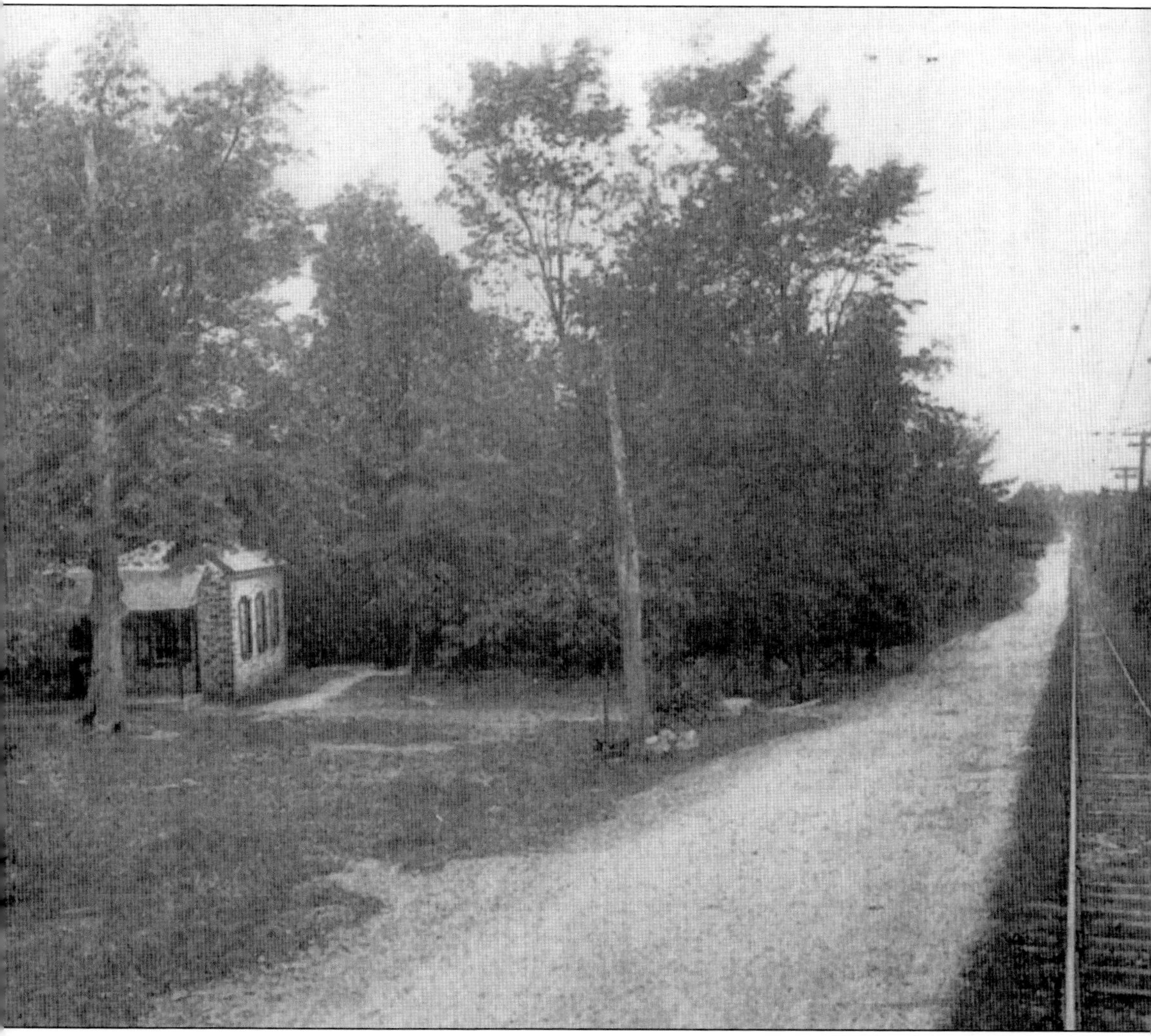

As it is known today, the Old Bethlehem Pike was once a major thoroughfare between Philadelphia and the Lehigh Valley. Pictured in this c. 1910 photograph, the stretch of road north of Perkasie continues to serve as a boundary line dividing East and West Rockhill. The trolley tracks following the Liberty Bell's route utilized the pike's right-of-way to traverse the countryside. On the left is the Rockwild Union Sunday school. (Courtesy of Timothy D. Hufnagle.)

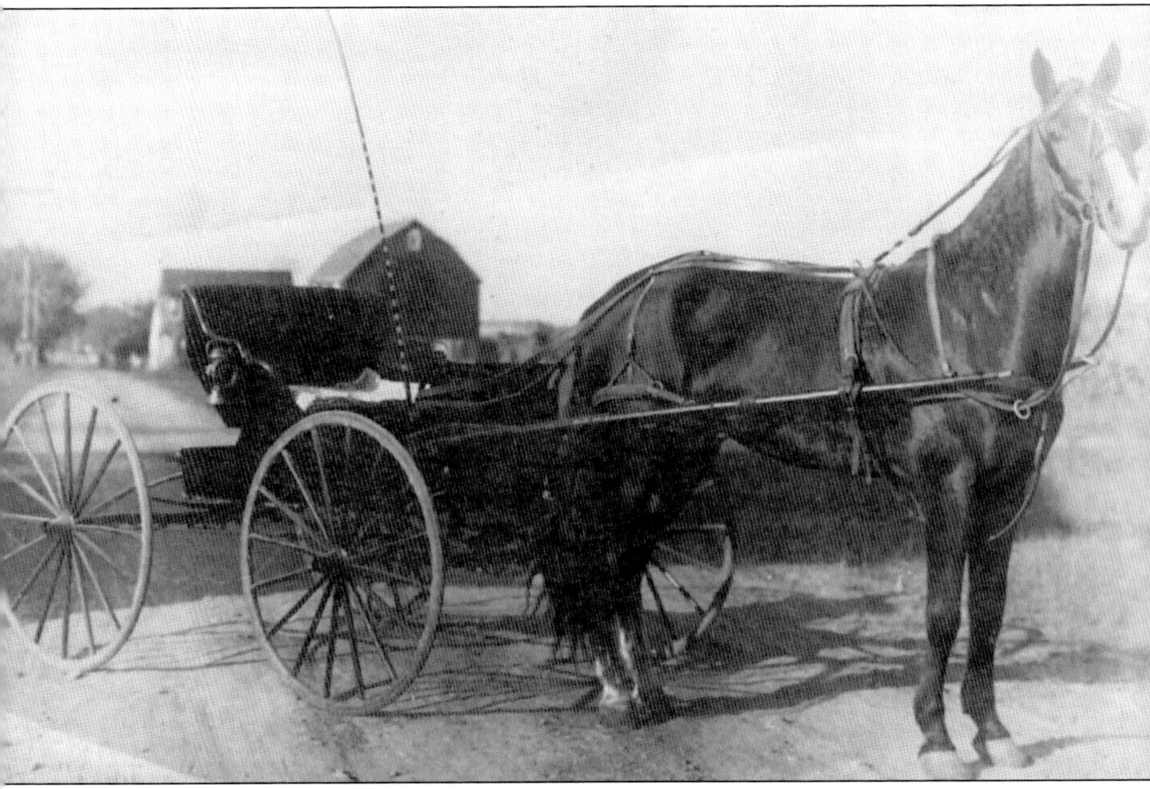

In 1915, Charles Batman of West Rockhill took this photograph, had it printed as a postcard, and sent it to his Perkasie friend, Howard Long. The horse and carriage are posed on the Ridge Road in front of Batman's house in West Rockhill. This view faces west towards the Naceville Hotel. The large barn and house in the background once stood near the intersection of Ridge and County Line Roads. (Courtesy of Timothy D. Hufnagle.)

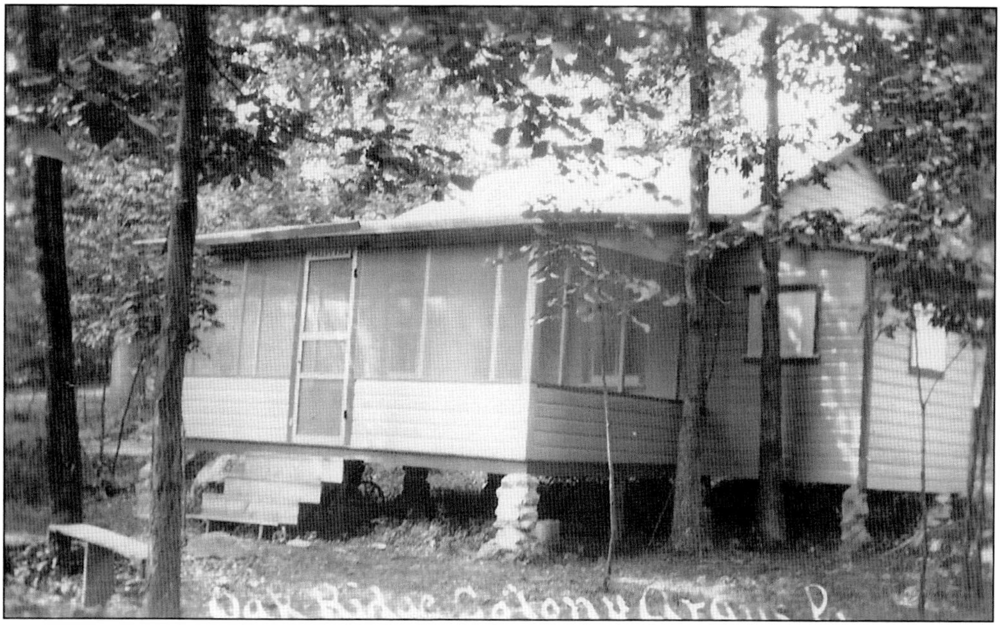

The Oak Ridge Colony located in Argus was a retreat like many in the Rockhill area. Pictured above is one of the many cabins at Oak Ridge Colony. Pictured below is the scene from Oak Ridge Colony; the twin churches of Ridge Valley can be seen in the background. (Courtesy of Timothy D. Hufnagle.)

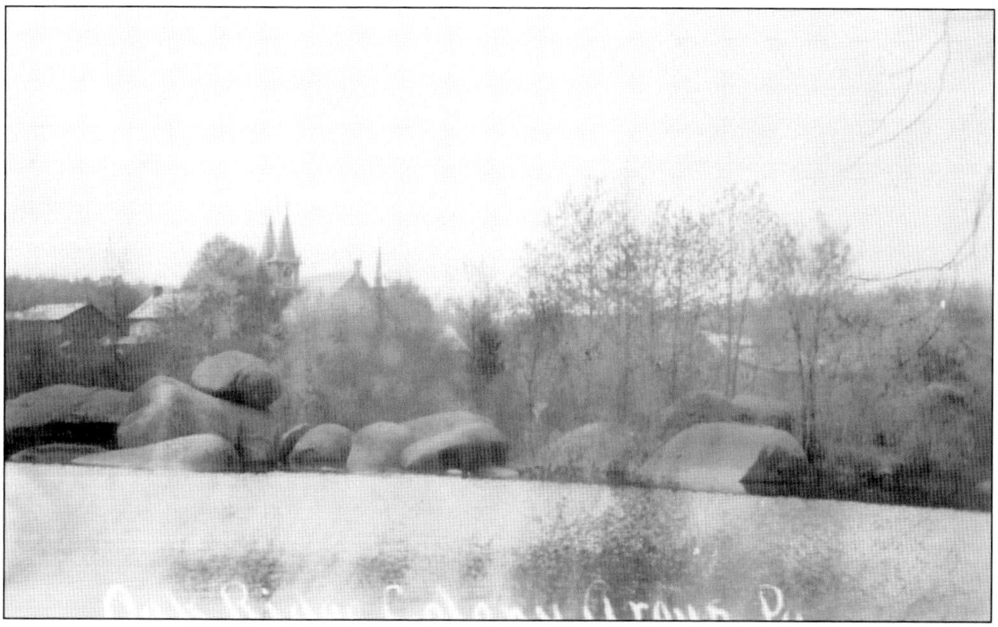

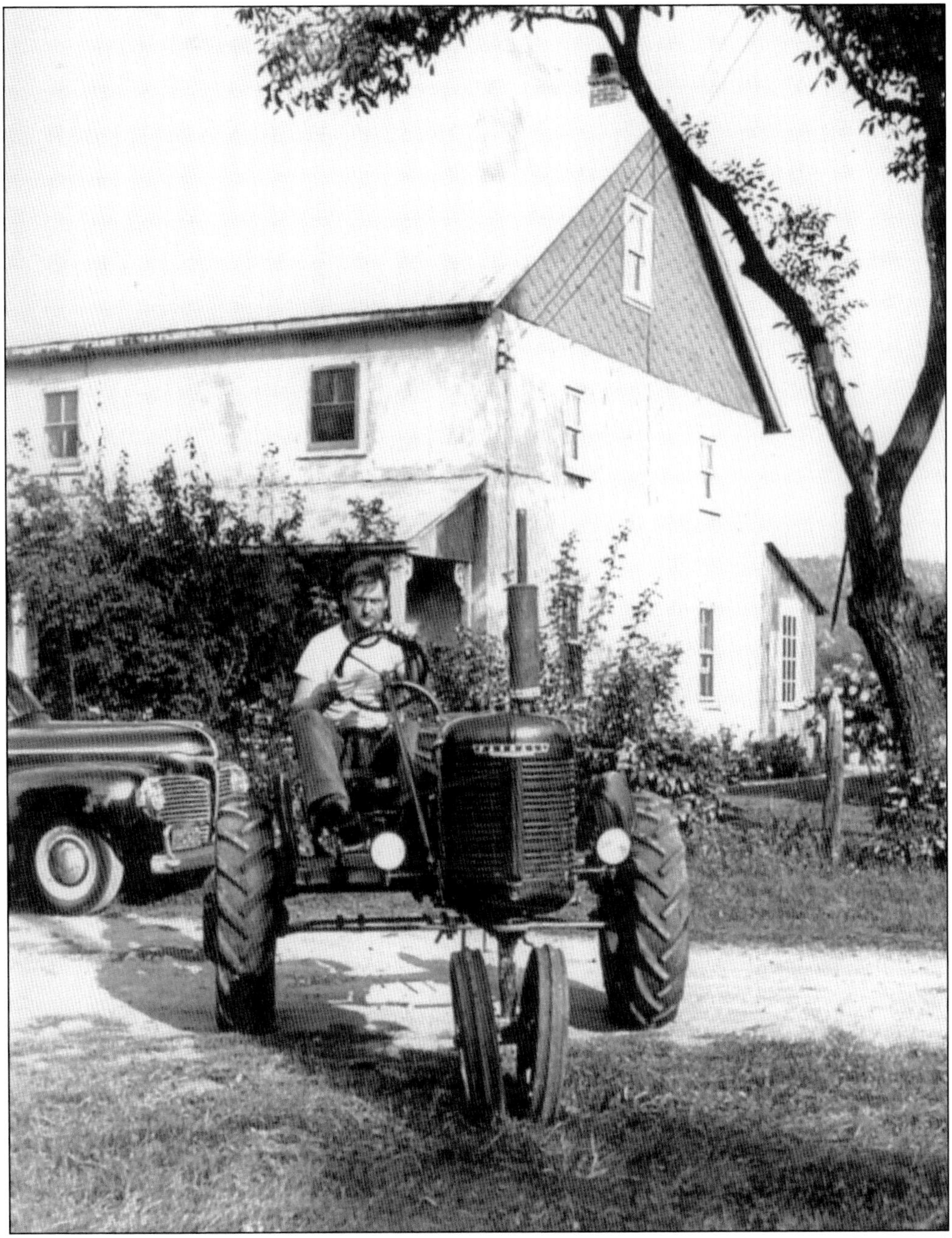

In this c. 1950 photograph is a farm on Schukraft Road in West Rockhill. (Courtesy of WRHS.)

Four

Taverns, Mills, and Bridges

Hotels and eateries were not just a fixture of the past; they are common today. Many are small, quaint establishments providing personal home-style meals with a touch of history. These establishments have often been in the townships for more than a century. Some are here a much shorter time, but they all provide an opportunity to socialize, relax, and enjoy a home-cooked meal.

What comes to mind when thinking of the tranquility of the past and the scenic beauty of the countryside? Covered bridges are the essence of days gone by—days of innocence. Known as "kissing bridges," they were shadowy havens where lovers could steal a kiss. Unfortunately, these bridges have been disappearing because of arson and natural weathering. Pennsylvania has 197 covered bridges, more than any other state. Bucks County had 50, but today, only 12 remain. Of those 12, two are located in East Rockhill—Moods Bridge and Sheards Mill Bridge.

Once the mainstay of rural living, mills are also becoming a thing of the past. A typical grain mill had two parts—the actual building and the waterworks. Essential to their operation were streams, which, once dammed, provided the power that ran the waterwheels. What makes a mill recognizable to the general public is usually not the building but the waterwheel. Aside from a waterwheel, there was a millrace, pond, and dam. Ponds had multiple uses, including fishing, swimming, and bathing. The Guenst family was just one family in the area that ran a mill. They ran different types of mills, fully using what was provided by nature. They also sold the goods to the community. The sawmill they operated was rare because it was powered by water; generally only grain mills used water for power. The Guenst family not only milled wood, they also milled and crushed rock. They sold wood to build homes and barns as well as rock for paving.

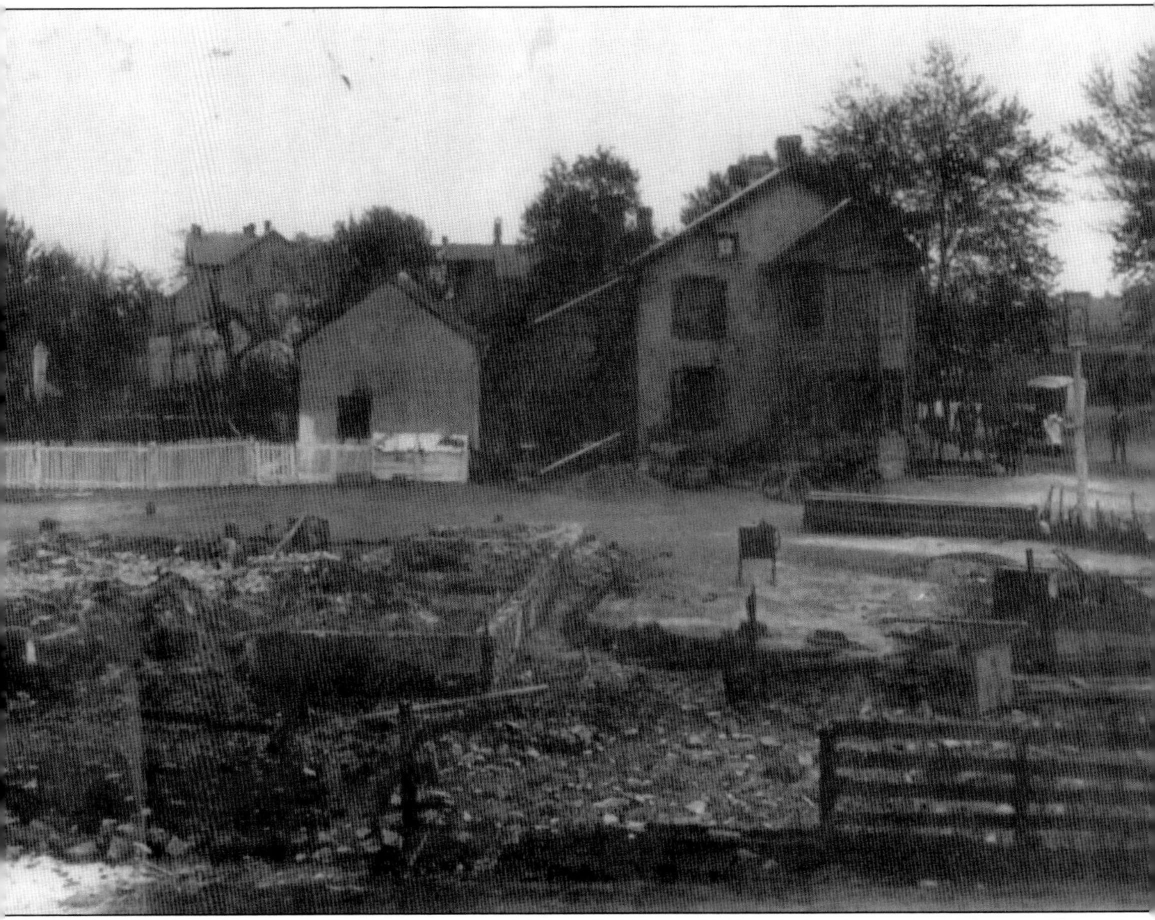

When this photograph was taken in 1898, the livery stable owned by Samuel Smith next door to the Almont Hotel was completely destroyed by fire. The night of the fire, a Rosebud ball was being held in the second story of the building. At 8:30, the fire alarm was given, and the building was evacuated. Luckily, no one was hurt. (Courtesy of WRHS.)

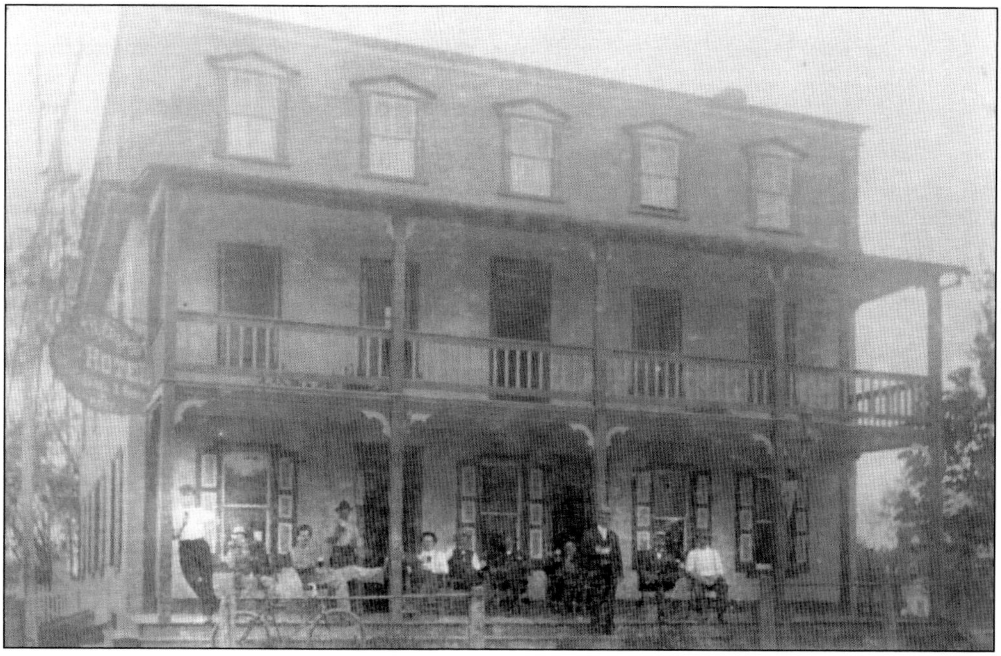

These c. 1900 photographs of the Tylersport Inn, located on the corner of Allentown and Ridge Roads, depict life in this rural township in the late 19th and early 20th centuries. Although the Tylersport Inn was just outside West Rockhill Township, it was well known to all the residents and a place for travelers to stop and get a much needed respite from the dusty road. Tylersport Hotel burned in the early half of the 20th century and was not reconstructed. Today, there is a restaurant on the site. (Both, courtesy of Stella Crouthamel.)

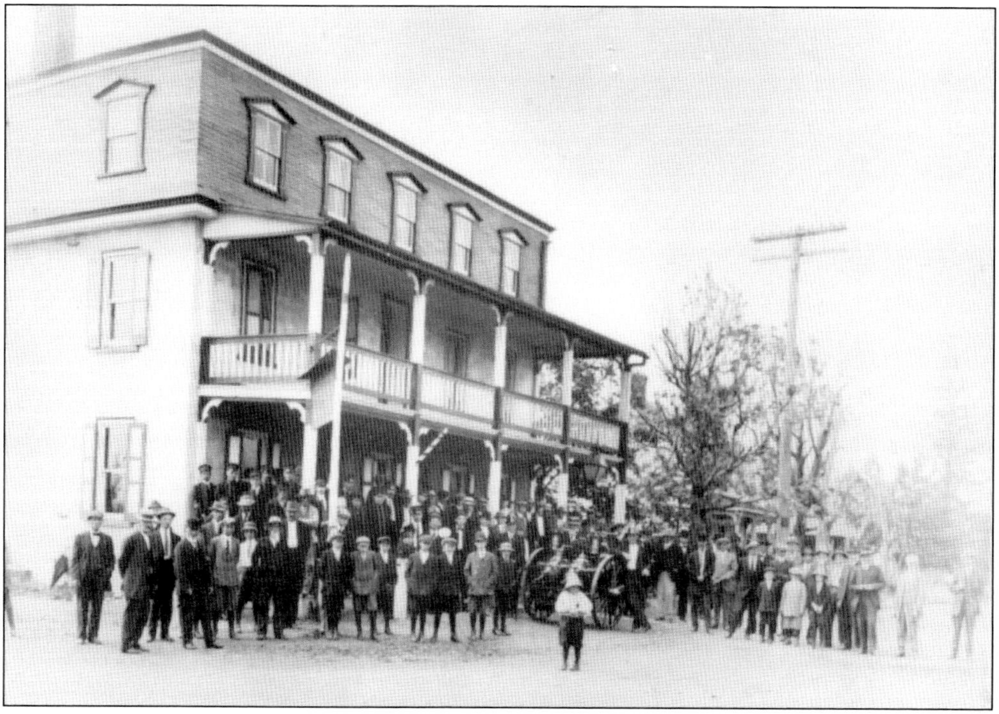

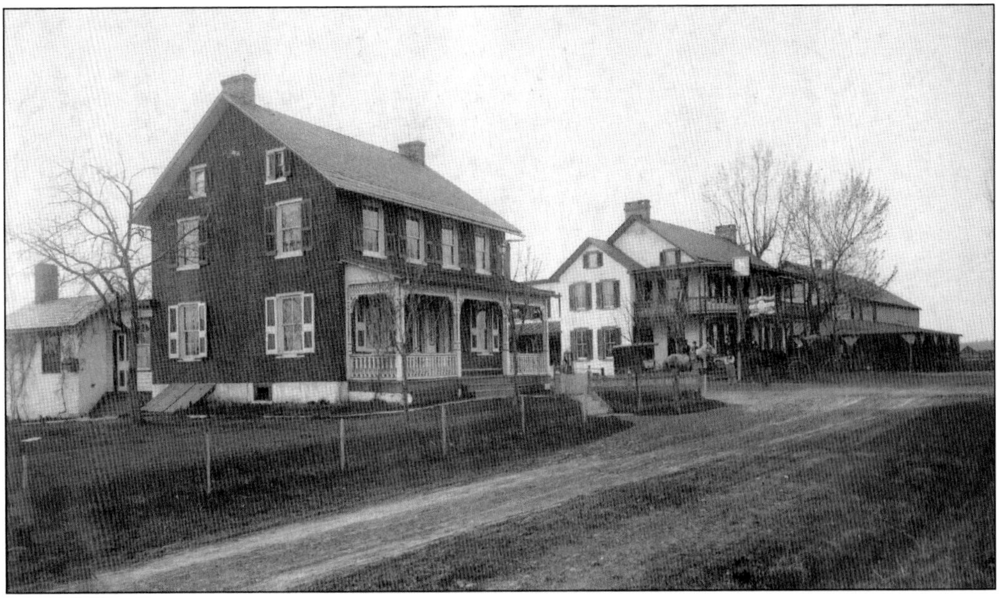

The White Horse Hotel has been a fixture on the corner of Ridge Road and Old Bethlehem Pike since 1757. It has been a gathering place for both locals and travelers from the Revolutionary and Civil Wars up through World War I and World War II and to the present day. The innkeeper's motto was "keep the lights on, the food hot, and the beer cold." Present owners Mike Carey and Dave Aldelsberger have changed the establishment's name to Horse Tavern and Grill, but the traditions remain the same. (Courtesy of Charles Guenst.)

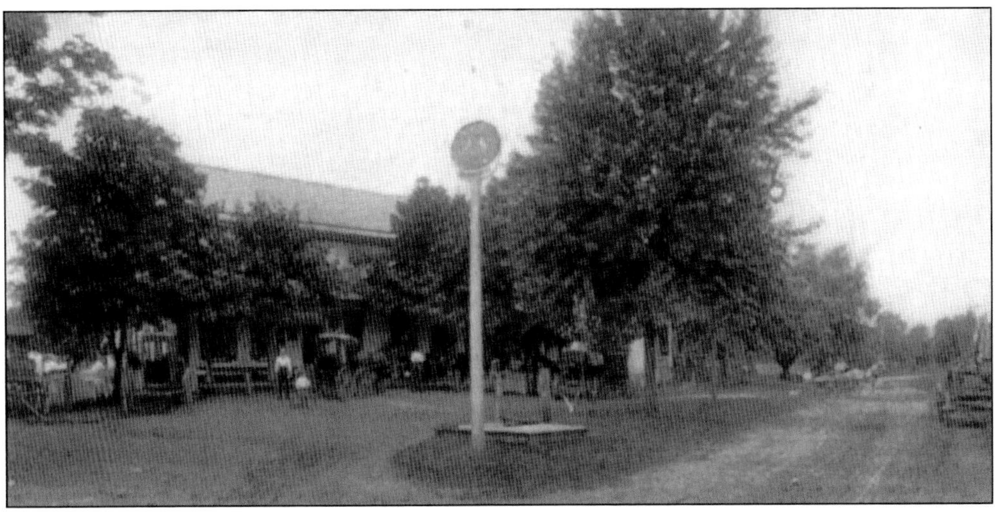

Argus Hotel proprietor William J. Sweeten is pictured around 1900. (Courtesy of Rhoda Clark.)

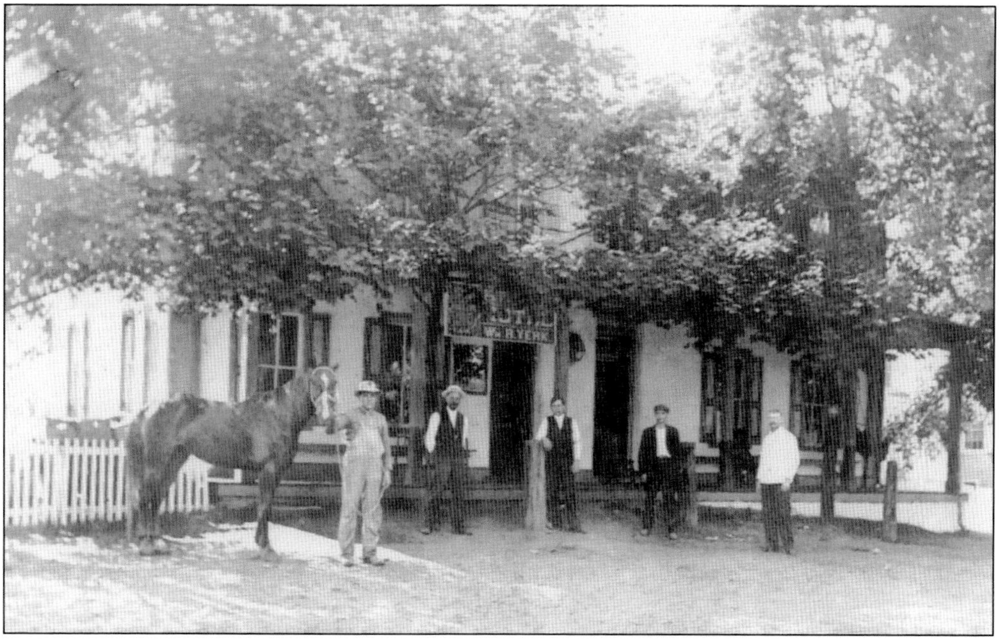

Patrons stand in front of the Argus Hotel; hitching posts line the front of the hotel. (Courtesy of Charles Guenst.)

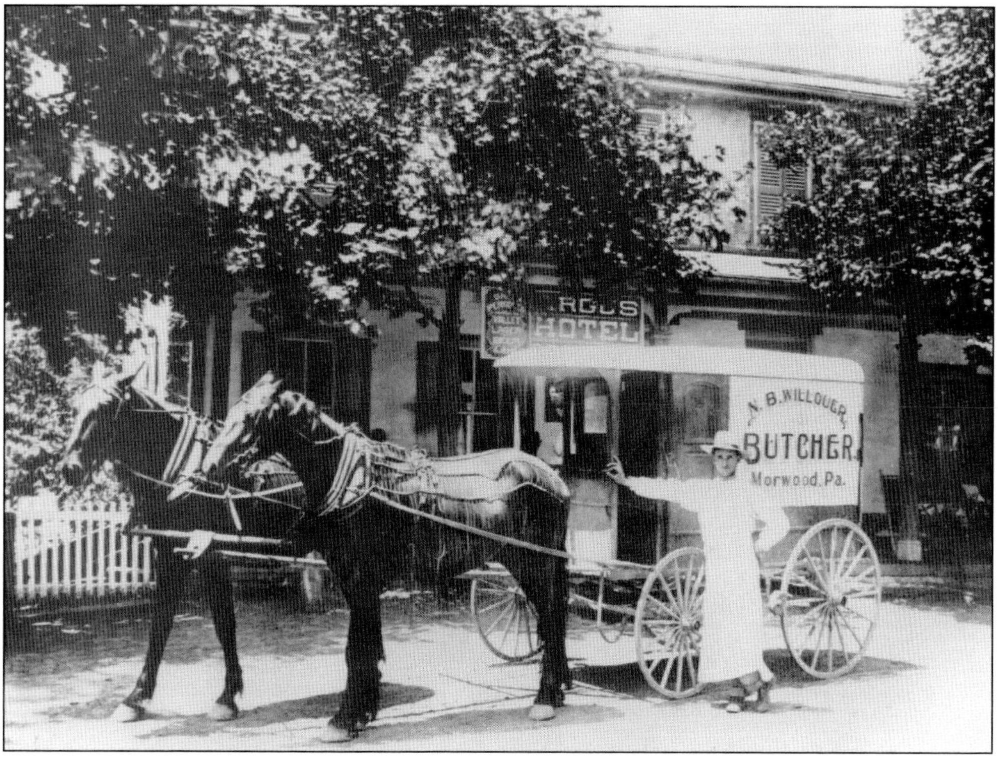

This photograph, taken in the late 1800s, depicts a local butcher from Morwood delivering goods to the Argus Hotel. The hotel, located on Allentown Road, was a frequent stop for locals and travelers alike. (Courtesy of WRHS.)

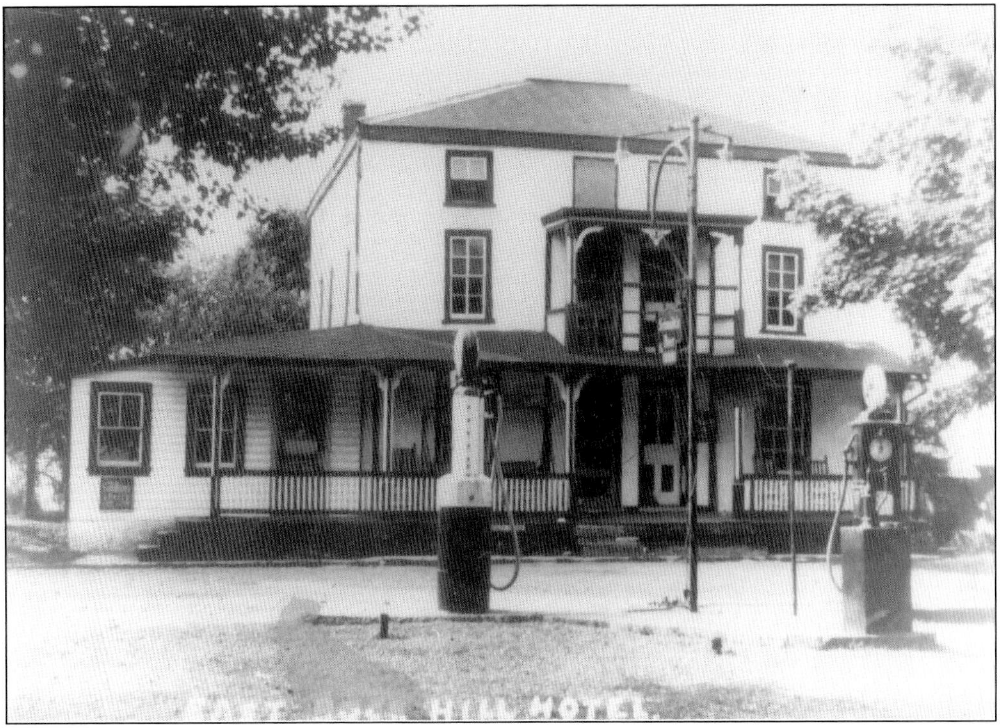

The photograph above was taken in 1948 of the East Rockhill Hotel on Ridge Road in East Rockhill Township. It was owned by Emily and Albert Kaupp. In the photograph above, taken around 1950, the hotel is pictured with its new gas pumps installed. The hotel was purchased by Mr. and Mrs. Emil Jacoby Sr., and became the locally famous Emil's restaurant known for its famous Pennsylvania Dutch dish, oyster pie. Emil Jacoby Jr. later took over from his father. (Both, courtesy Emil Jacoby Jr.)

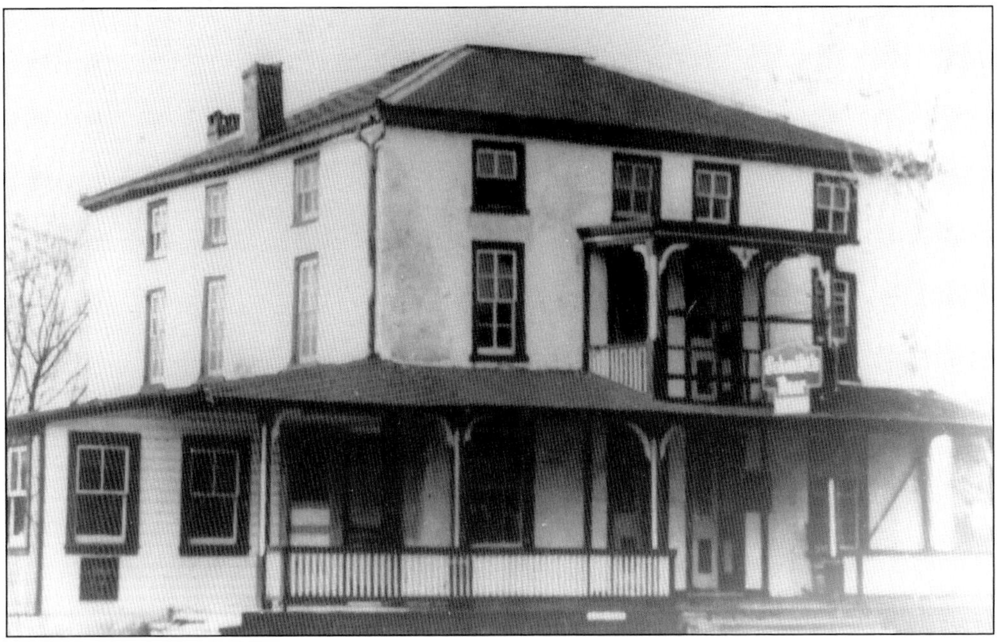

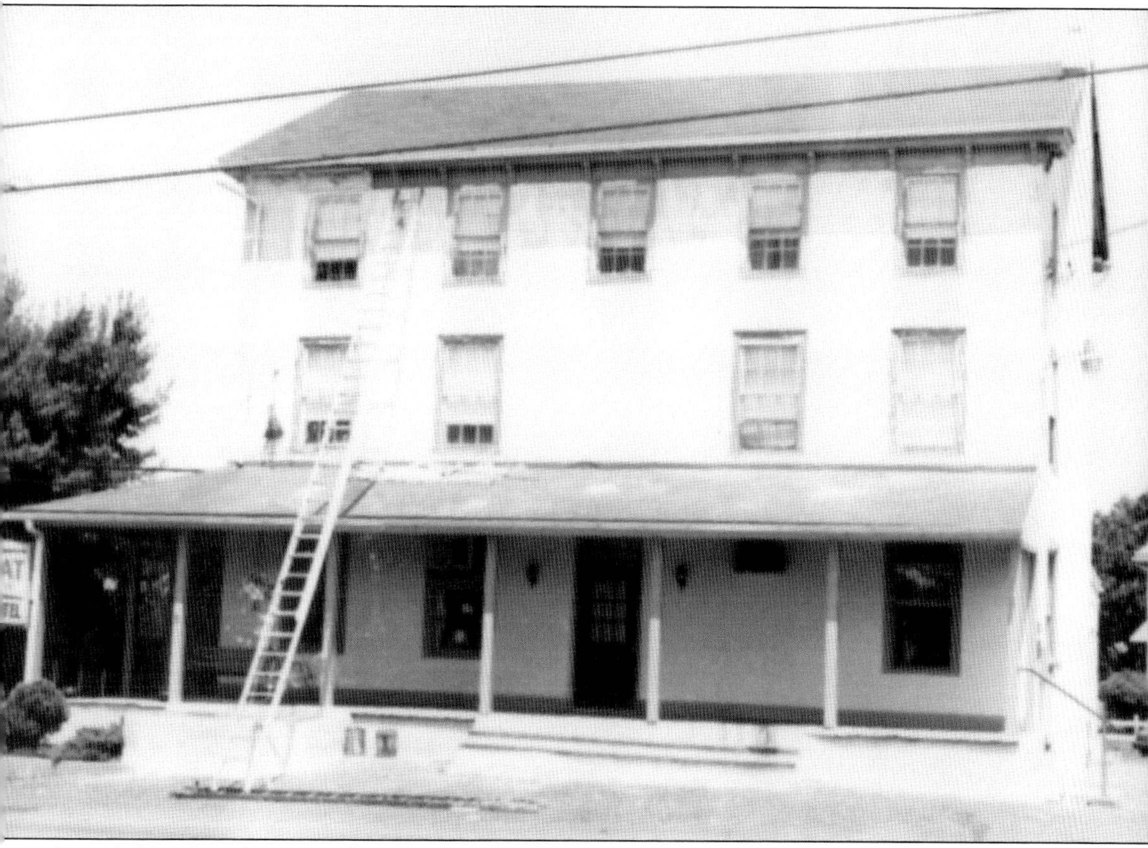

Founded in 1841, the Naceville Hotel, located on Ridge Road in Sellersville, is currently owned by Jim And Zori Croissette III. In this photograph, taken in the late 20th century, repairs are being done to the exterior. At one time, the Naceville Hotel served as a stagecoach stop for travelers to and from Philadelphia. (Courtesy of Charles Guenst.)

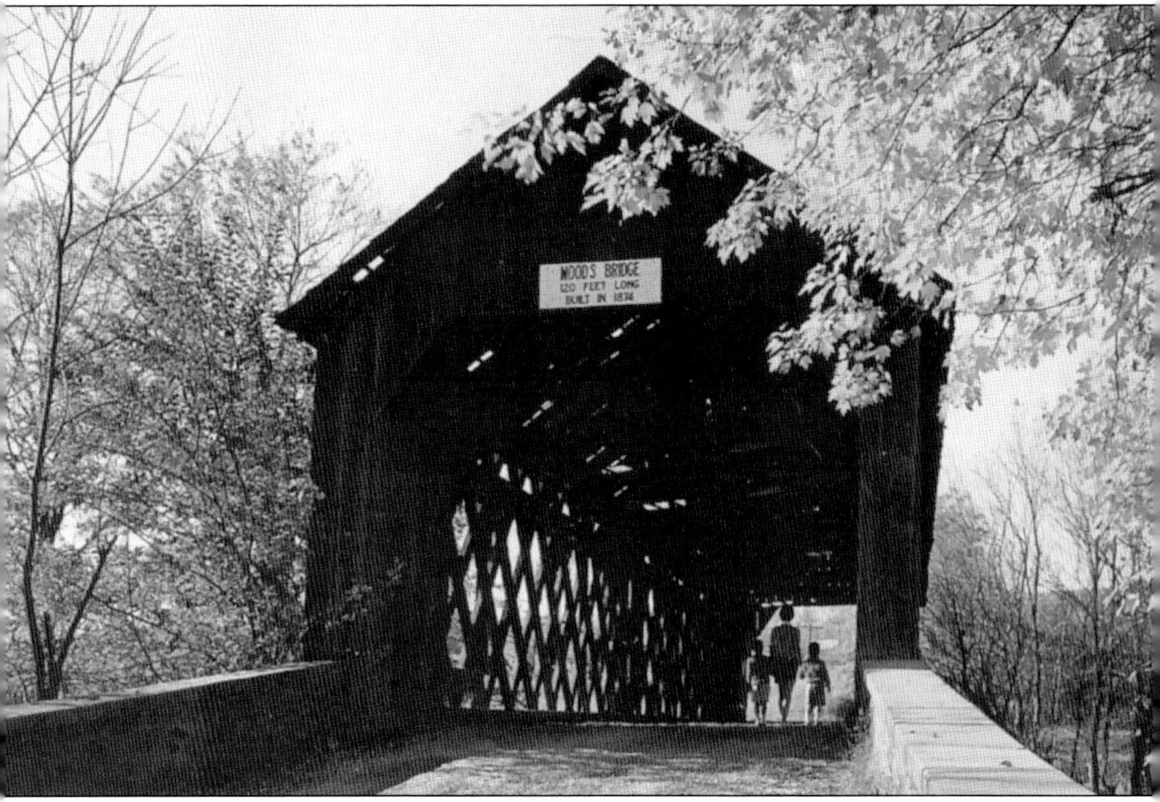

This is a 1962 postcard of Mood's Bridge, built in 1874 and spanning the Perkiomen Creek (northeast branch). Mood's is located just outside Perkasie, and over the years it has been heavily used, sustaining much damage and many repairs. Its timbers were damaged by a truck in 1993, and Mood's was subsequently restored, only to be struck again by a trash truck in January 2004. Finally repaired, in June 2004, it was completely destroyed by arson. Preserving local heritage, a new replica covered bridge has been built by PennDOT using period-type framework. Rededication of the bridge took place in 2008. (Courtesy of Petrona Charles.)

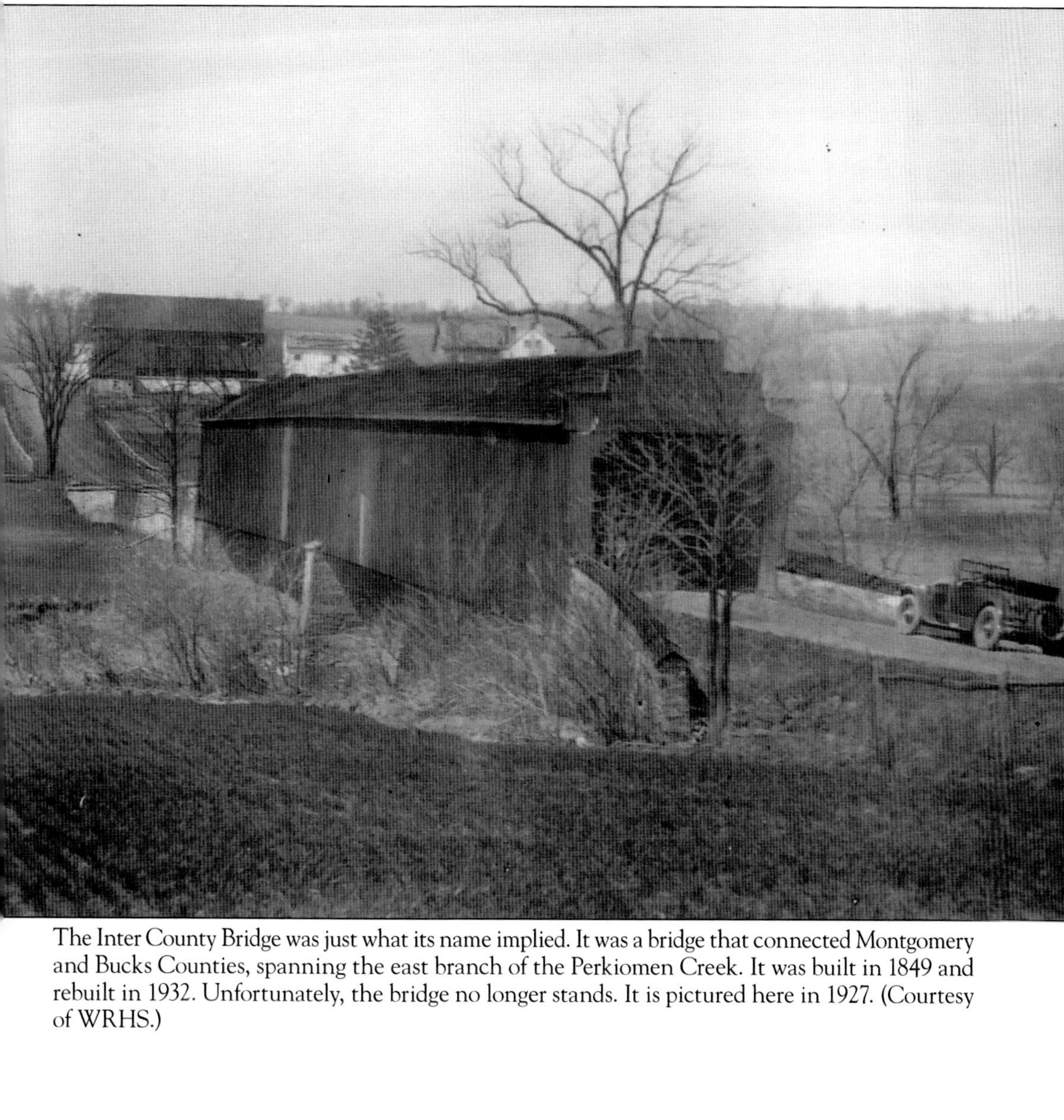

The Inter County Bridge was just what its name implied. It was a bridge that connected Montgomery and Bucks Counties, spanning the east branch of the Perkiomen Creek. It was built in 1849 and rebuilt in 1932. Unfortunately, the bridge no longer stands. It is pictured here in 1927. (Courtesy of WRHS.)

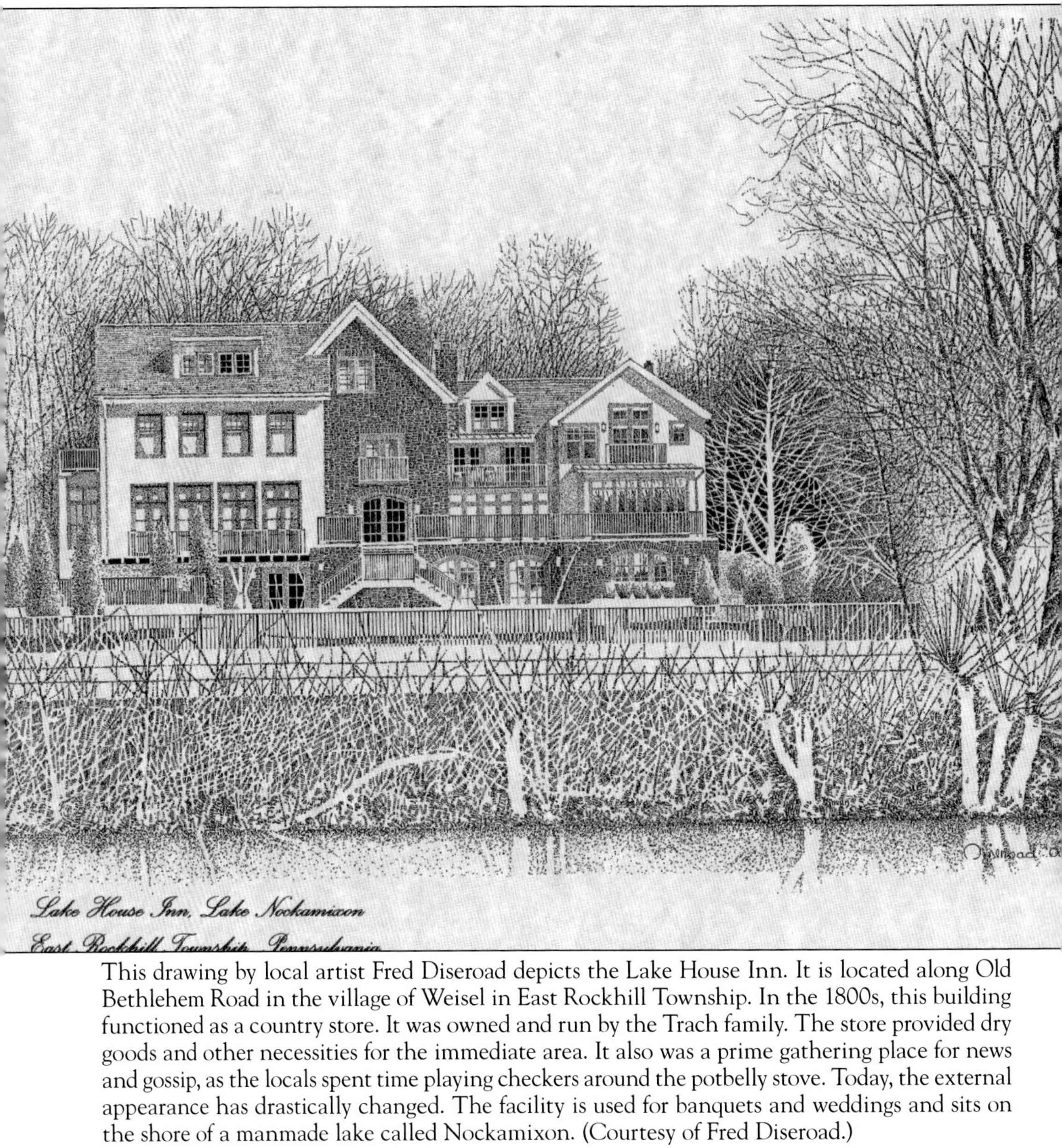

This drawing by local artist Fred Diseroad depicts the Lake House Inn. It is located along Old Bethlehem Road in the village of Weisel in East Rockhill Township. In the 1800s, this building functioned as a country store. It was owned and run by the Trach family. The store provided dry goods and other necessities for the immediate area. It also was a prime gathering place for news and gossip, as the locals spent time playing checkers around the potbelly stove. Today, the external appearance has drastically changed. The facility is used for banquets and weddings and sits on the shore of a manmade lake called Nockamixon. (Courtesy of Fred Diseroad.)

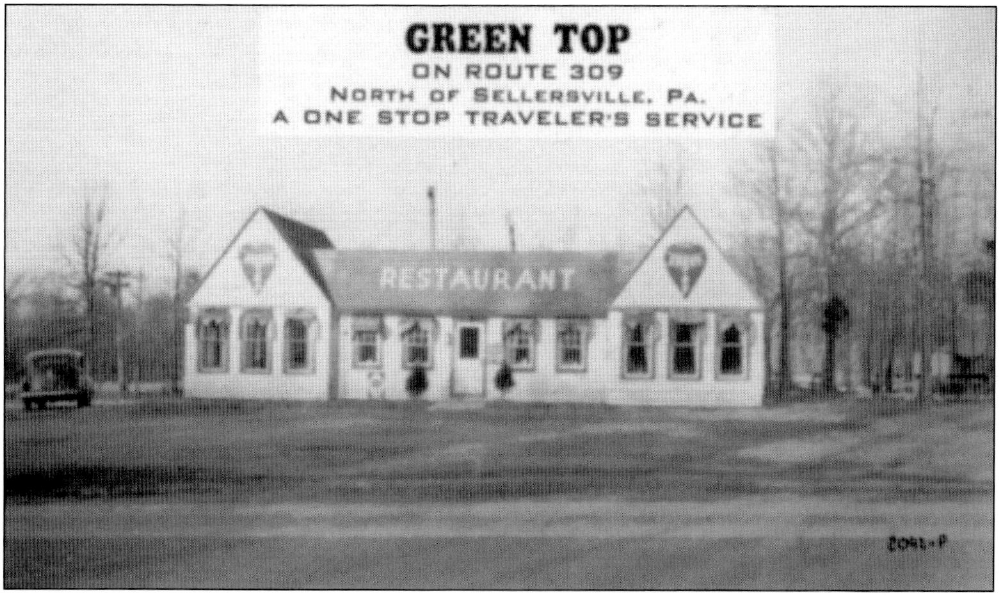

Like many US highways, Route 309 had its share of roadside attractions and businesses. Before the Sellersville Bypass opened in 1969, the long stretch of road north of the borough in West Rockhill had several luncheonettes and eateries, including the Green Top Restaurant. Besides serving up short-order meals, it also doubled as a motor lodge. The establishment was destroyed by fire in 1949. (Courtesy of Timothy D. Hufnagle.)

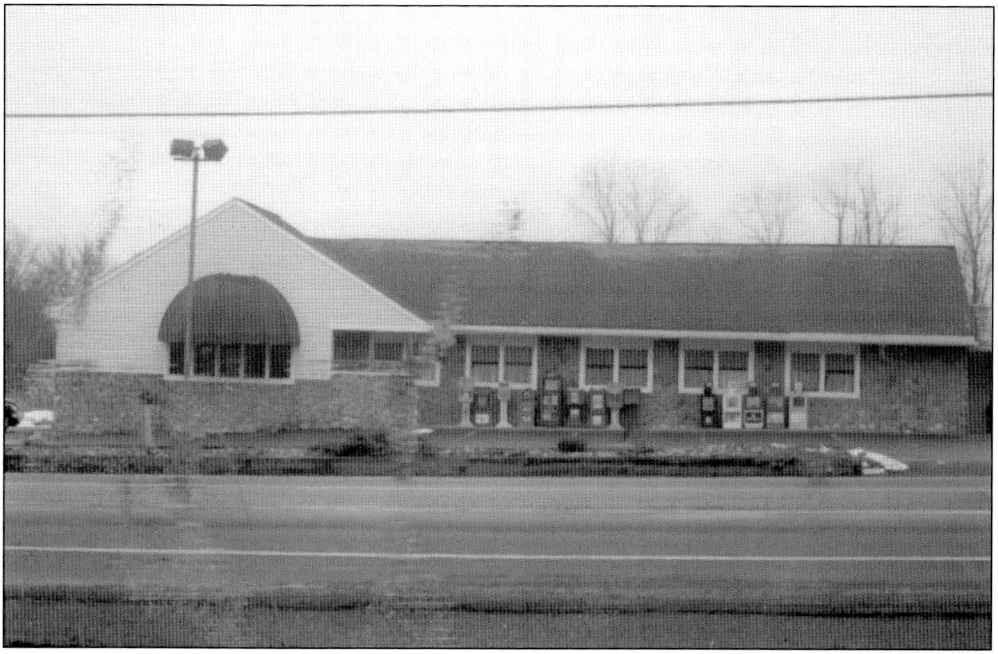
This is a current photograph of Roy Ann's Diner located on Route 309. Roy Ann's Diner was started by Leroy and Annie Smith and has been owned and operated by the Smith family for four generations. Roy Ann's had its humble beginnings in 1953, when it opened as a hotdog and hamburger stand along Old Bethlehem Pike prior to the construction of Route 309. It currently is a well-known and frequently visited dinner spot for residents. (Author's collection.)

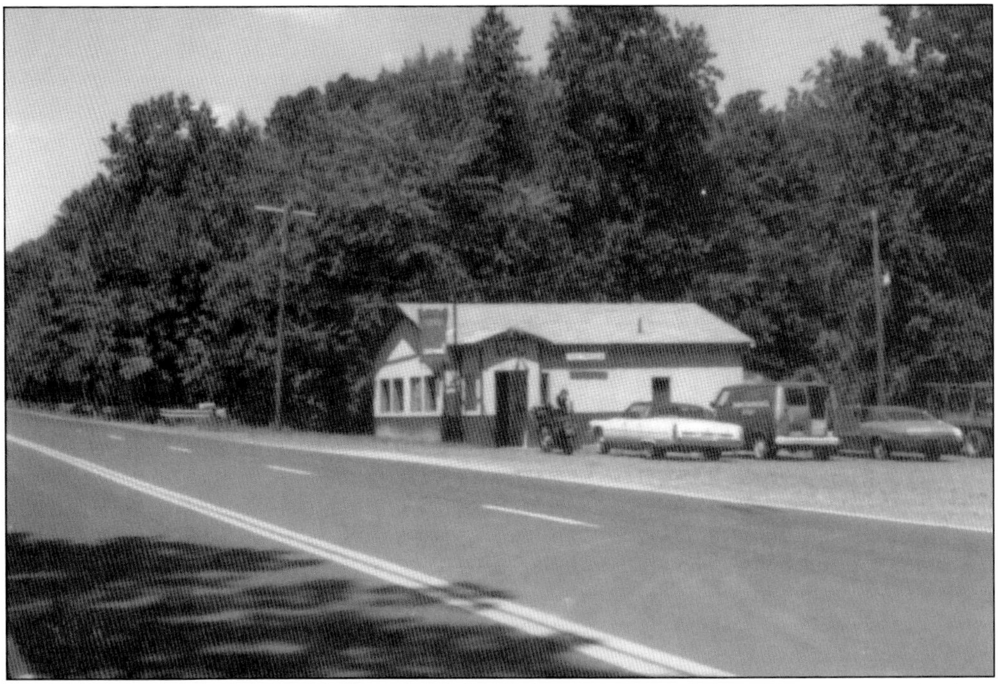

These photographs of an establishment the locals know as Gracie's has a history going back to 1960, when the proprietors sold chestnuts to local campers. The establishment was also known as the Jungle Hunt in the 1970s. The building was vacant for 10 years, but with the construction of Rout 309 and new patrons, it reopened in the 1980s and was known as Mary's Place, then Gracie's in the 1990s, and is known today as Nick's Café. Owner Jim Detweiler has maintained its reputation for fine breakfast and lunch dining with a quaint atmosphere and many friendly patrons. Whatever its name, when visiting, it is like going home. (Both, courtesy of Jim Detwieler.)

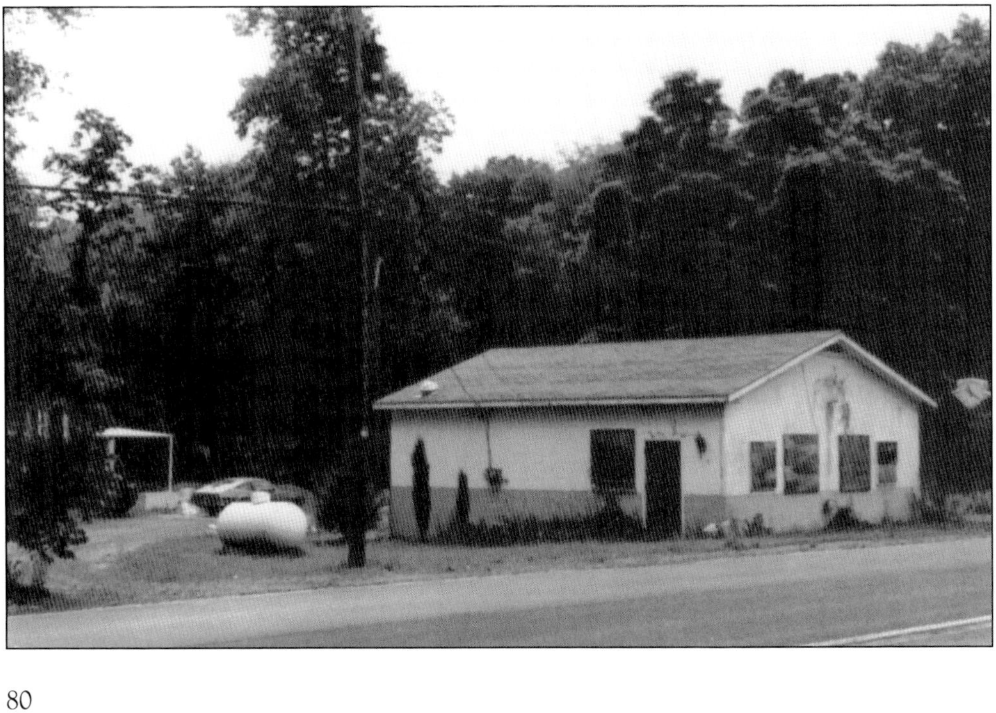

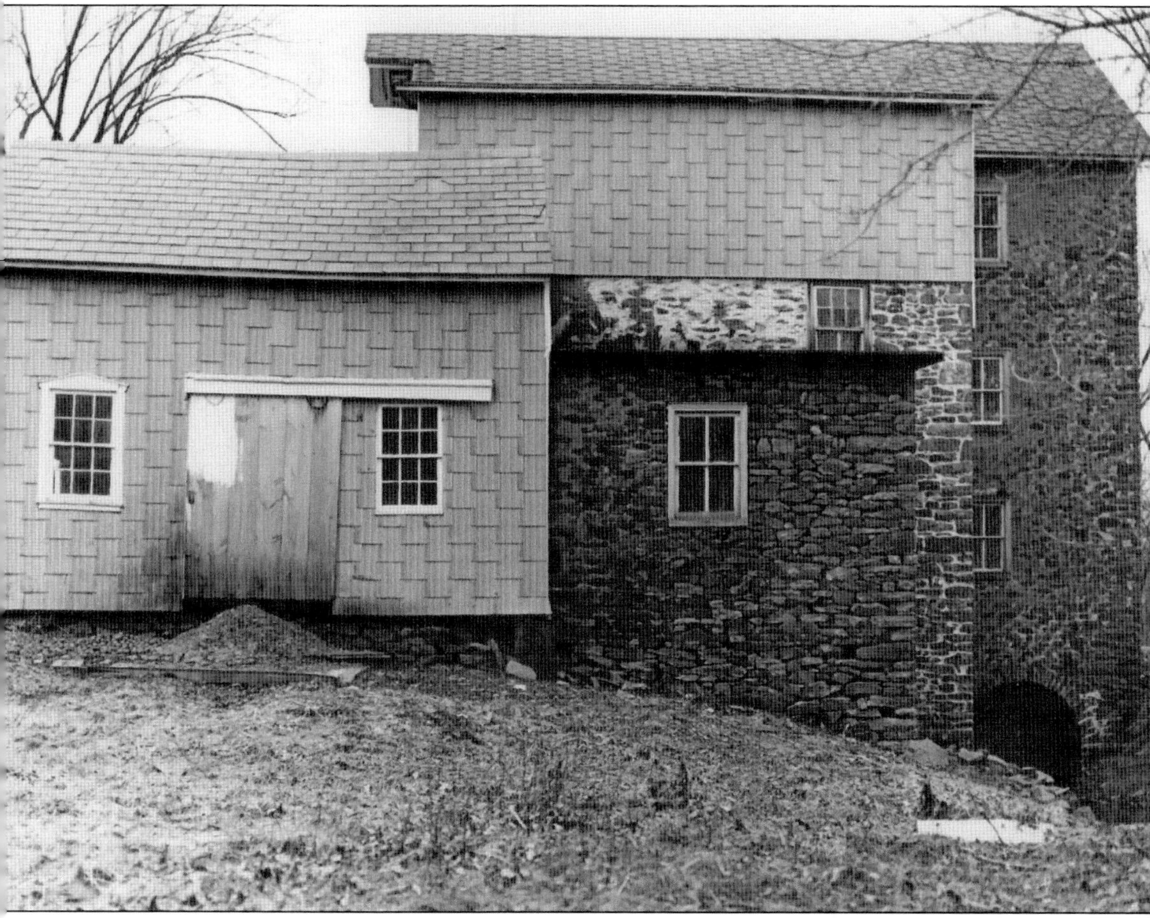

The earliest deeds of this mill date back to 1798. In 1844, Levi Sheard purchased the gristmill, pictured here around 1950. This is an example of a waterwheel mill, used to grind grain such as corn, rye, and wheat. The grain was than sold to local farmers or the general public. This mill was bought by John Clymer and was in operation until 1971, when its waterwheel fell silent forever. (Courtesy of Jim Deegan.)

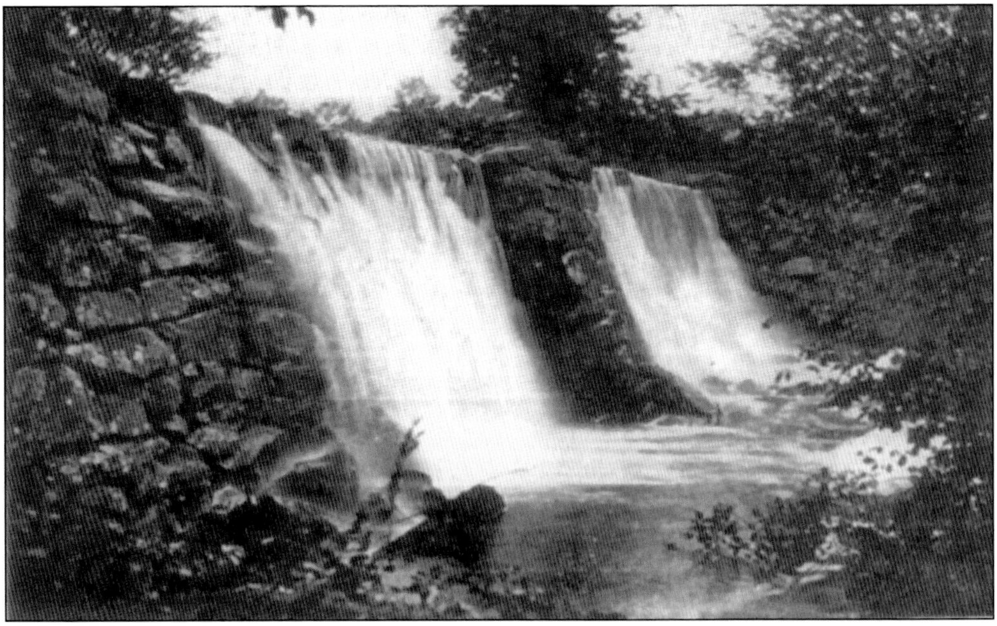

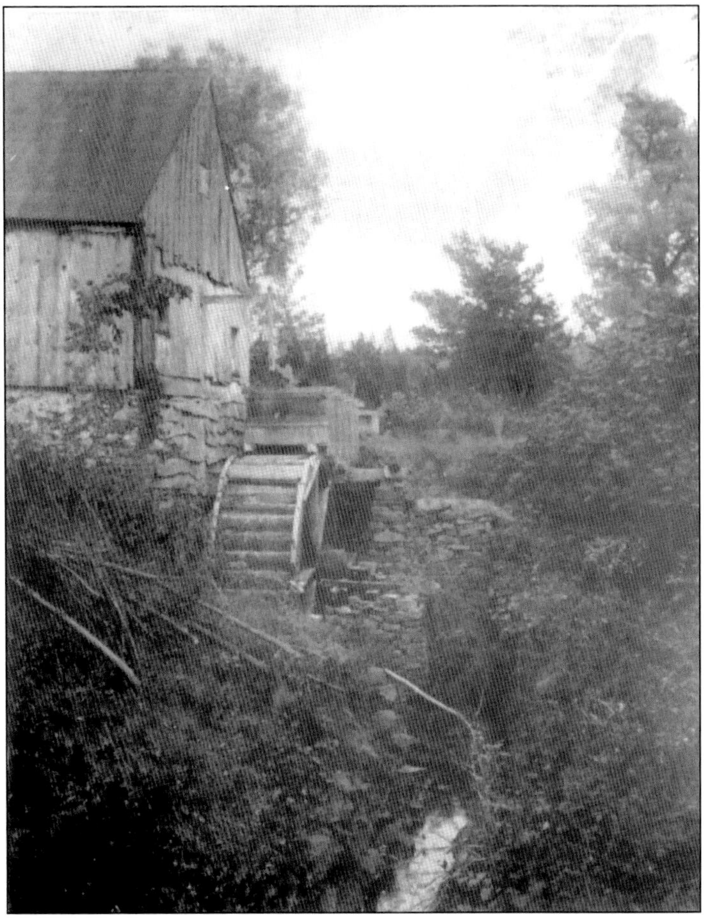

Hoot's mill and dam are pictured around 1900. Theodore Hartley took over Hoot's Mill in Rocky Dale in West Rockhill after leaving his employment at White's Mill. Old deeds indicate that Hoot's, which was also known as the "little red mill," may have been in existence since the 1730s. Hoot's was an unsophisticated mill with old machinery, which meant it could only grind meal and animal feed, not refined flours. After a few years, Hartley could not compete with the surrounding mills and returned to White's Mill. (Above, courtesy of WRHS; left, courtesy of Rhoda Clark.)

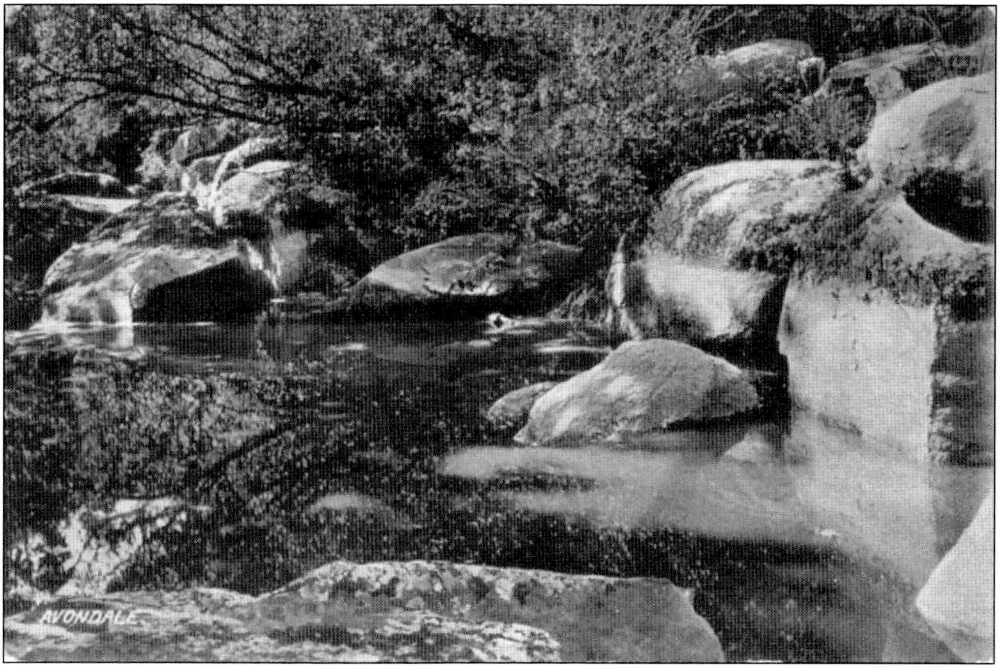

Peace, beauty, and tranquility drew travelers and campers alike. All were ready to enjoy fishing, hiking, and relaxing in beautiful Avondale, located in West Rockhill. (Both, courtesy of Tim Hufnagel.)

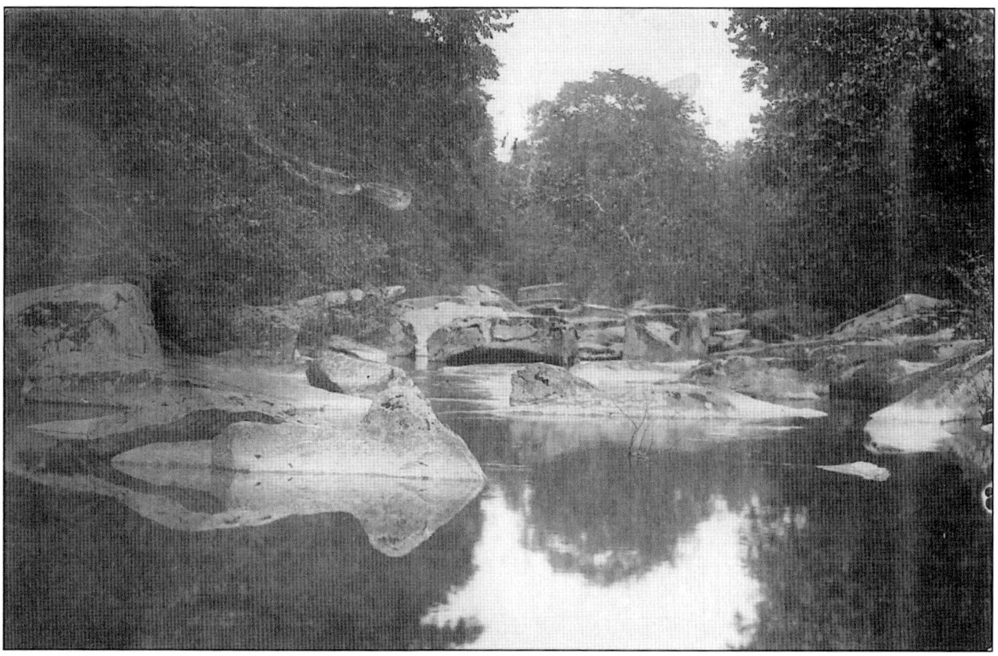

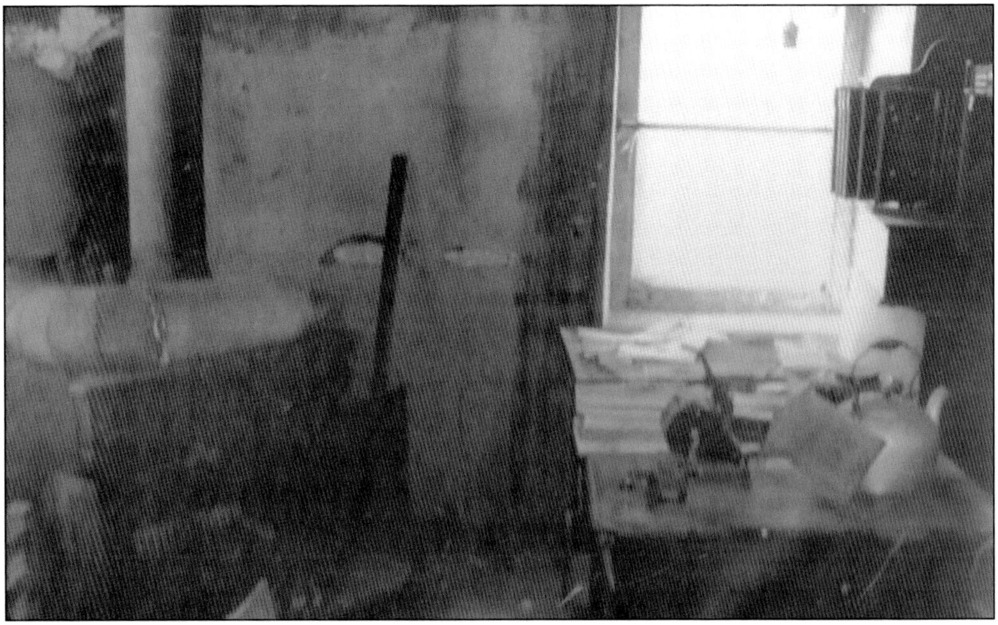

The interior mill office of the Sheard's Mill is pictured in this undated photograph. The mill office was the only place heat would be found in any mill. It was also a place for the miller to sit and take a break from the arduous work of the day. Here is where the miller would keep his tolling records. Tolling was the amount of money charged for grinding a person's grain. (Courtesy of Jim Deegan.)

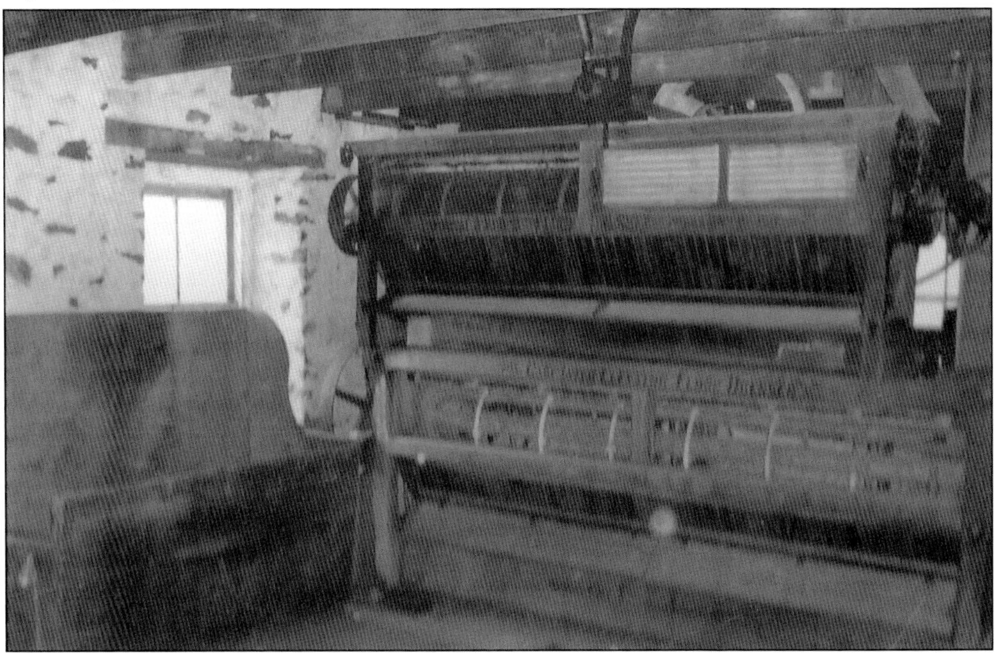

This is the interior of the Sheard/Clymer Mill. The mill was purchased by the late Gerard F. Deegan, who worked tirelessly to have the site placed in the National Register of Historic Places. The mill stands as a memorial in his honor. Deegan made the mill part of the Tohickon Campgrounds. His son Jim is the present owner of the property. (Courtesy of Jim Deegan.)

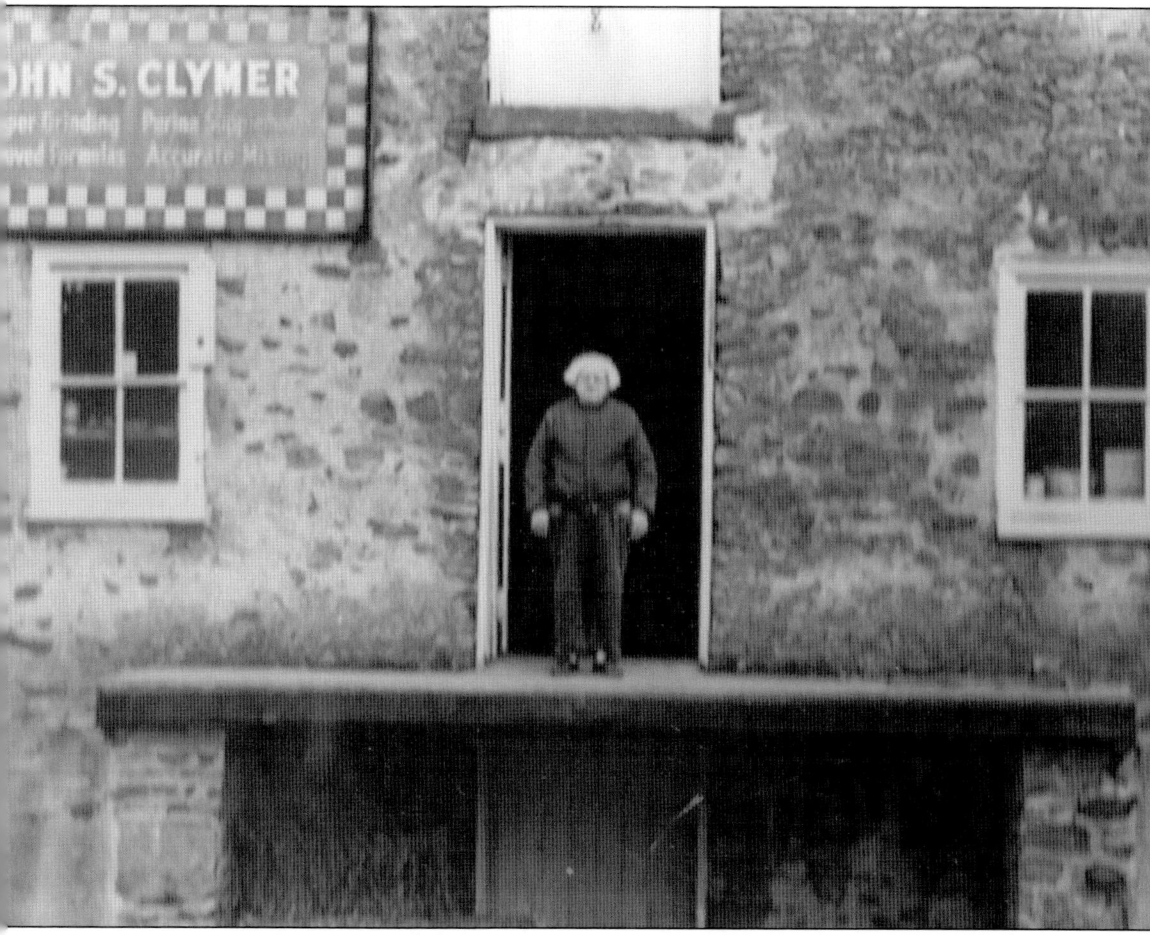

The caption of this photograph simply reads, "Mama Clymer." She stands on the loading dock of the mill after completing a hard day's work. After purchasing the mill, the Clymers continued to operate it until 1971. They ran a cider business until 1985. The mill would later become known as Sheard's Mill. (Courtesy of Jim Deegan.)

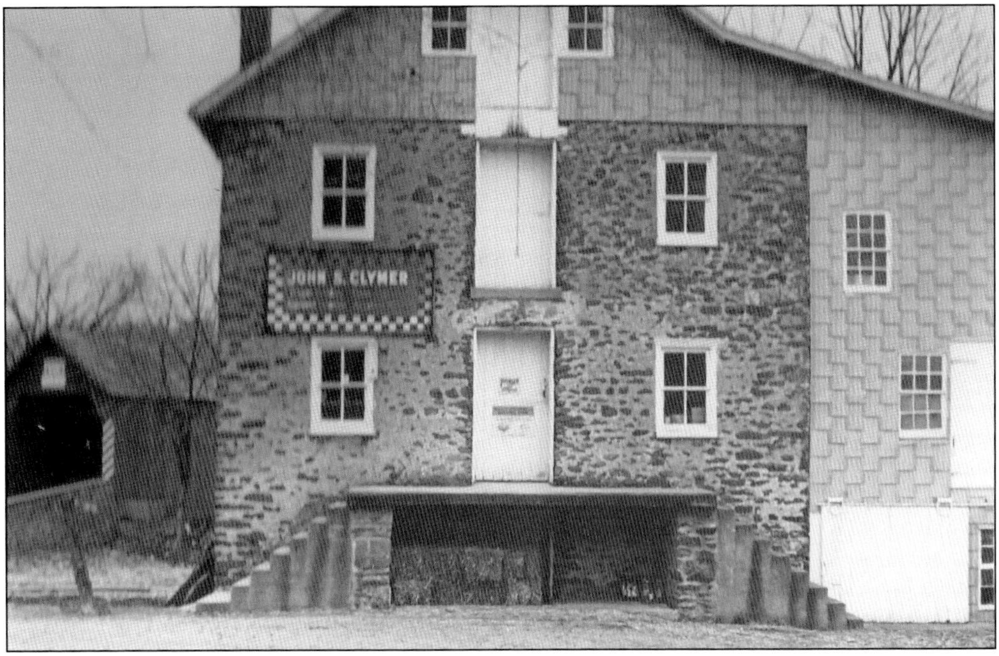

Sheard's Mill covered bridge was built in 1835 and crosses the Tohickon Creek just upstream from manmade Lake Nockamixon at the border of Haycock and East Rockhill Townships. The bridge is located just behind the old mill and was named after Levi Sheard, owner of the mill. This small valley once contained not only the mill, but also a general store. The bridge and mill are located on Covered Bridge Road and Thatcher Road. (Courtesy of Jim Deegan.)

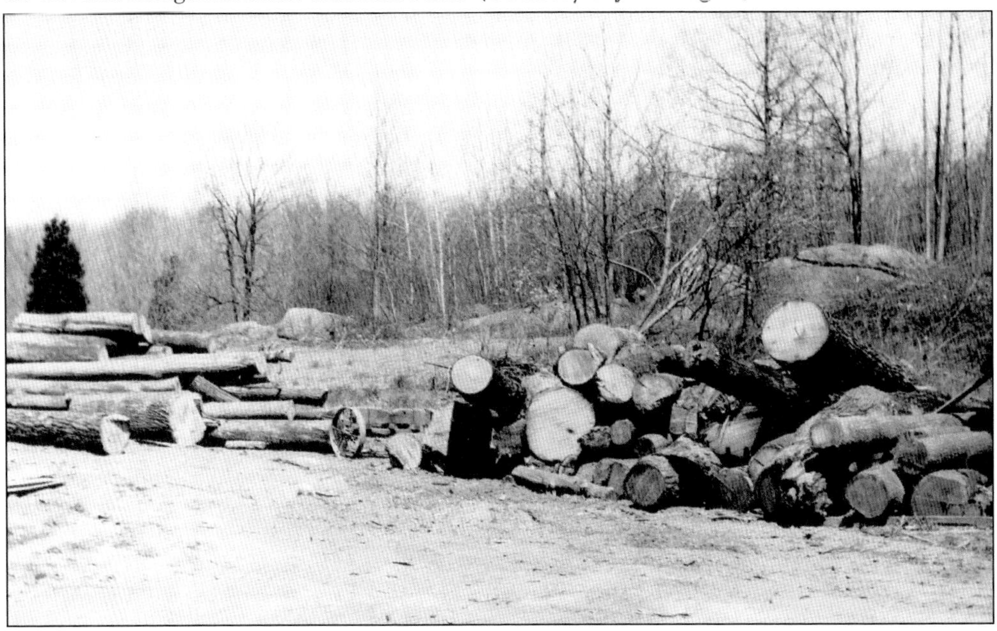

This photograph of the Guenst family sawmill was taken in 1940. The original sawmill was located on Buttercreek Road. The mill, however, was mobile. It could be taken down and moved to another location. The mill is currently located on Shucraft Road in West Rockhill and is still operated by Charles Guenst, great-grandson of the original owner. (Courtesy of Charles Guenst.)

Five

Grand View Hospital's Beginnings

The origins of Grand View Hospital can be traced to a conversation between Dr. Walter J. Brown (1876–1963), Dr. William J. Wilkinson (1866–1934), and Dr. Alfred Fretz. They decided to present their ideas to the medical members of the North Penn Clinical Society, which covered an area from Quakertown to Lansdale. The interest in the establishment of a hospital was widespread, and the result was the purchasing of Dr. Pursell's property in August 1913.

In September 1913, the Grand View Hospital Association was founded, and $8,000 worth of renovations began on the former Pursell house to create a community hospital in Bucks County. It is said that the statue of William Penn in Philadelphia could be seen from the upper quarters of the Pursell house. What a grand view it was, which is why the Pursells called their estate Grand View. Thus, the hospital acquired its name.

The new facility had eight patient rooms, one operating room, a bathroom, an office, and a kitchen. In 1914, the newly formed hospital admitted 101 patients.

Undoubtedly, the most dramatic event of 1913 was the outbreak of typhoid fever in Sellersville. Several patients where treated at Grand View, including one of their own physicians, who recovered. World War I created acute shortages. Local farmers donated food, and housewives donated canned goods to keep the hospital going. In 1918, Spanish influenza struck Grand View, and the entire region was quarantined. During World War II, the staff was depleted when 14 physicians and 23 nurses answered the call to duty. As in World War I, there were extreme shortages, and again, the residents donated food, supplies, and textiles. As witnessed through their long history, the people of this region and the hospital are intricately entwined.

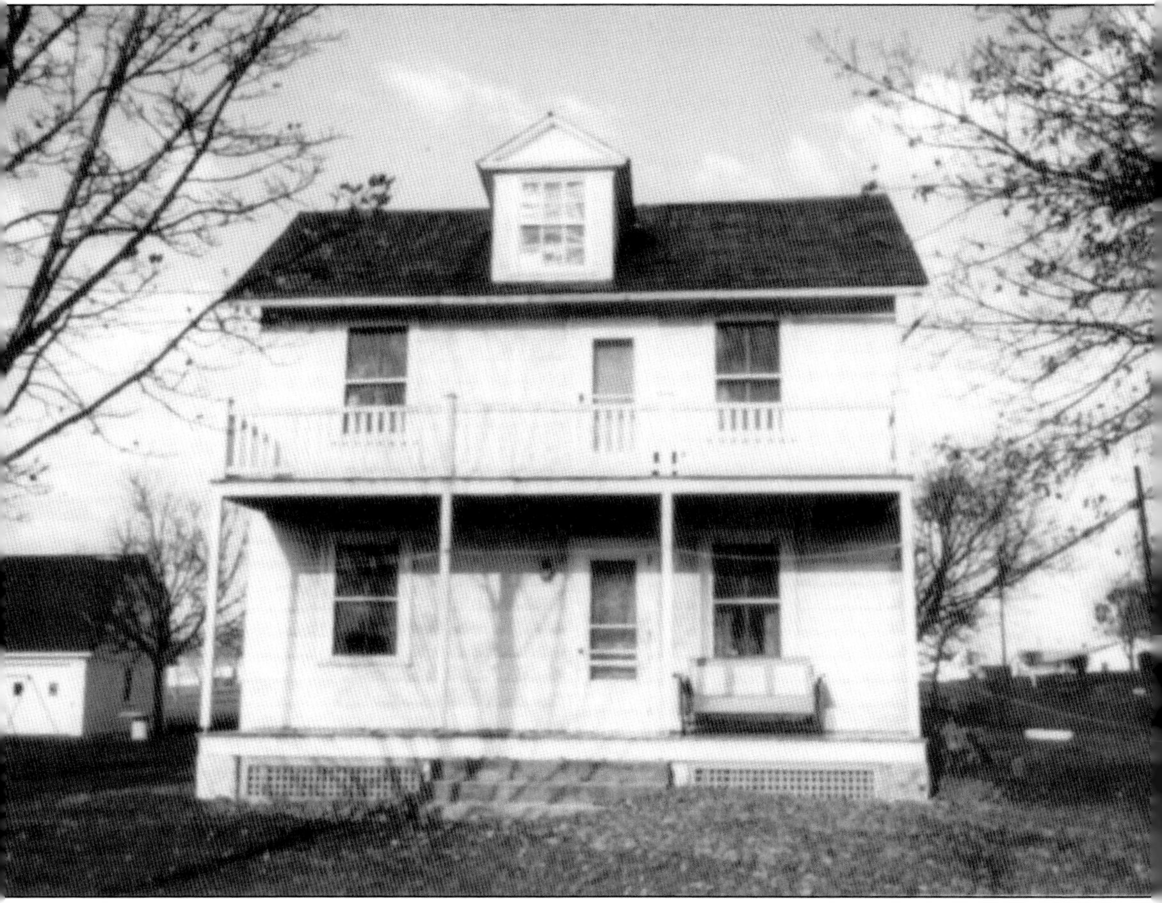

This is the original property that Dr. James Pursell donated to create the first sanitarium and hospital. Dr. Pursell was an eye specialist and also conducted a convalescent home. After years of labor, he decided to retire and sell his property, which included a large house, a small-framed dwelling, a storage house, a barn, and the surrounding land. In the first hospital, there were no established fees or charges for rooms, nursing services, operating rooms, surgical fees, or other medical attention. Each patient's fee was adjusted to fit his or her financial rating. The hospital staff in 1914 consisted of Dr. William J. Wilkinson, MD, who served as superintendent and surgeon; H.C. Grim, MD, assistant surgeon; and Mrs. Wilkinson and Mrs. Walter Brown, who served as nurse superintendents. The nurses only worked the day shift. The physicians worked the night shift and were subject to be on-call at all hours. (Courtesy of Grand View Hospital Archives/Sellersville Museum.)

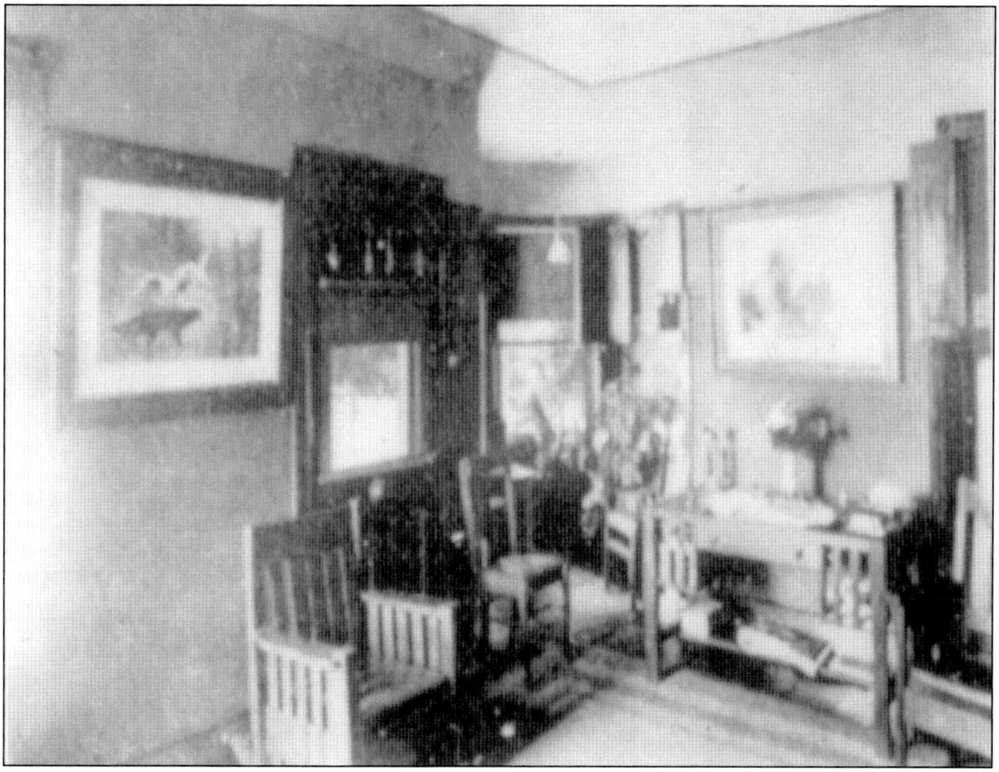

These c. 1915 photographs show the resting rooms. All of the furniture was donated by local businesses. On several occasions, the physicians themselves donated furniture. There were no telephones in the facility at this time, and only one restroom. They did the best they could with what little they had. (Courtesy of Grand View Hospital Archives/Sellersville Museum.)

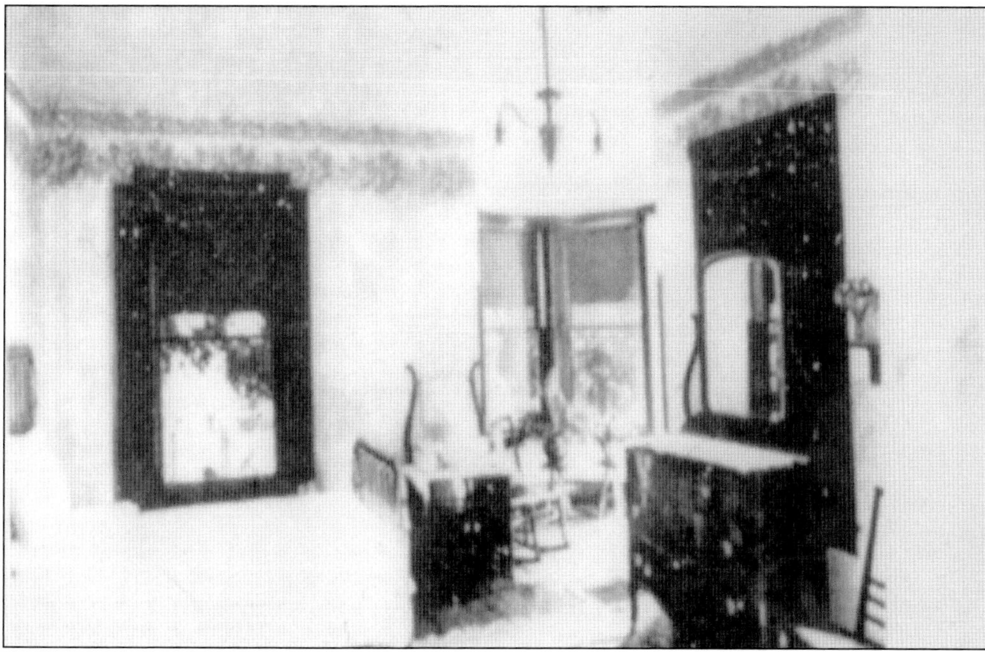

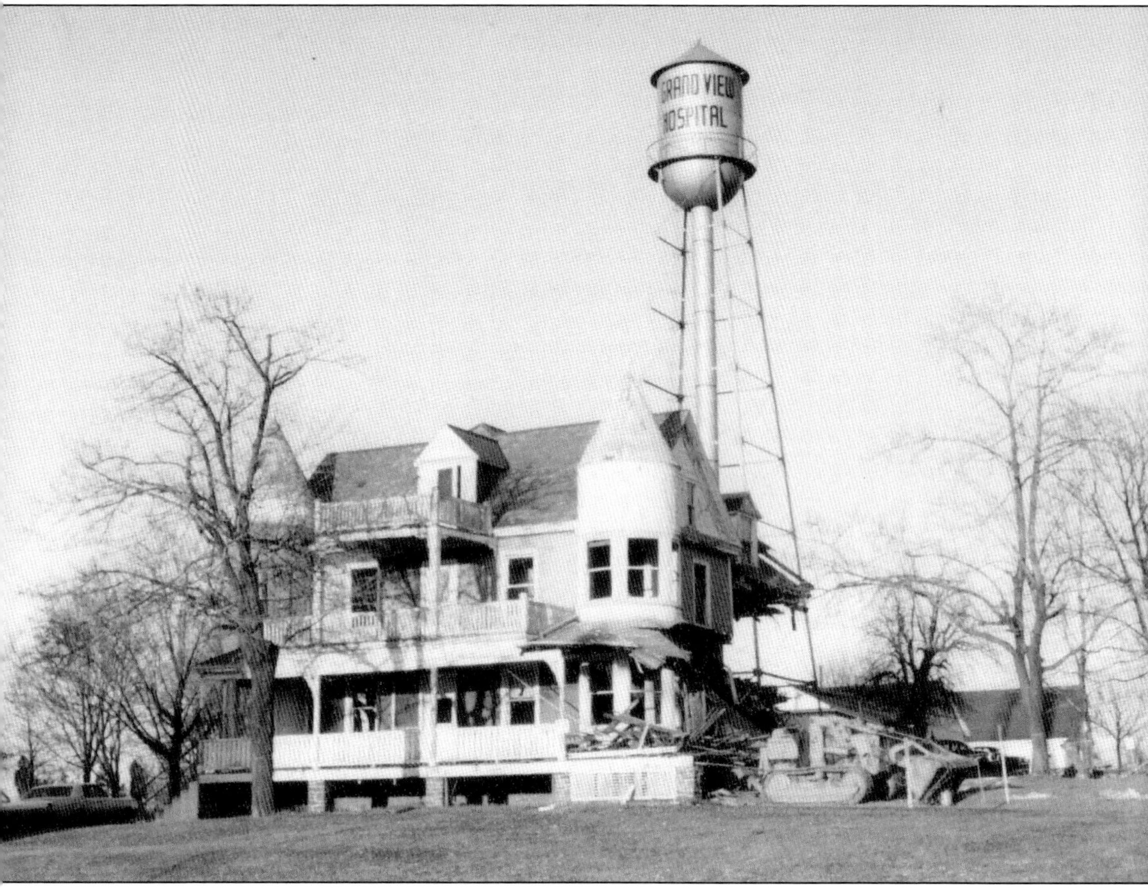

This c. 1970 photograph shows the demolition of the 1905 home of Dr. Purcell, which was the original Grand View Hospital and Sanitarium. The water tower in the background was also demolished and replaced with a more modern tower. (Courtesy of Grand View Hospital Archives/Sellersville Museum.)

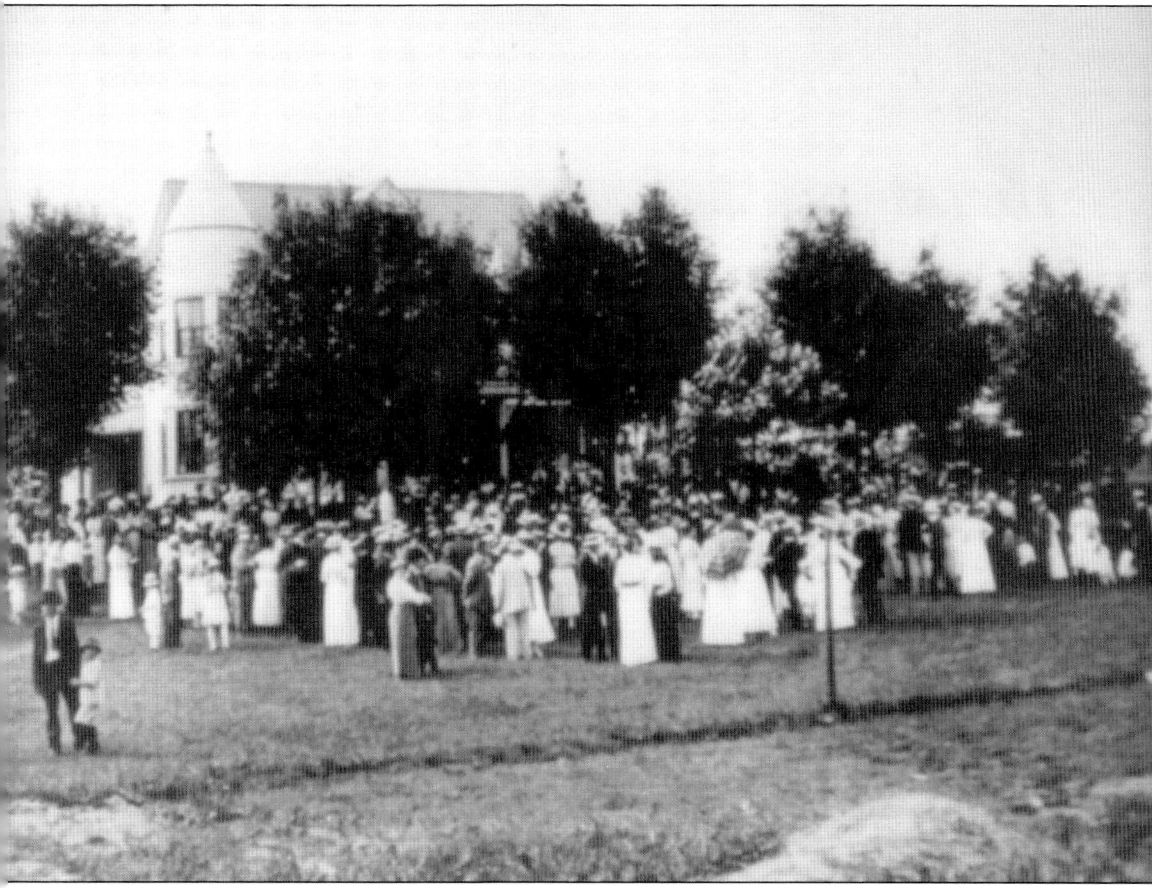

This photograph was taken in December 1913. Over 200 guests arrived for the grand opening of Grand View Hospital. Some residents came by horse and buggy, but most came on foot. The event brought together physicians and guests to inspect the new hospital. The guests expressed their pleasure at the general appearance of the facility and its equipment. (Courtesy of Grand View Hospital Archives/Sellersville Museum.)

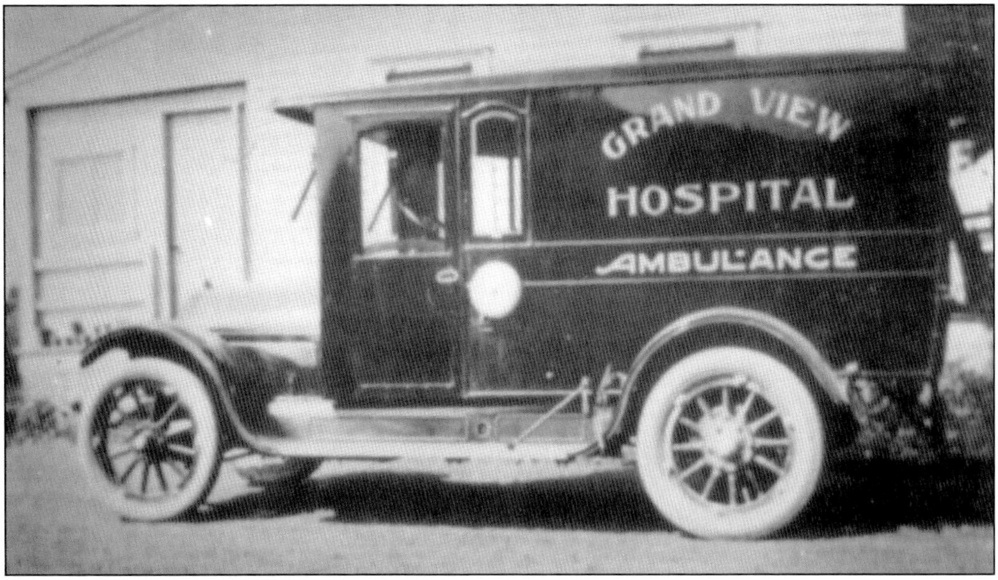

This photograph, taken in 1915, shows the first ambulance Grand View Hospital used to bring patients to the hospital for care. The automobile was an REO Speed Wagon. REO stood for Ransom E. Olds, the owner of the company that made these vehicles. The REO Speed Wagon was in production for 10 years. They were used as fire trucks, hearses, buses, and ambulances. The original REO Speed Wagons sold for about $300 and are worth about $15,000 today. (Courtesy Grand View Hospital Archives/Sellersville Museum.)

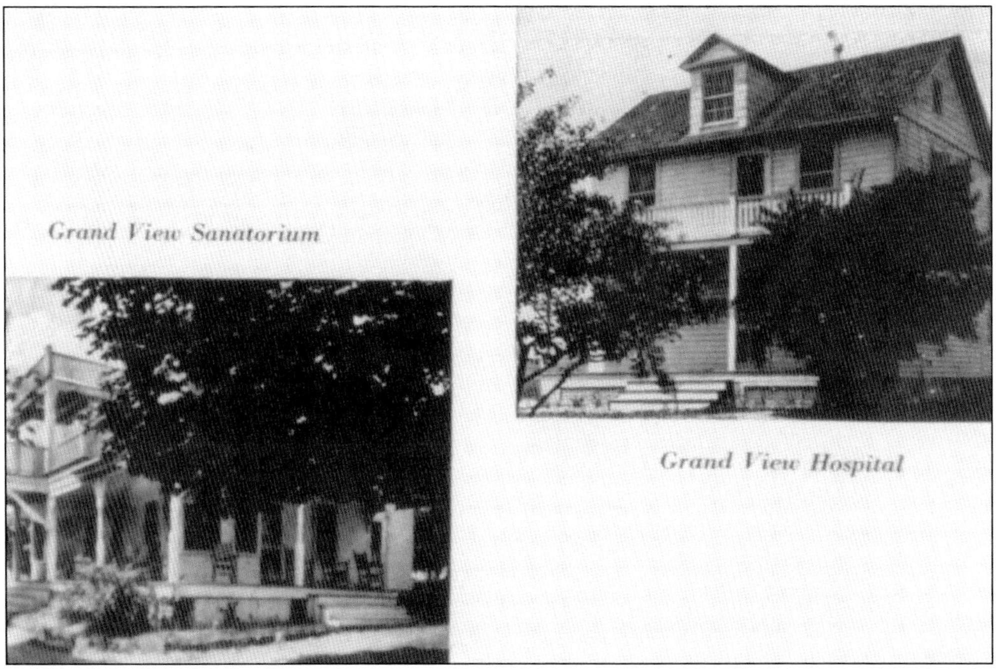

This c. 1900 Berkemeyer postcard is one of only a few Berkemeyers that contain two photographs on the front. Photographs for the postcards were taken by local photographer Daniel Zeigler, from Souderton. These postcards were collected by local residents. (Courtesy of Grand View Hospital Archives/Sellersville Museum.)

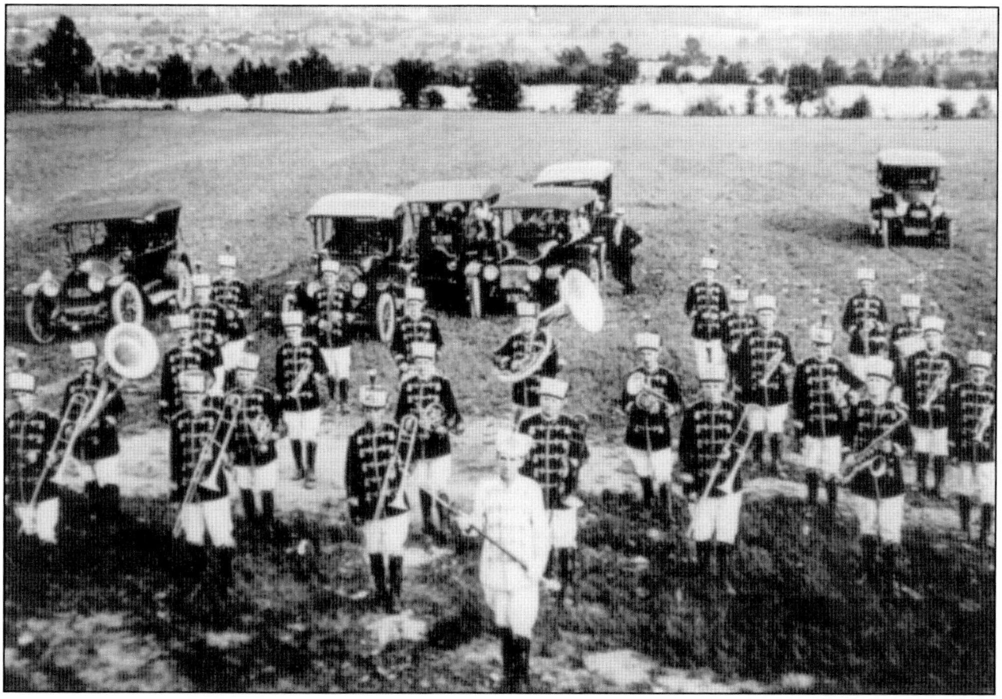

Pictured is the 1915 dedication of the newly formed Grand View Hospital. Grand View would have many more dedications and celebrations. One such celebration became a yearly event and was known as the Lawn Fete. The dedications and fetes were for the purpose of necessary fundraising. (Courtesy of Grand View Hospital Archives/Sellersville Museum.)

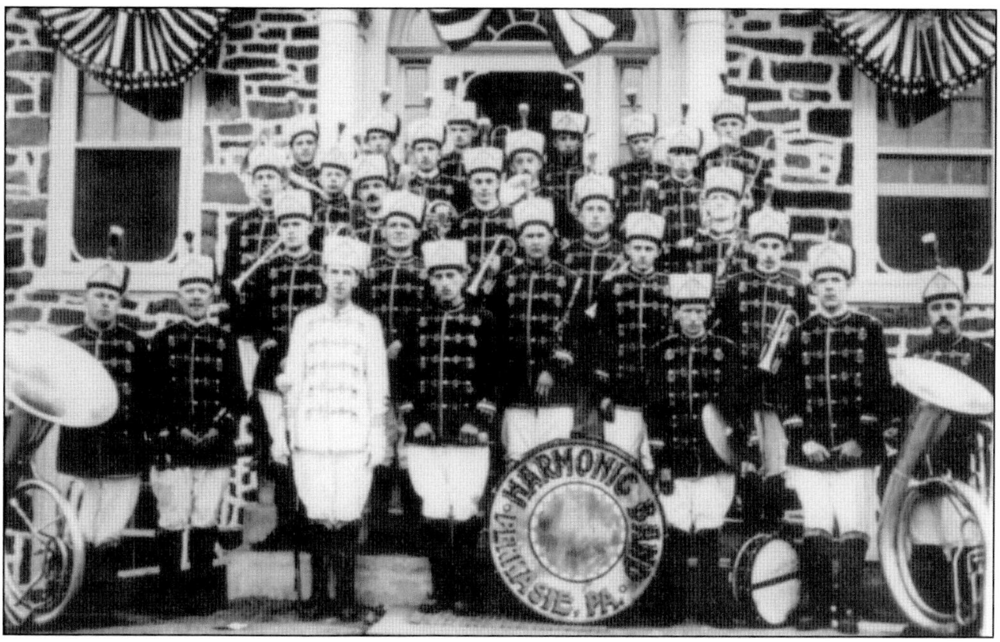

This photograph was taken in June 1918 for a dedication ceremony at Grand View Hospital. The Perkasie Harmonic Band also came to entertain the gatherers at one of the earlier dedications. (Courtesy of Grand View Hospital Archives/Sellersville Museum.)

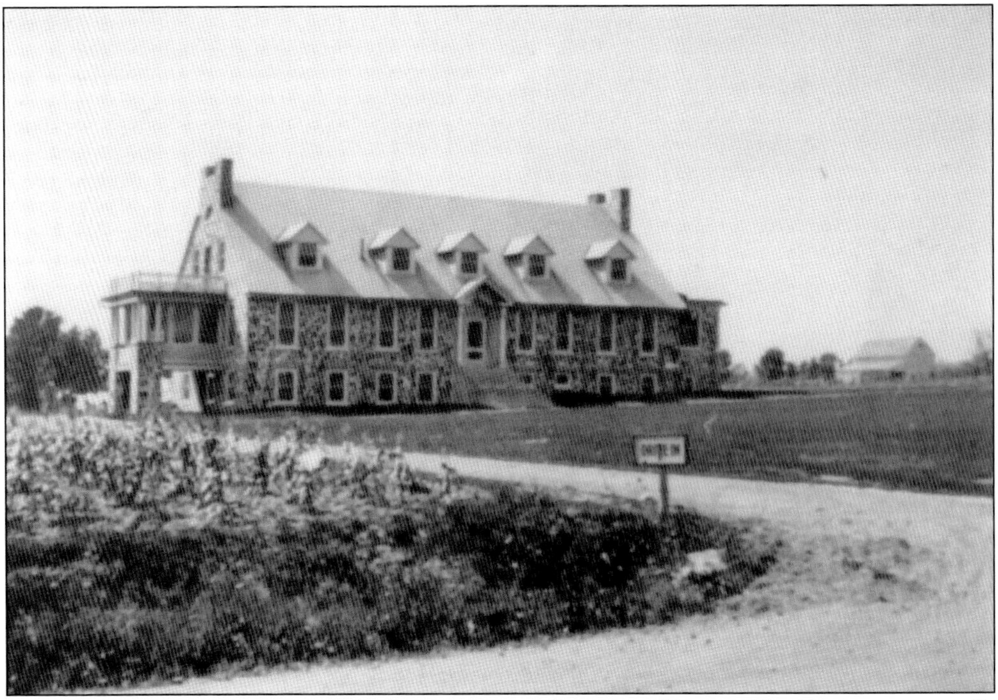

These c. 1920 photographs show the first new unit. The original hospital had become too small, having only eight rooms for patients, an operating room, a bathroom, an office, and a kitchen. More rooms and extra help were needed. It would be the first of many upgrades to the hospital, and residents would witness this evolution over the next 100 years. (Both, courtesy of Grand View Hospital Archives/Sellersville Museum.)

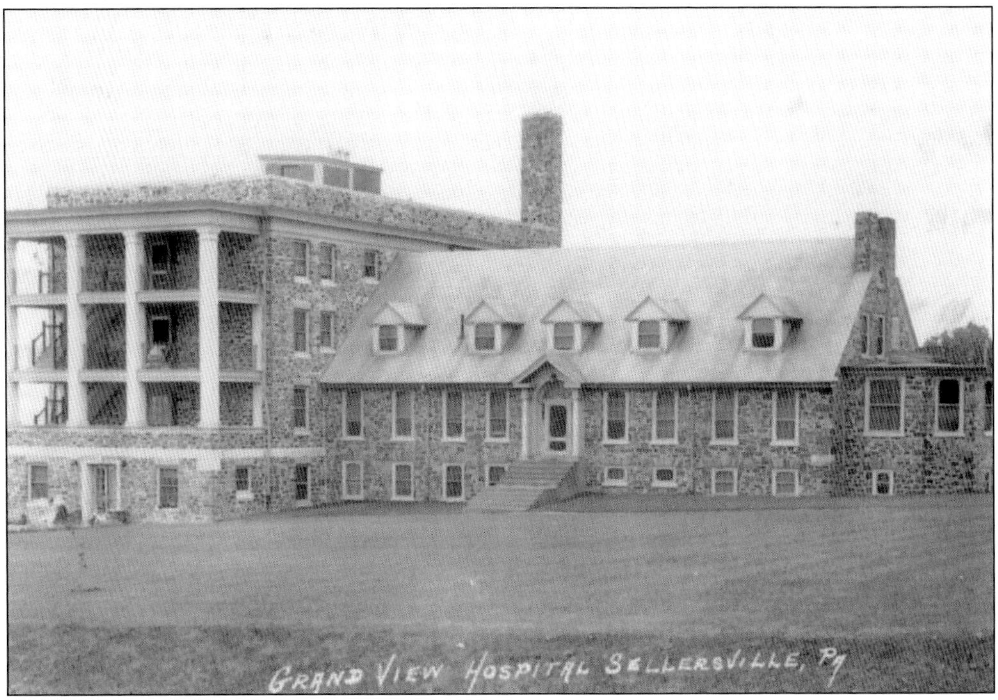

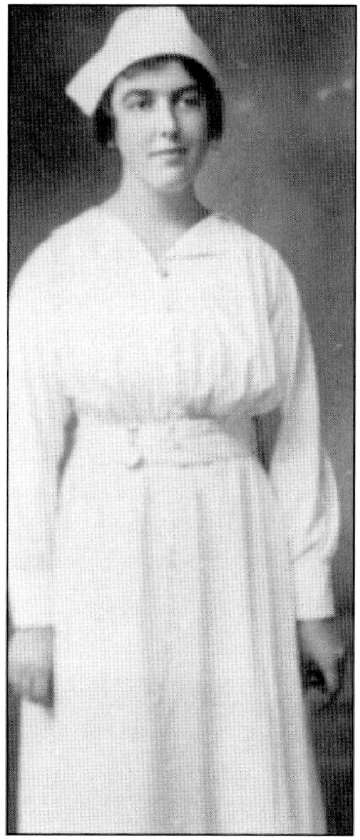

Pictured are Anna Ohm (below) and Sara Buzby (right), graduates of the nursing class of 1916. The original school of nursing provided only a one-year course consisting of practical work and little theory. In 1917, a two-year course began, and by 1923, it had increased to three years. By 1923, theory had been included in the curriculum, and the number of students began to increase yearly. (Both, courtesy of Grand View Hospital Archives/Sellersville Museum.)

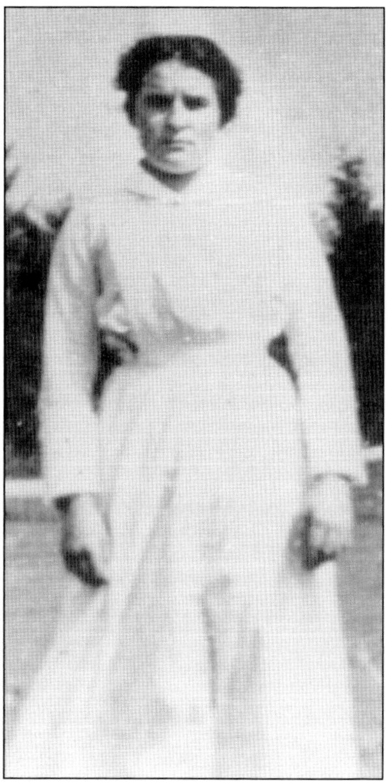

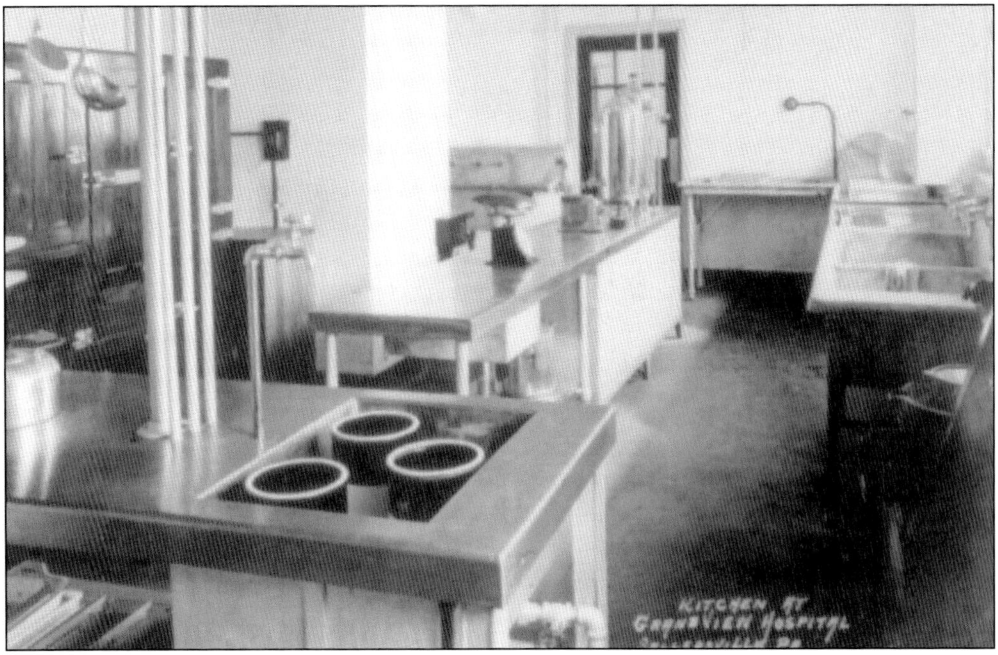

The kitchen at Grand View is pictured in this 1929 photograph. This was a great improvement over the original kitchen from 1915, which was used for sterilization of instruments. Food was not cooked there at that time, but was prepared and brought to the hospital from a nearby residence. (Courtesy of Grand View Hospital Archives/Sellersville Museum.)

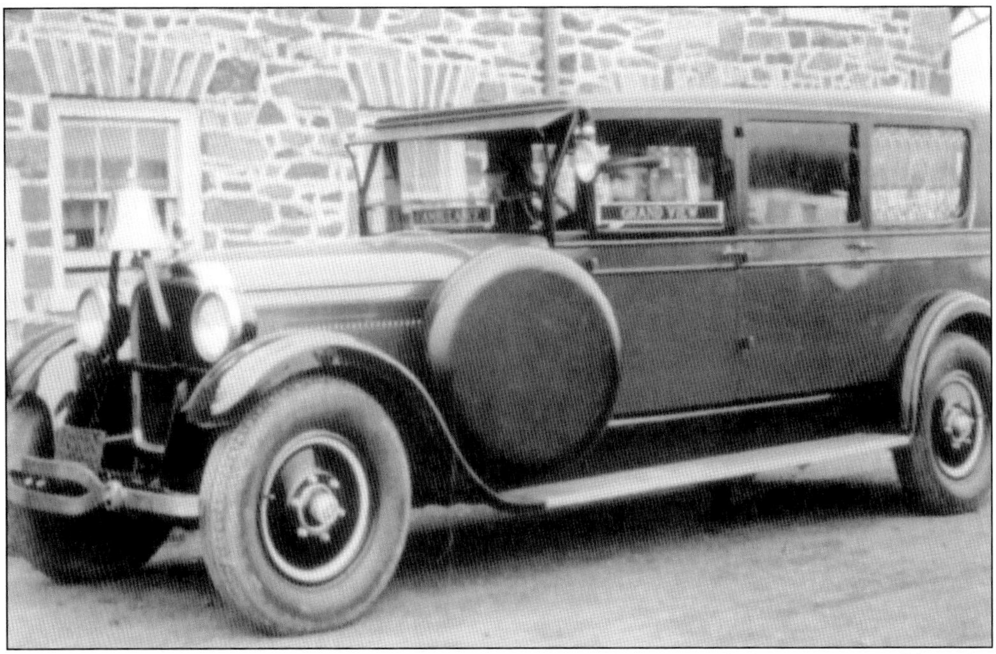

This 1929 ambulance is a Flexible/Buick Paddy Wagon. The first ambulances were sold to the hospital by Fred C. Young, who owned the dealership. Because of a lack of drivers, he also became the first person to deliver patients to the hospital. He drove the ambulance until a permanent driver could be found. (Courtesy of Grand View Hospital Archives/Sellersville Museum.)

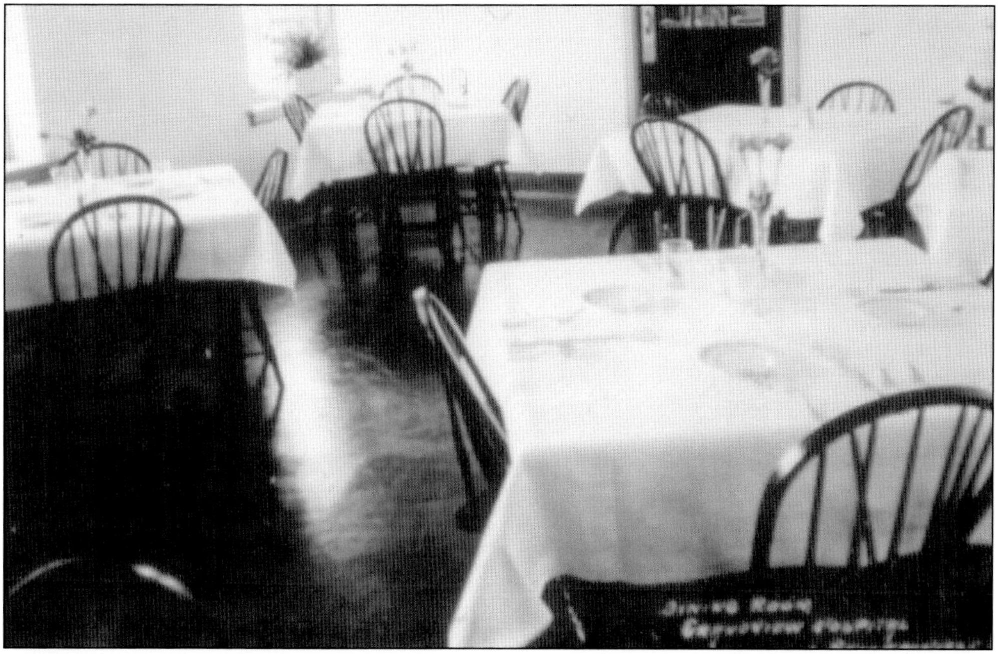

In 1913, the first hospital had no dining facility and often meals were prepared off site and transported by foot to their destination. In 1929, for the first time, trays and racks were used on every floor. Food was transported by dumbwaiter from the kitchen to the dining hall (pictured). Dishes were still washed by hand. (Courtesy of Grand View Hospital Archives/Sellersville Museum.)

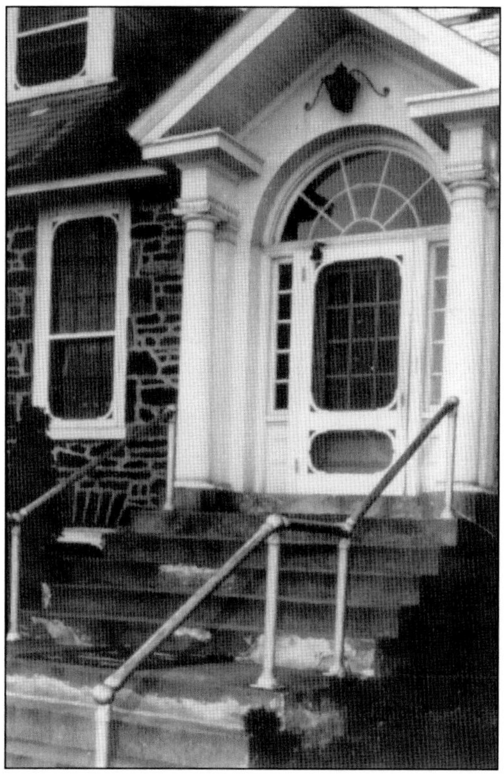

This photograph shows the entrance to Grand View Hospital as it looked in 1929. The unit, which included this entrance, was built with native stones. (Courtesy of Grand View Hospital Archives/Sellersville Museum.)

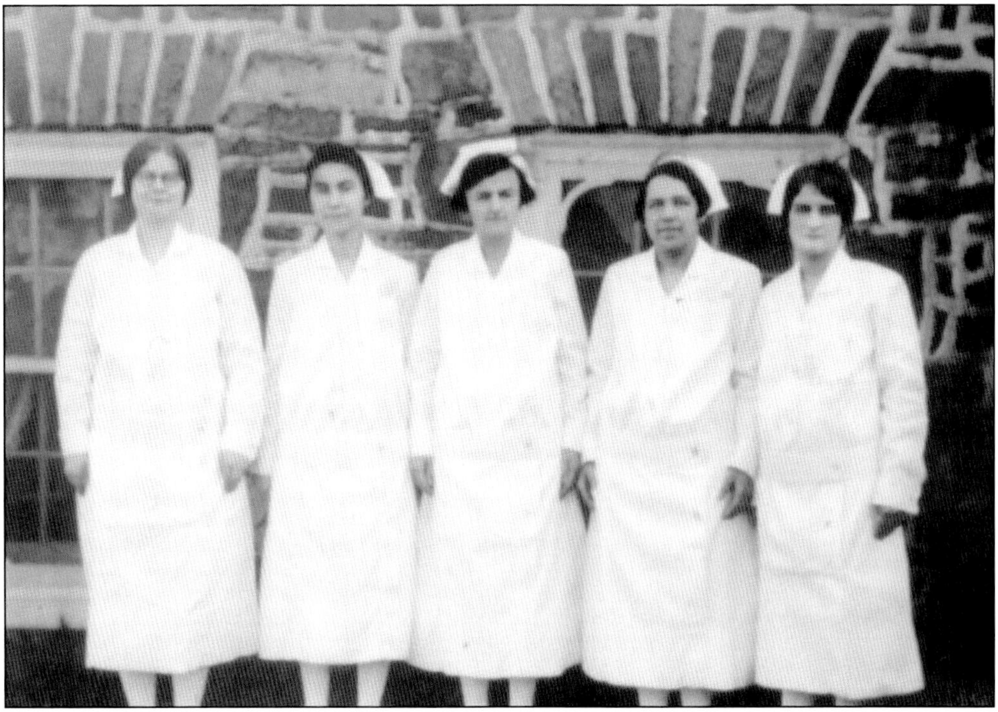

These nursing school graduates from the class of 1928 are, from left to right, Grace Nicholas, Verda Moyer, Eleanor Plant, Margaret Schell, and Mildred Souder. (Courtesy of Grand View Hospital Archives/Sellersville Museum.)

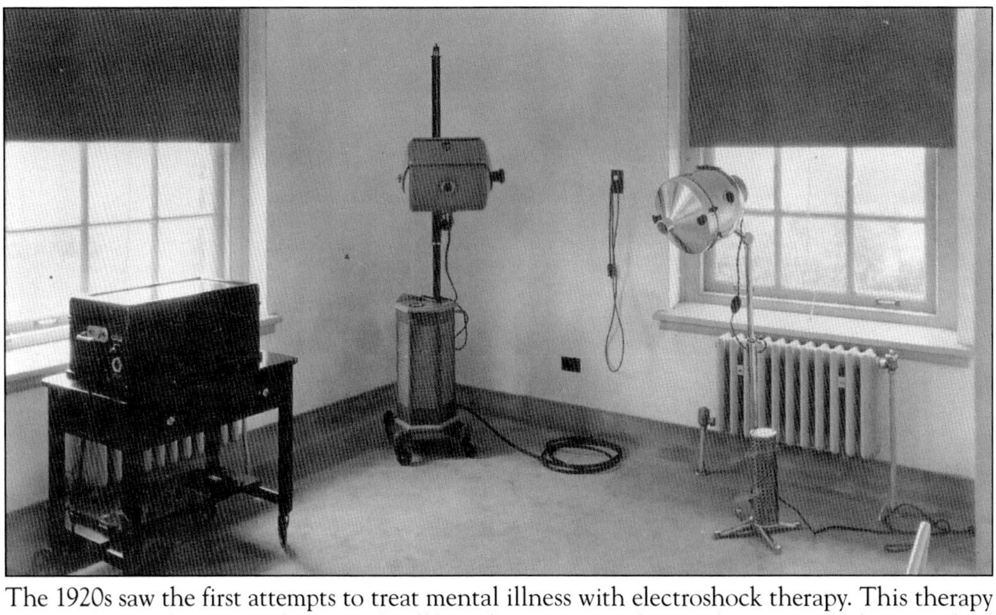

The 1920s saw the first attempts to treat mental illness with electroshock therapy. This therapy was used not only to treat the mentally ill but also to treat epilepsy. This is a 1929 photograph of the Electro Therapy room at Grand View Hospital. (Courtesy of Grand View Hospital Archives/ Sellersville Museum.)

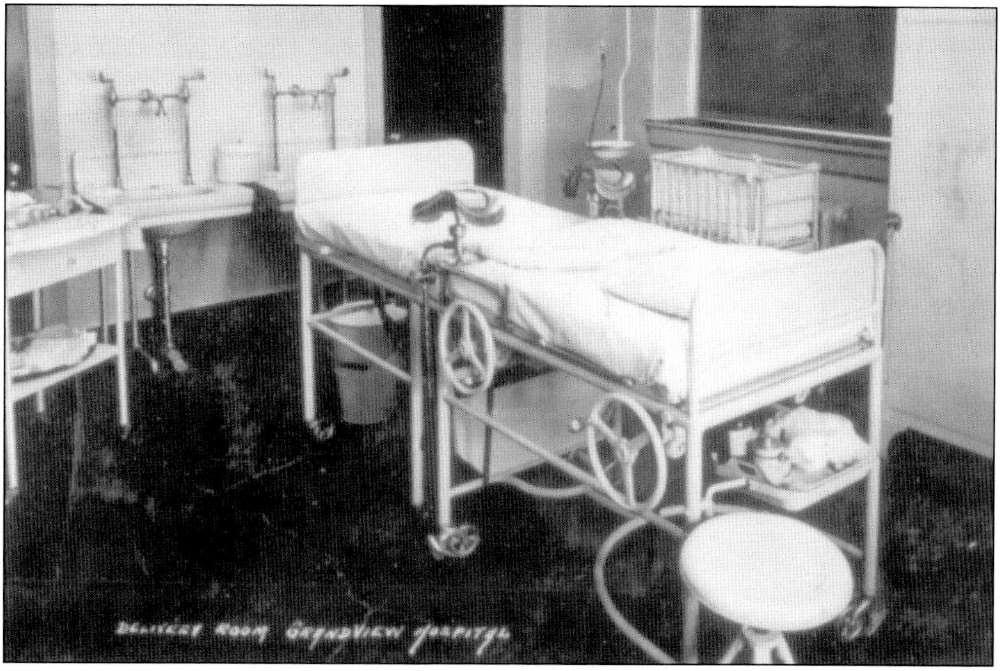

This is a 1929 photograph of a Grand View Hospital delivery room. The first cesarean section was performed on May 13, 1926, and both mother and baby were fine. By 1939, there was a great demand for maternity services, and by 1940, a maternity wing opened. In its first year of operation, there were 337 infants born and cared for in the new wing. (Courtesy of Grand View Hospital Archives/Sellersville Museum.)

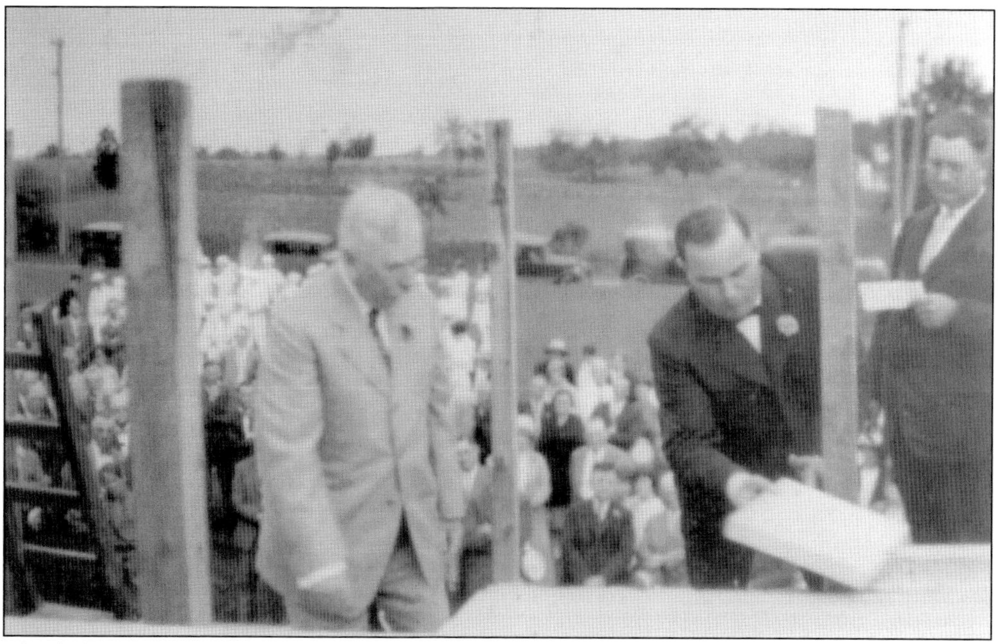

The dedication of a new unit is pictured around 1920. Grand View Hospital had many dedications over the years to let the community know of its progress and for much-needed fundraising. (Courtesy of Grand View Hospital Archives/Sellersville Museum.)

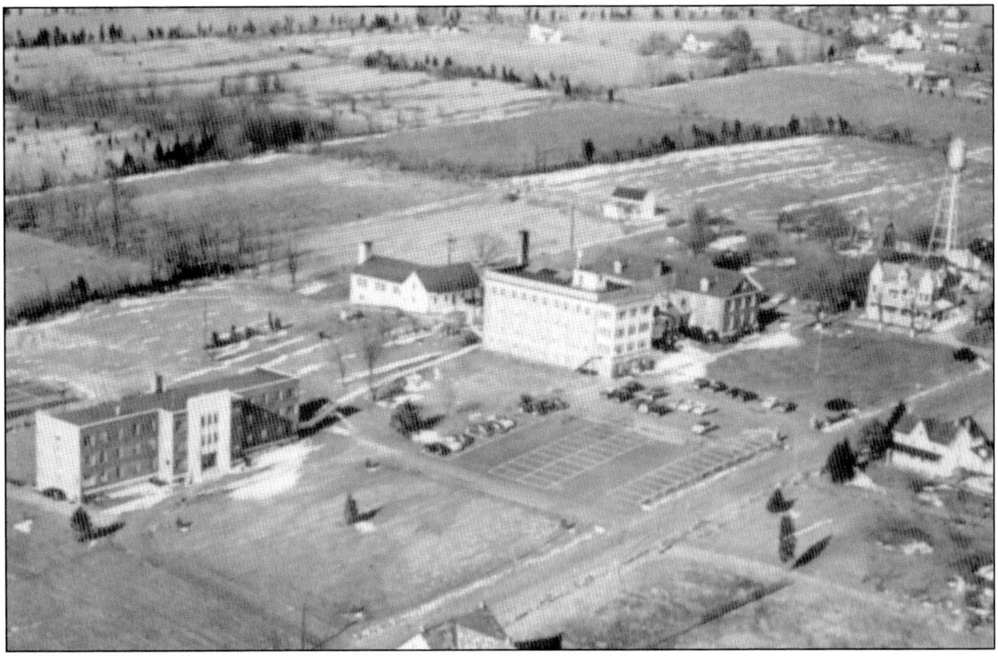

This is a c. 1950 aerial view of Grand View Hospital. Located at the upper right corner below the water tower is the original sanitarium. In the middle of the photograph stands the new unit of the hospital, and to the left is the nursing school. (Courtesy of Grand View Hospital Archives/Sellersville Museum.)

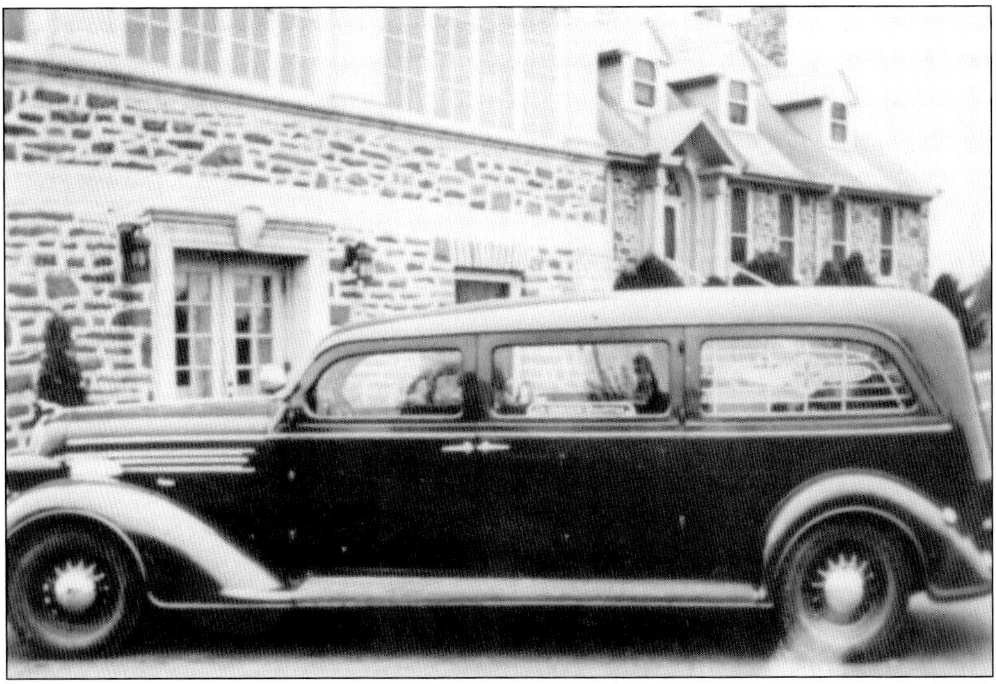

Pictured is a 1936 ambulance. Grand View Hospital continued its own ambulance service until 1945. At that time, a volunteer community ambulance service assumed responsibility for transporting patients. (Courtesy of Grand View Hospital Archives/Sellersville Museum.)

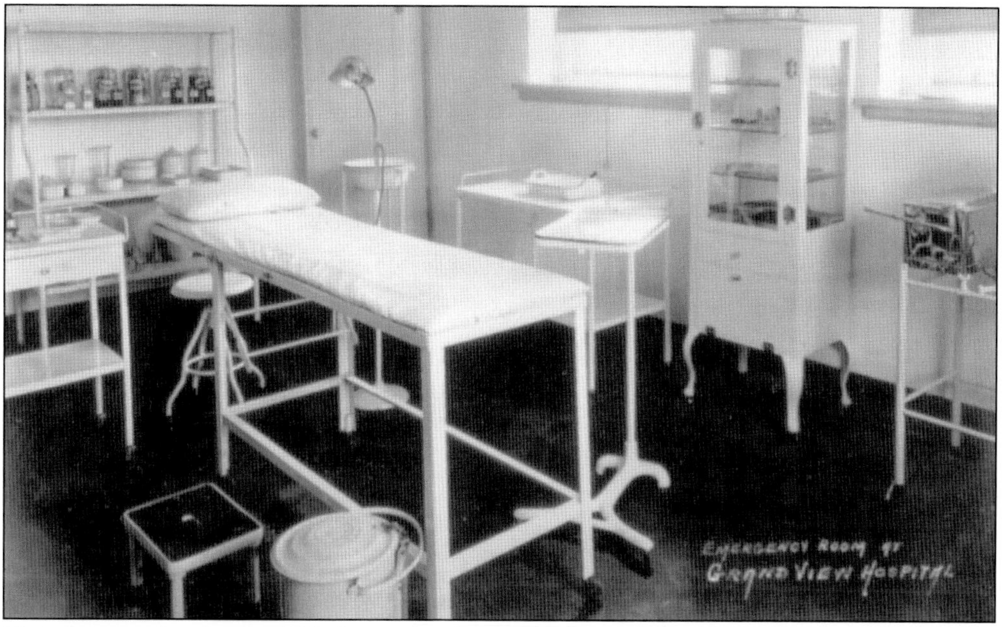

This photograph, taken in 1929, shows a vastly improved emergency room. Previously, instruments were brought from a nearby physician's office. Sterilization of instruments took place in the kitchen on a coal stove; sponges, pads, and other dressings were washed, dried, and sterilized for use on the next patient. Gowns were washed in the physician's home because their number was limited. (Courtesy of Grand View Hospital Archives/Sellersville Museum.)

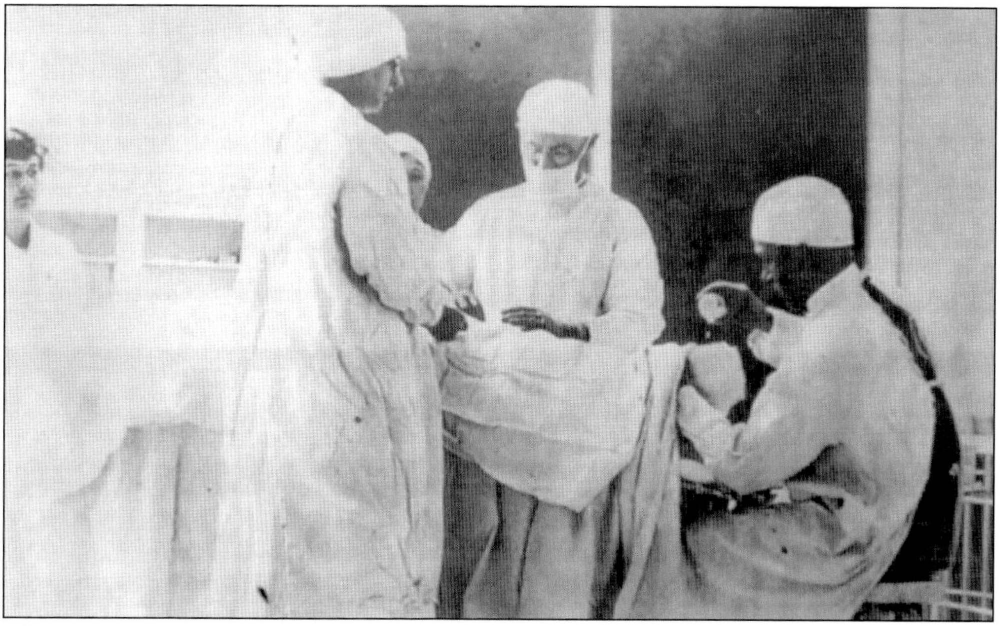

This 1929 surgery was preformed at Grand View Hospital by Dr. Stanley Moyer and Dr. H.C. Grim. Assisting were Helen Grim and Mary Layacn. This was a big improvement over the first surgeries in the earlier part of the century, when the doctors did not wear surgical gloves. One doctor even contracted an infection that left him unable to work for weeks. (Courtesy of Grand View Hospital Archives/Sellersville Museum.)

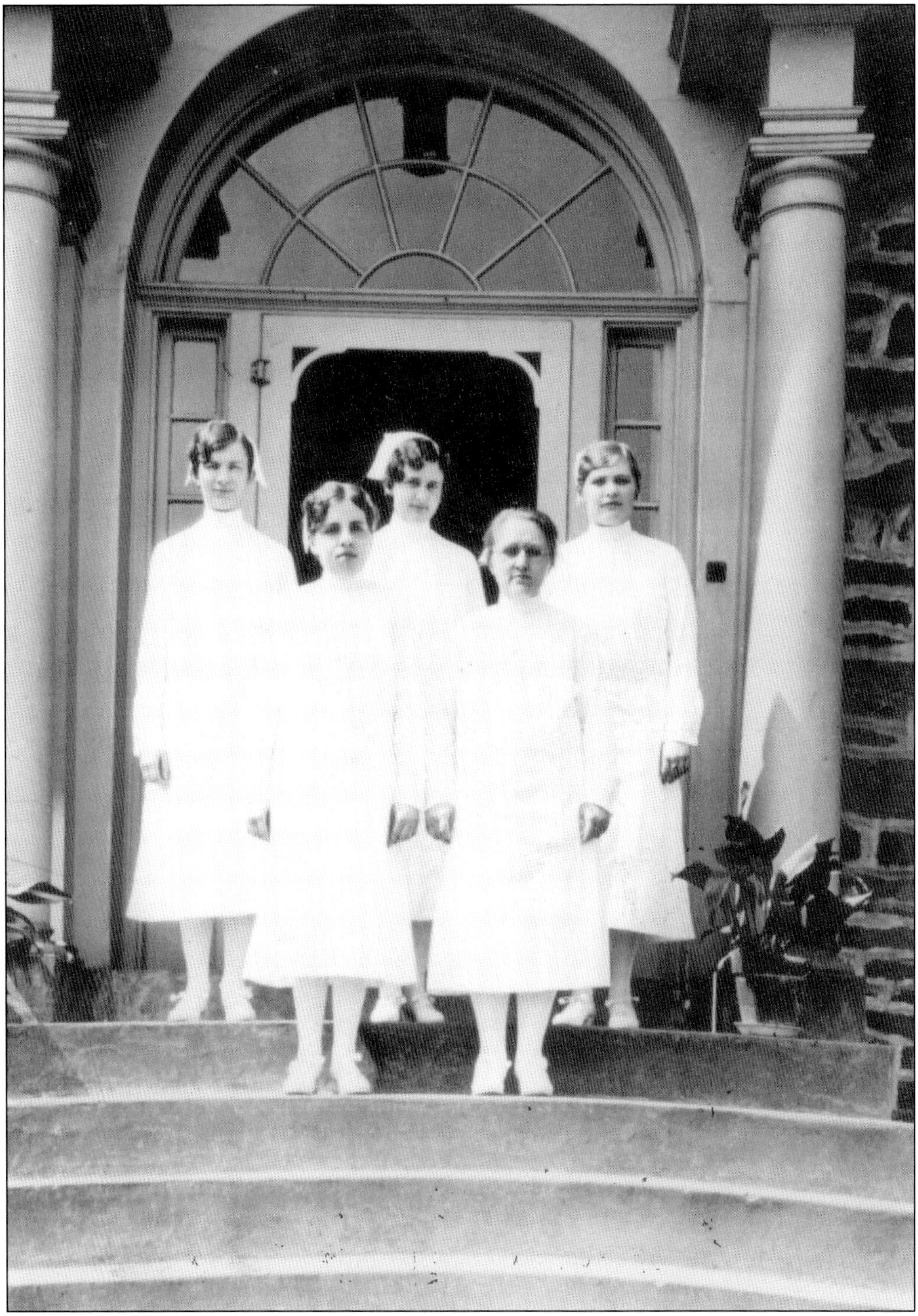

Shown is the graduating class of 1932 standing at the entrance of Grand View Hospital. Pictured are, from left to right, Evelyn Fredrick, Kathryn Rickert, Laura Moyer, Helen Bergstresser, and Helen Faulkner. (Courtesy of Grand View Hospital Archives/Sellersville Museum.)

Six

Grand View Hospital into the Future

Grand View Hospital saw rapid growth from the 1950s on. Medical technology was about to take a great leap. By this time, antibiotic and chemotherapeutic drugs were widely used to fight diseases. No longer did patients have to rely on home remedies and antiquated drugs and equipment. Life could be prolonged. Heart disease, cancer, and degenerative diseases would occupy the future of health care.

The hospital staff also had to adjust to the changing times. Grand View Hospital began to break down its services into specialized fields. Several departments were created, including surgery, urology, obstetrics, pediatrics, and orthopedics. Landmarks such as modern incubators were installed in the nursery, which helped the survival rate of many premature infants.

In 1955, Grand View Hospital marked the 10,000th birth at its facility. In 1966, Medicare became a reality for residents. The 1970s saw the demolition of the first unit, built in 1917, to make room for a new x-ray expansion. The 1980s and 1990s saw the beginning of managed care, which brought many changes to the hospital. Outpatient services increased, and subsequently inpatient bed space decreased. Today, Grand View Hospital covers 70 acres and employees 1,500 people, including a medical staff of 200. In 2012, Grand View Hospital will celebrate its 100th year of service to the community.

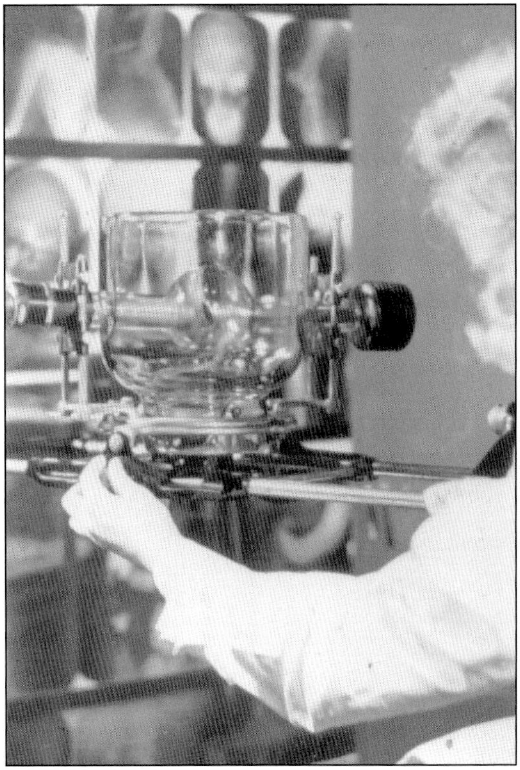

The radiology department at Grand View Hospital is pictured around 1943. In the very early days of x-ray, the equipment could actually burn a patient's skin. Medical advances changed that, and by the 1940s, x-rays were becoming an increasingly important tool for many medical specialties. (Courtesy of Grand View Hospital Archives/Sellersville Museum.)

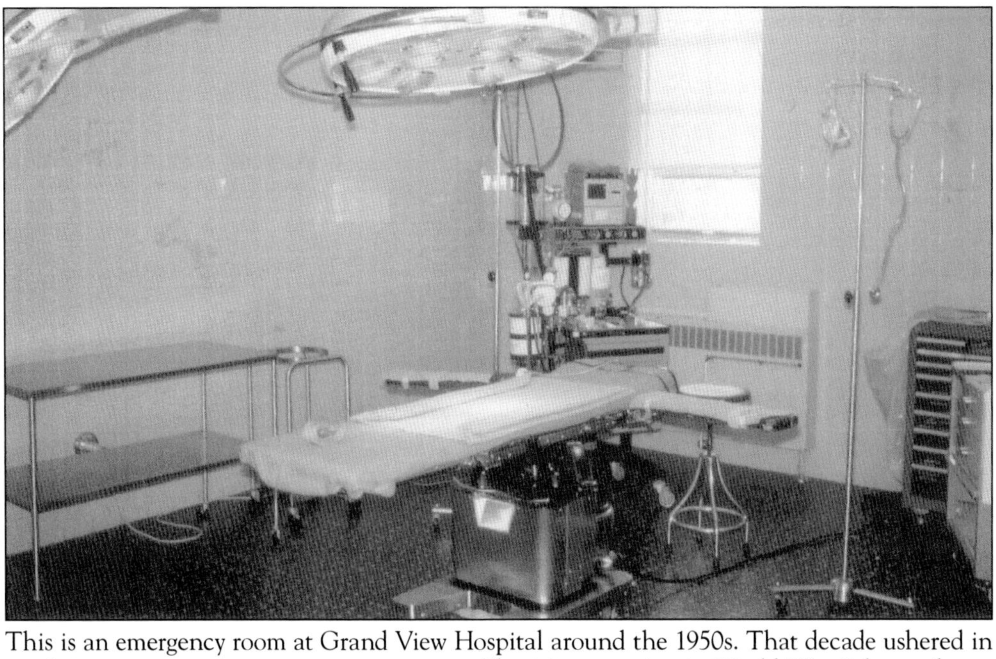

This is an emergency room at Grand View Hospital around the 1950s. That decade ushered in much improvement in emergency-room care. Physicians serving in World War II learned new battlefield techniques and brought them home, employing them in the local emergency rooms. Physicians found they could treat more patients effectively and efficiently with the new devices and knowledge available. (Courtesy of Grand View Hospital Archives/Sellersville Museum.)

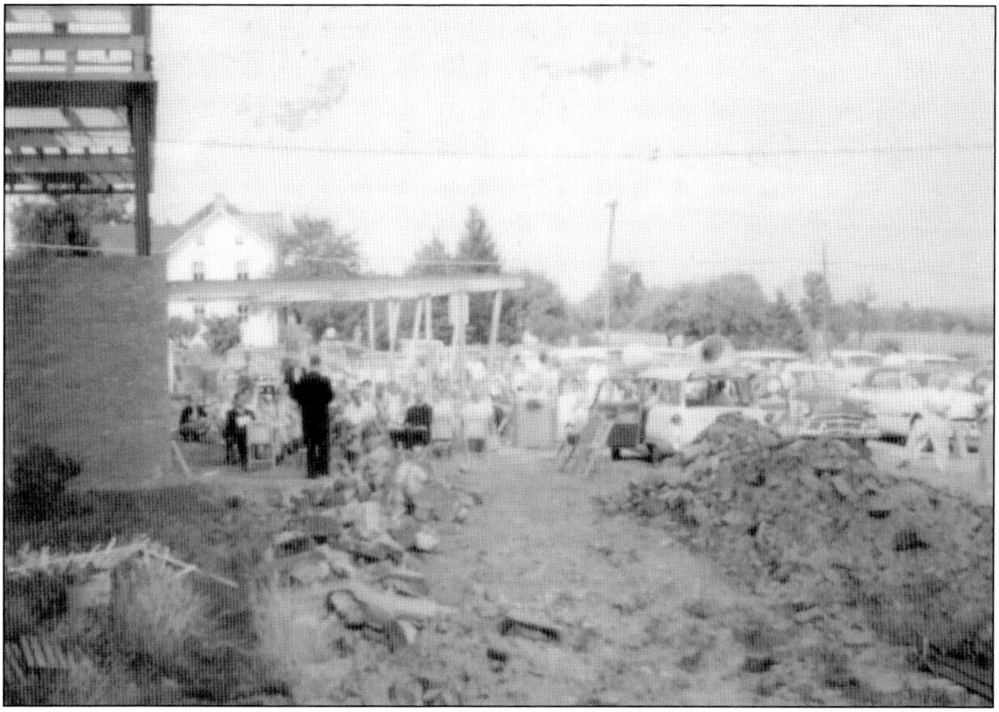
The construction and groundbreaking of the hospital in 1950 is pictured. (Courtesy of Grand View Hospital Archives/Sellersville Museum.)

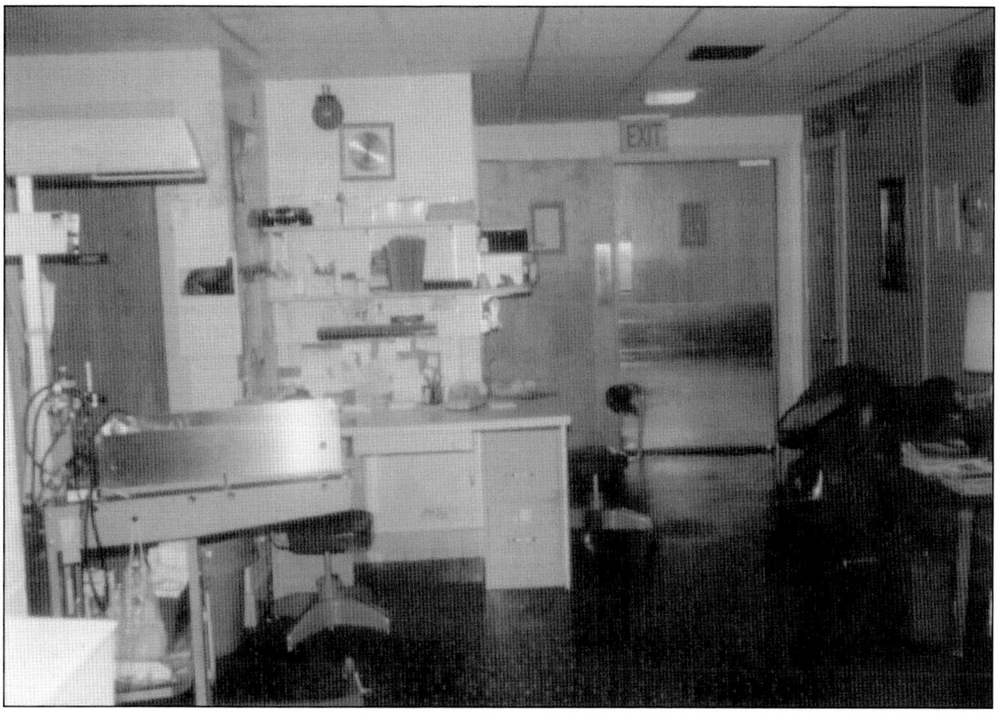

The entrance to Grand View Hospital is pictured around 1950. (Courtesy of Grand View Hospital Archives/Sellersville Museum.)

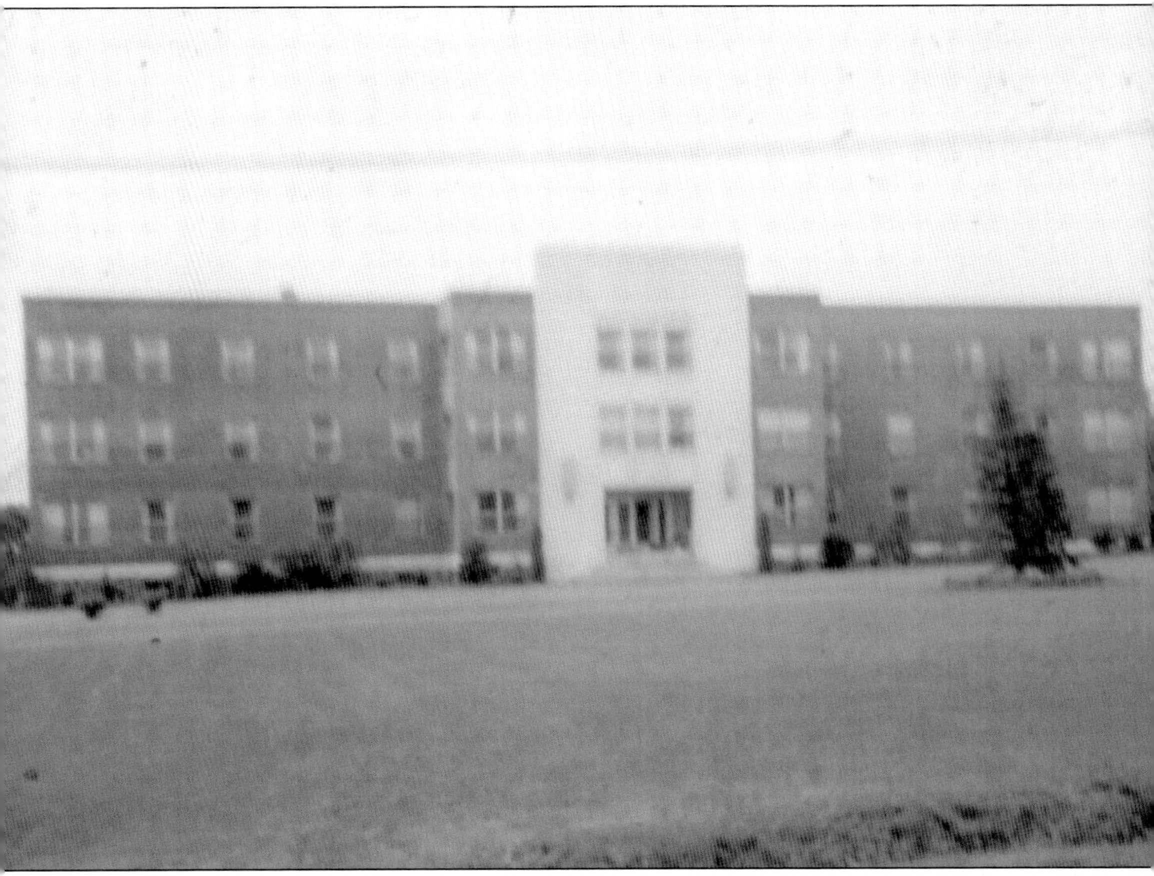

In the early years, nurses lived in and attended classes at the Pursell home. In this 1951 photograph, the new nurses' facility on Lawn Avenue is pictured. It was a vast improvement over what the earlier nurses experienced. This facility was a three-story structure with several classrooms, a library, a laboratory, a recreation room, and individual living quarters for 60 nurses. (Courtesy of Grand View Hospital Archives/Sellersville Museum.)

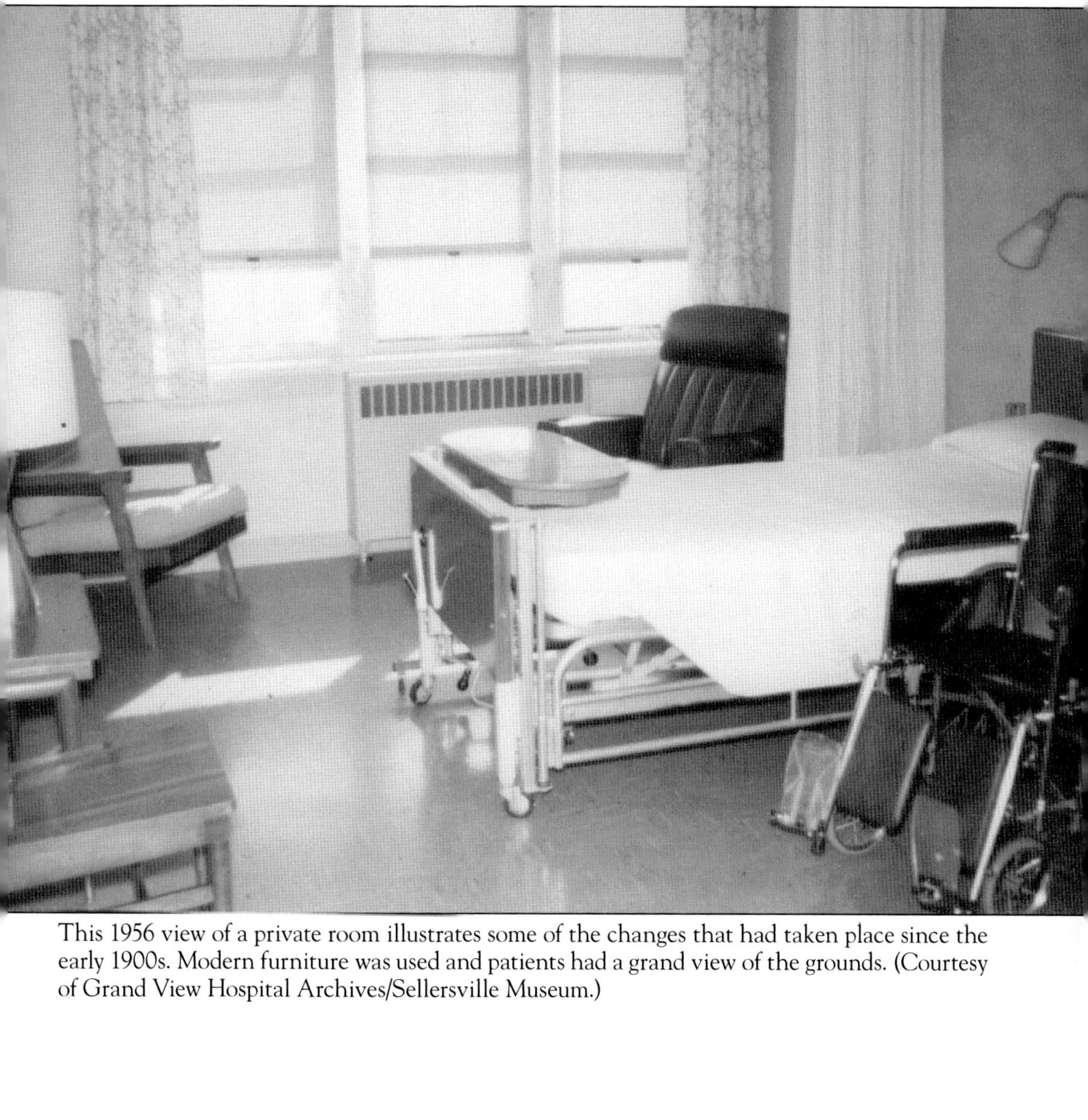

This 1956 view of a private room illustrates some of the changes that had taken place since the early 1900s. Modern furniture was used and patients had a grand view of the grounds. (Courtesy of Grand View Hospital Archives/Sellersville Museum.)

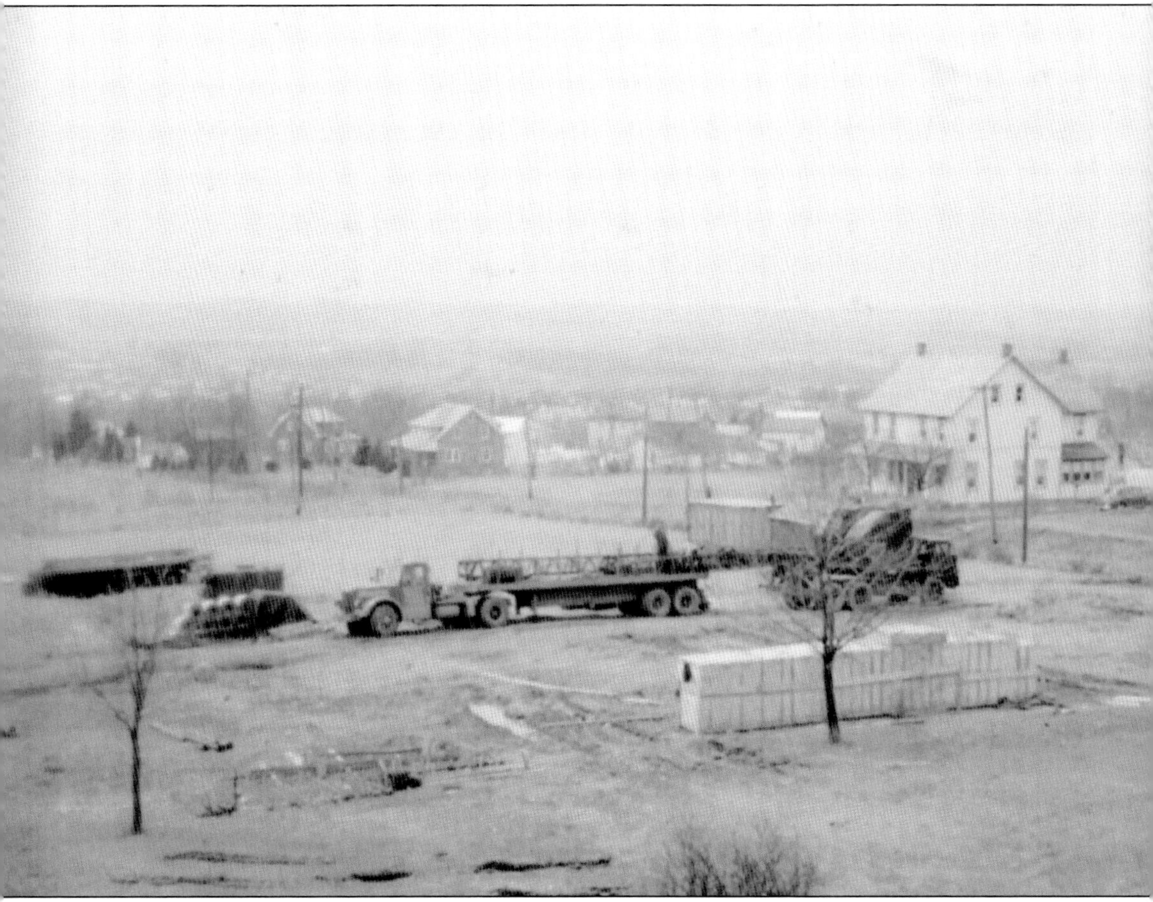

This c. 1969 photograph captures the destruction of the original Purcell home/sanitarium, which served as the first nurses' residence. The small water tower on the property was also demolished and replaced with a 150-foot, 100,000-gallon water tower. (Courtesy of Grand View Hospital Archives/Sellersville Museum.)

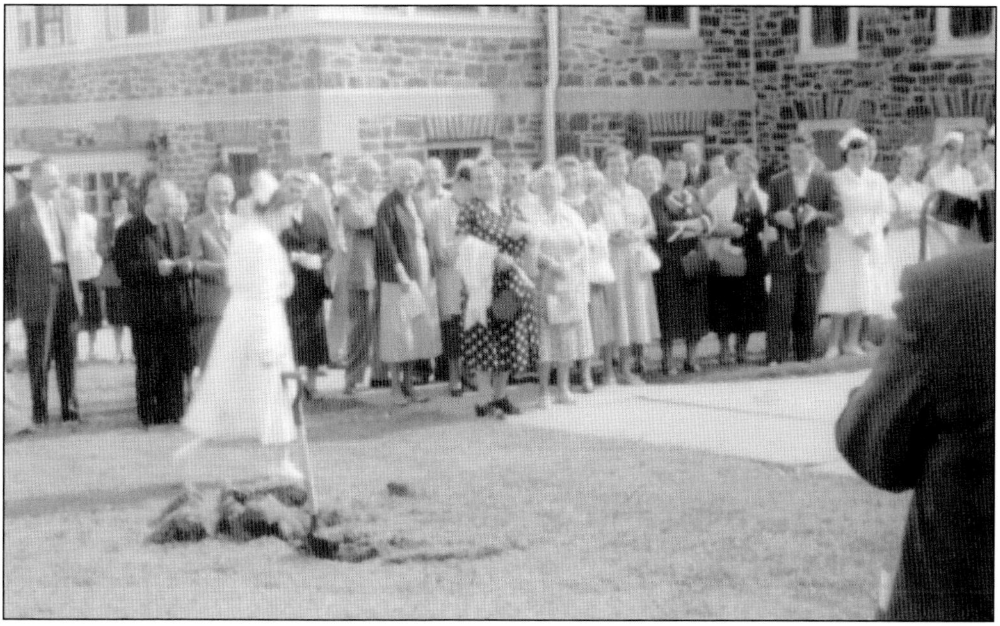

Nellie Hoffecker is pictured walking away after her groundbreaking moment at the 1956 dedication of the new unit. Hoffecker was the superintendent of nurses and completed 25 years of service to the hospital. Under her administration, Grand View had undergone two expansions, constructed and equipped a nurses' home, and dedicated a modern annex. She resigned her position in 1958. (Courtesy of Grand View Hospital Archives/Sellersville Museum.)

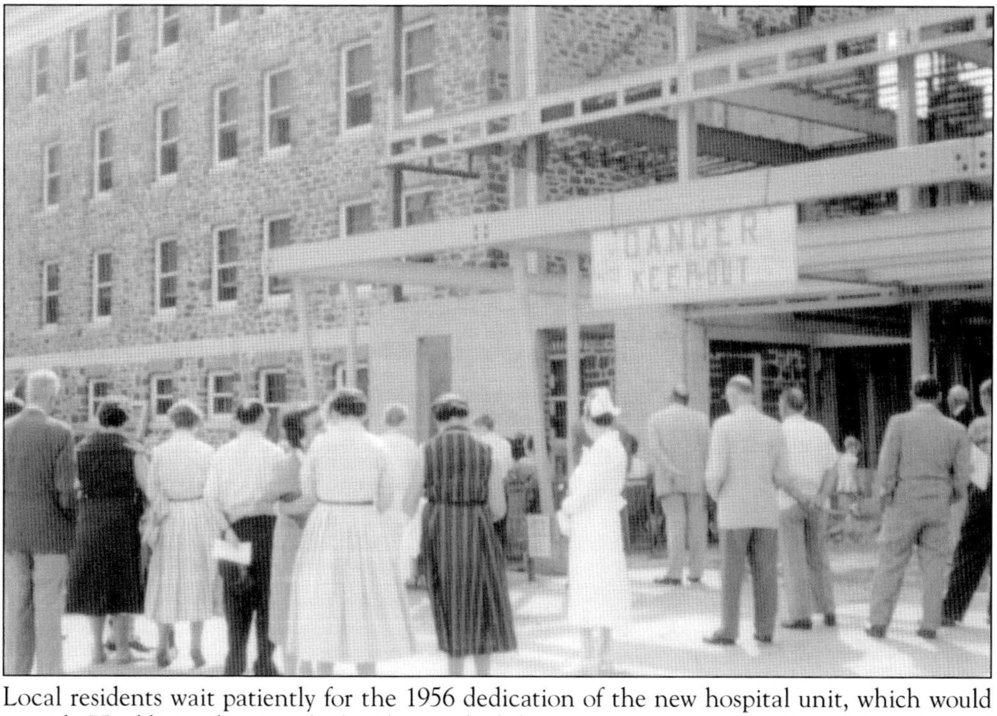

Local residents wait patiently for the 1956 dedication of the new hospital unit, which would provide 75 additional patient beds. This marked the most extensive expansion the hospital had seen to date. (Courtesy of Grand View Hospital Archives/Sellersville Museum.)

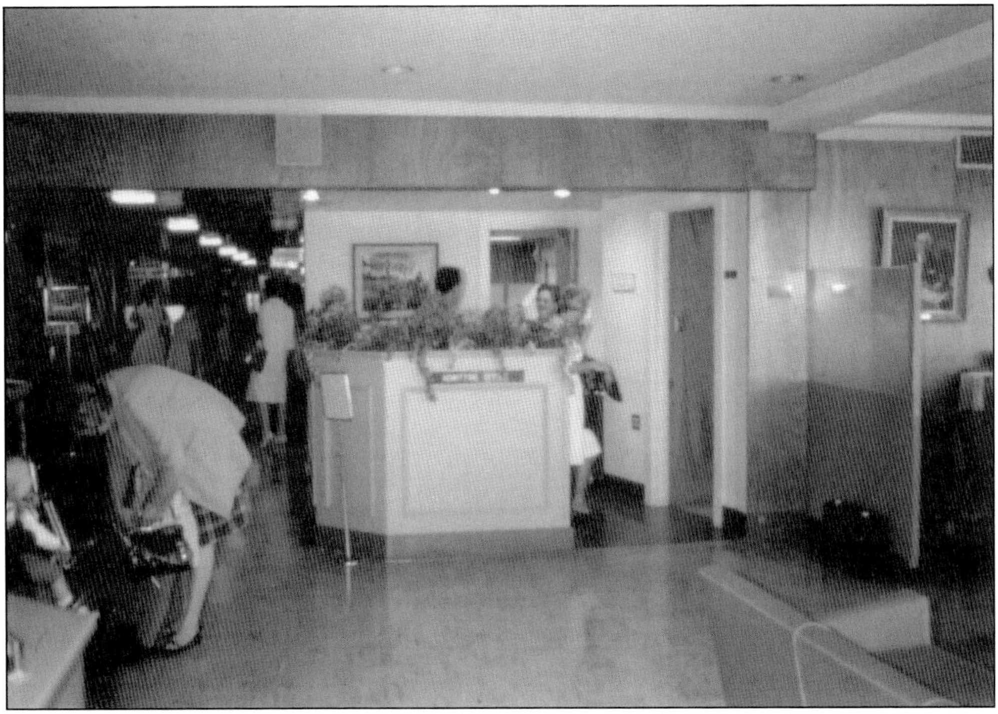

This is what the interior entrance of Grand View Hospital looked like in the 1950s. (Courtesy of Grand View Hospital Archives/Sellersville Museum.)

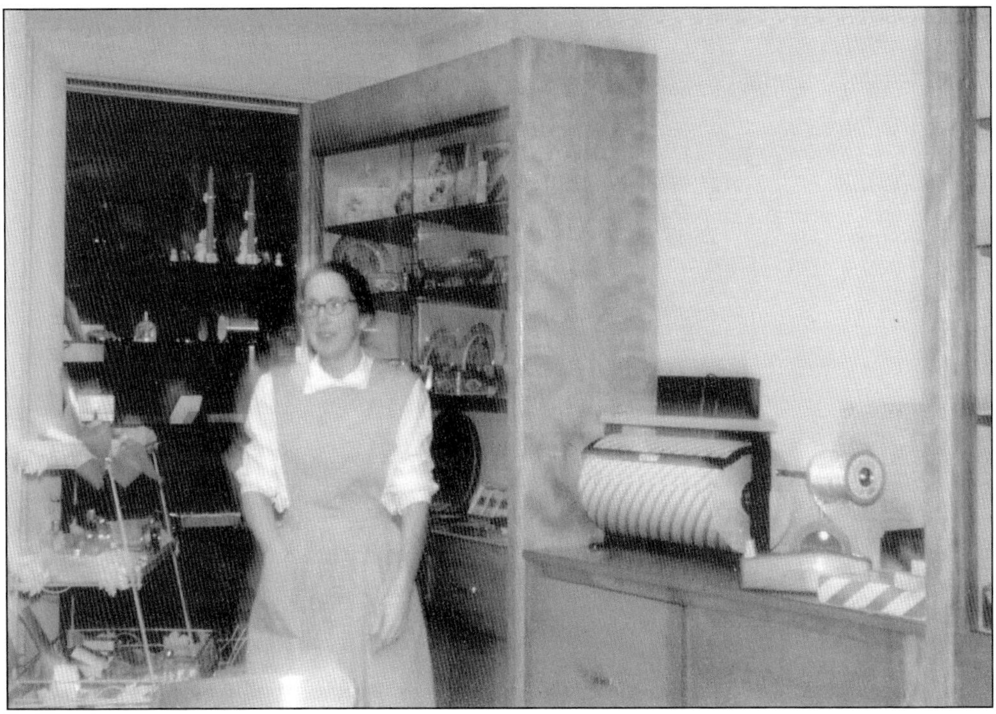

Pictured is the gift shop inside Grand View Hospital. (Courtesy of Grand View Hospital Archives/ Sellersville Museum.)

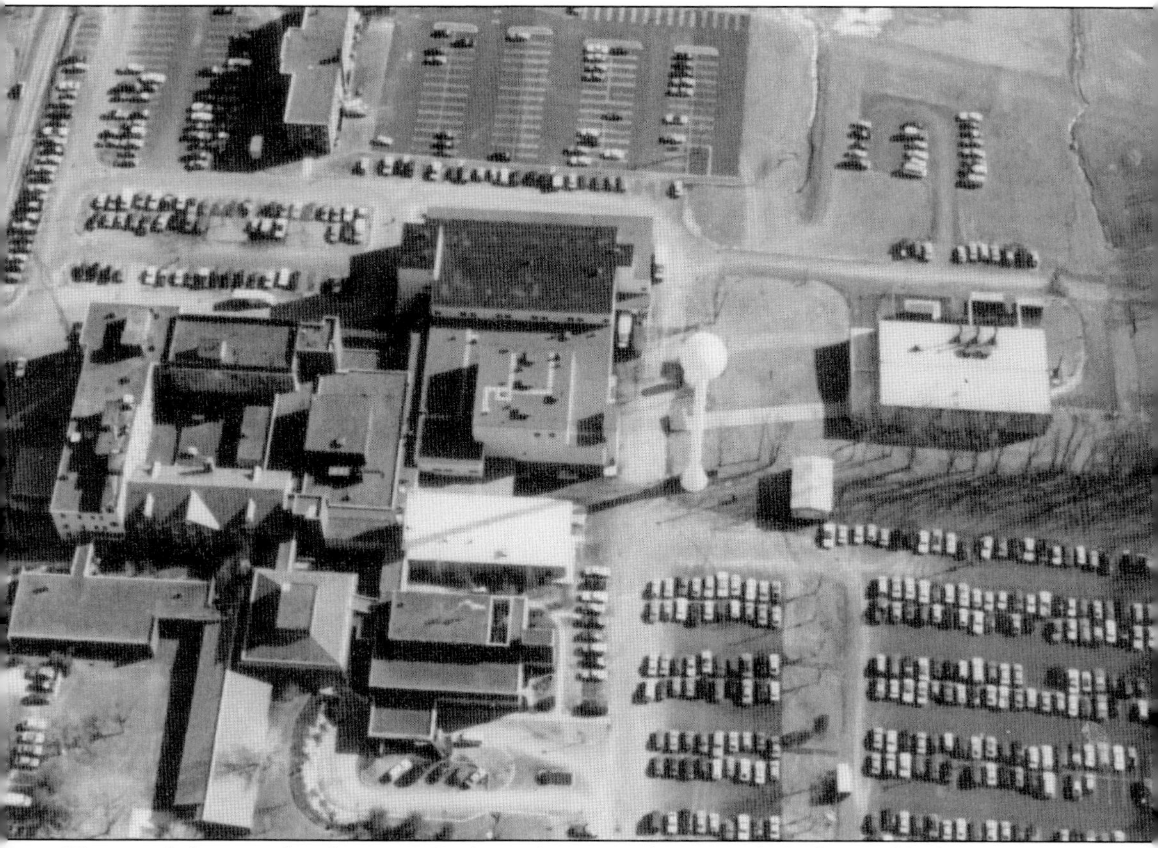

This aerial photograph, taken in 1969, shows the tremendous growth the hospital had seen since its beginnings. Note the new water tower at right center. (Courtesy of Grand View Hospital Archives/Sellersville Museum.)

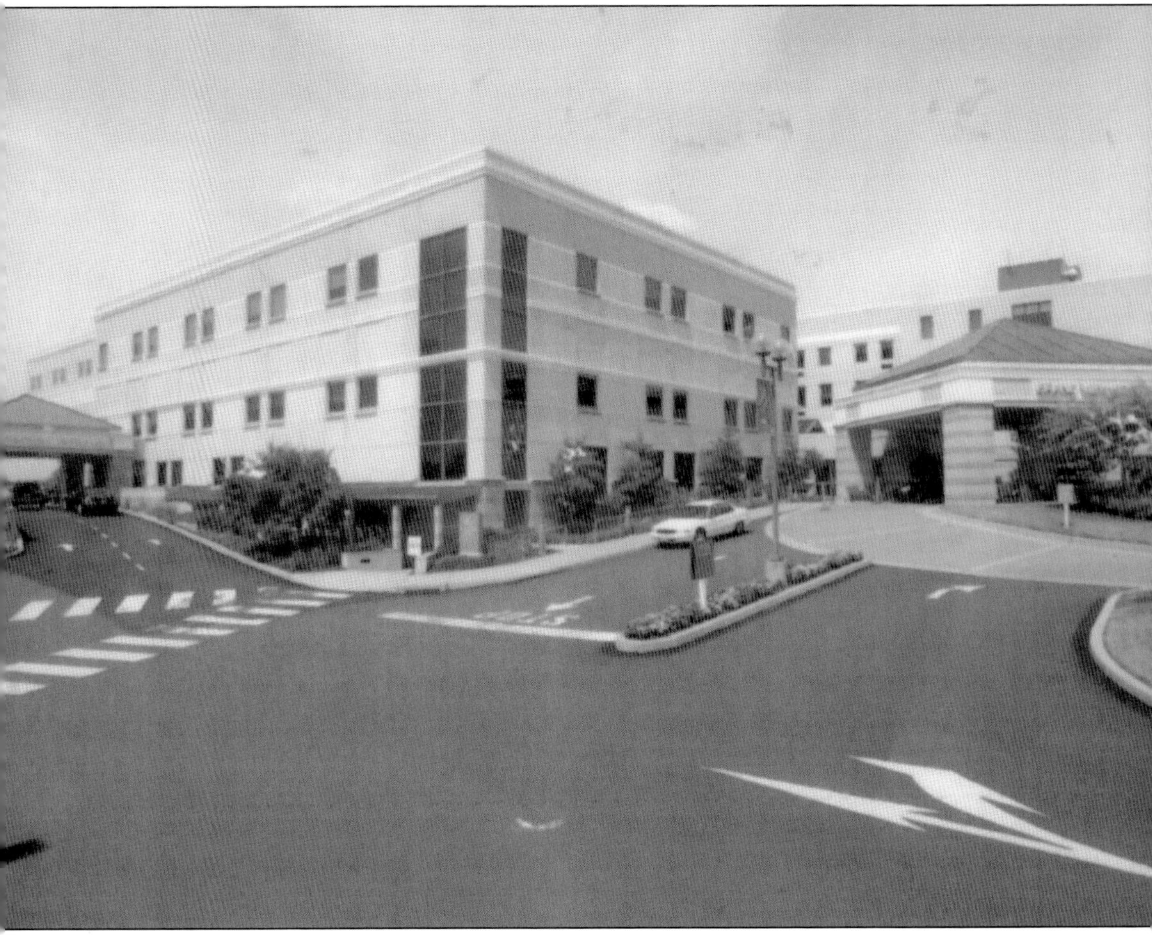

Grand View, on Lawn Avenue in Sellersville, is pictured as it looks today. The hospital has outpatient facilities in the surrounding areas of Harleysville, Sellersville, Pennsburg, Quakertown, and Upper Bucks. (Courtesy of Grand View Hospital Archives/Sellersville Museum.)

Seven

Rockhill's Brush with Fame

East and West Rockhill have seen a taste of both fame and infamy. Famous people traveling through likely do not realize the impact that they have on the residents. The infamous leave behind a silence and only whispers tell of their tales. The German-American Bund is an example of such dark and villainous action. Operating in West Rockhill without the knowledge of residents, Fritz Kuhn and his followers, supporters of Hitler, preached a doctrine of hatred and anti-Semitism. Soon, the law caught up with them; Kuhn was arrested and served five years in a New York state prison. Upon his release, he returned to Germany and died in obscurity.

John Fries and George Getman, West Rockhill residents, were heroes to some and criminals to others. Some thought they were standing up against taxation created to pay for a nonexistent war. Others felt they instigated rebellion and other treasonous acts. The idea of being taxed on the size of a house and the size and number of its windows was too much for most residents to bear. In 1798, Fries led a band of about 60 armed men around the countryside to intimidate, threaten, and run the assessors out of town. They were successful in keeping the assessors from doing their work in Milford and the surrounding areas. Similarly, armed intimidations occurred in the Northampton area. Fries and Getman were arrested, charged with treason, and sentenced to death. President Adams later pardoned them both.

There are also the daily silent heroes who are hardly recognized—firefighters, police, and soldiers. One such individual was Norris White, a soft-spoken gentleman known as a renowned wood turner. Norris could turn a piece of wood into an extraordinary piece of art. He also collected bells. What was not widely known was that Norris White was drafted into the Army in February 1943. A paratrooper, he served in the elite 82nd Airborne in Europe, where he participated in D-day, the Battle of the Bulge, and the standoff with the Germans at Nijmegen.

This chapter aims to honor and recognize those who have had an impact on the community, both the infamous and local heroes.

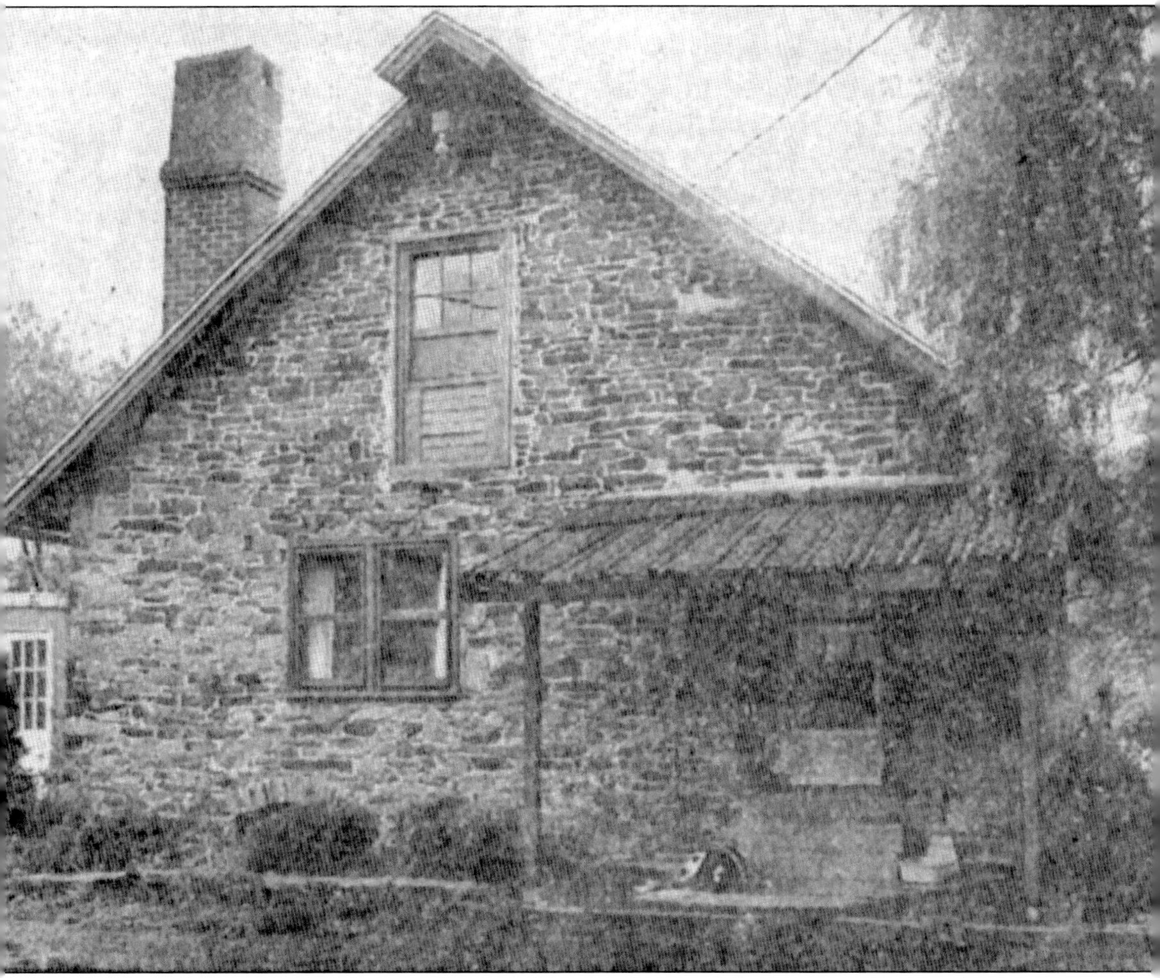

This old 40-acre farm with its small mill and German-style buildings seems peaceful and picturesque. In 1939, this property was bought from the Wilhelm family and became known as Deutschhorst Country Club. Most of the members of the country club where not local residents, though the club did sell property to local residents as a guise to hide their identity and to raise money for their nefarious cause. In reality, it was owned by the German-American Bund, supporters of Hitler and his 1,000-year reich. The bund was a rising force that preached racism and anti-Semitism. Fritz Kuhn, one of the Bund's leaders, was later arrested. The landscape has changed very little over the years, but very little physical evidence is left of the former country club. (Courtesy of WRHS.)

The photograph at right of Chief One Star with his horse Spotted Thunder was taken around 1940. Chief One Star was an Oklahoma Cherokee who came to live in this region. He put on shows for the locals and was a frequent customer at the local inns. The chief was also a well-known artist and would pay his outstanding tabs by painting murals on walls and rocks. The painting below is the last known mural of Chief One Star and is located on the wall of Emil's Restaurant on Ridge Road in East Rockhill. At the time the chief painted the mural, the establishment was known as the East Rockhill Hotel. (Courtesy of WRHS.)

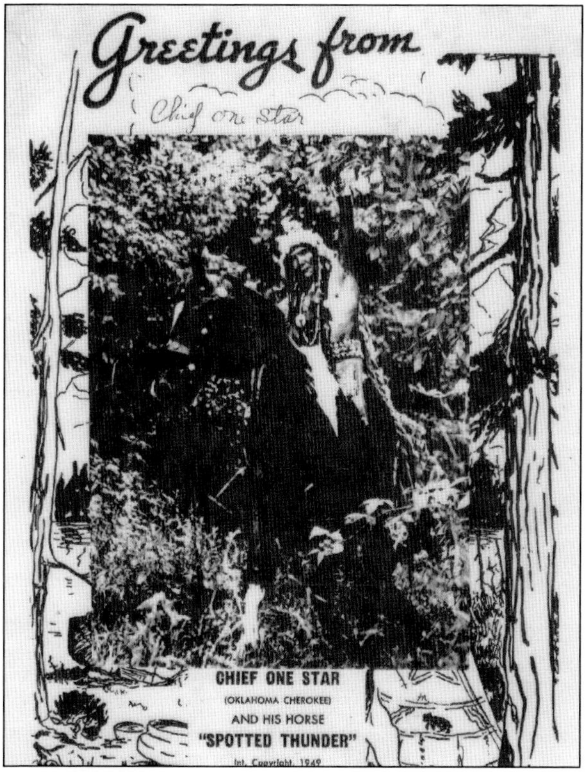

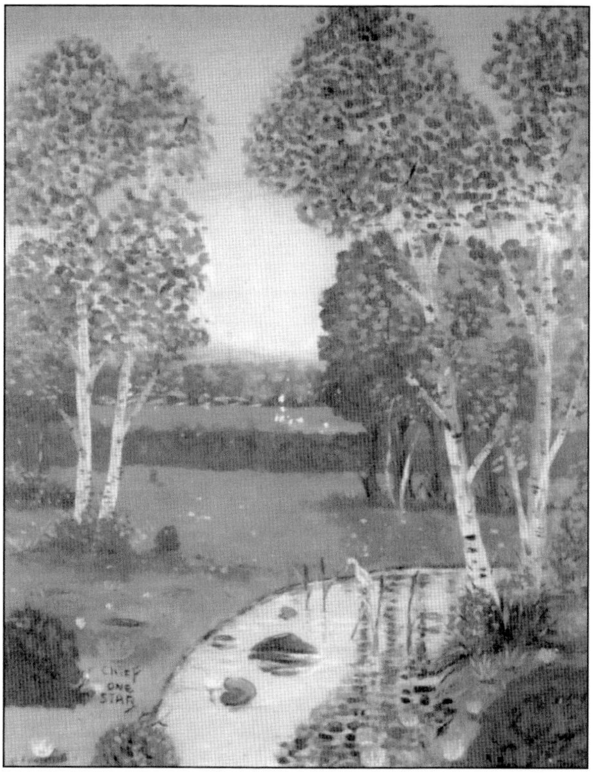

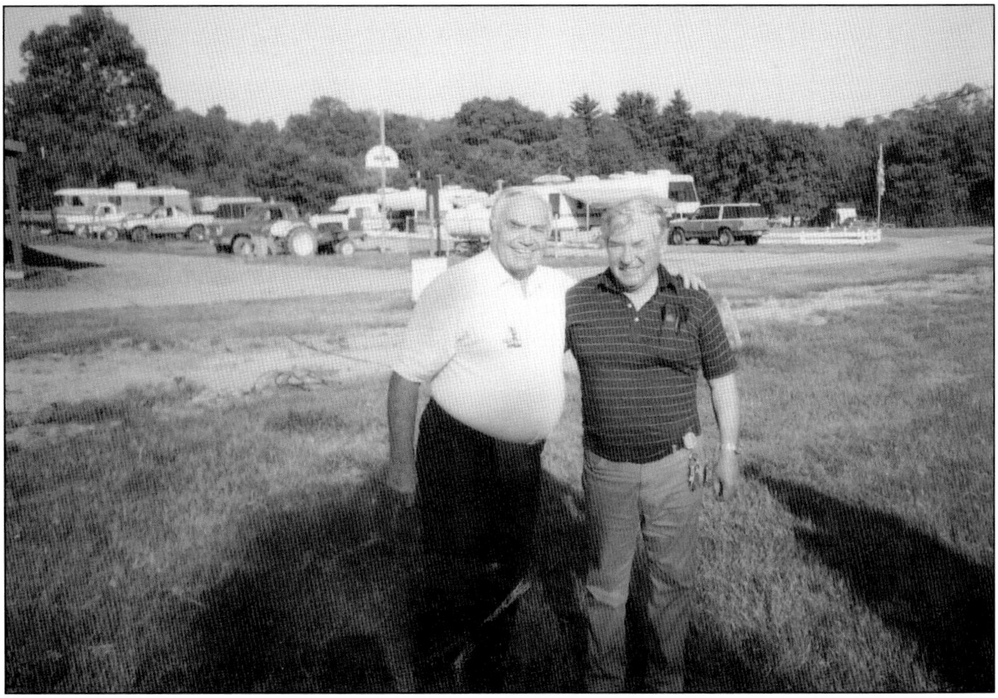

Ernest Borgnine visited the Homestead Farm Campground in West Rockhill Township off Allentown Road. He appears here with the current owner, Whitey Hager. Below, Borgnine poses with Earl Bachamn, friend of Whitey Hager and longtime visitor of the Homestead Farm Campground. (Both, courtesy of Whitey Hager.)

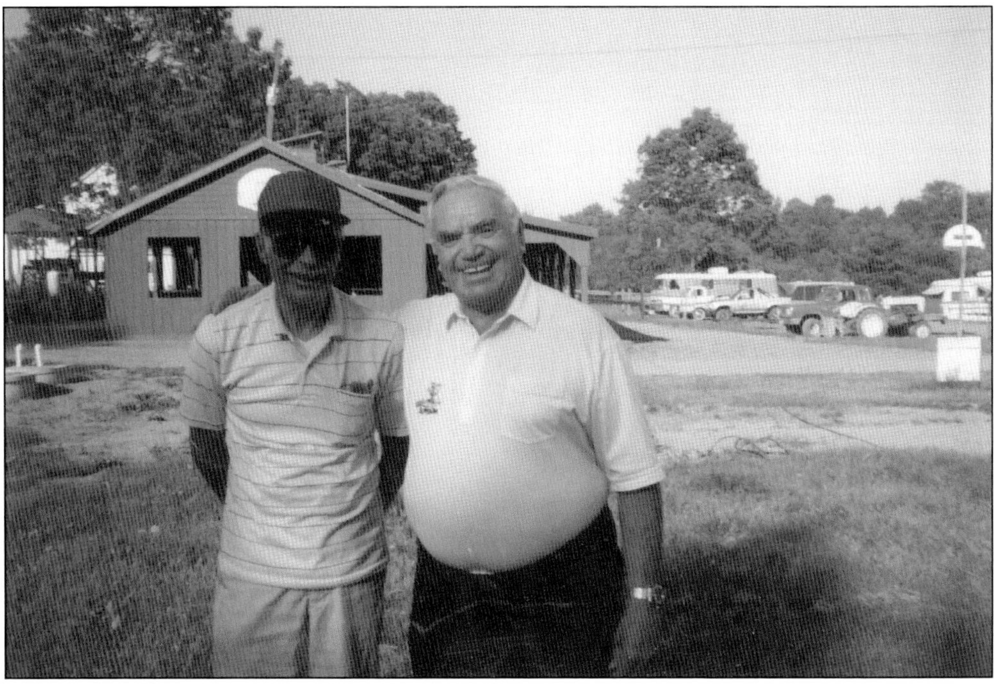

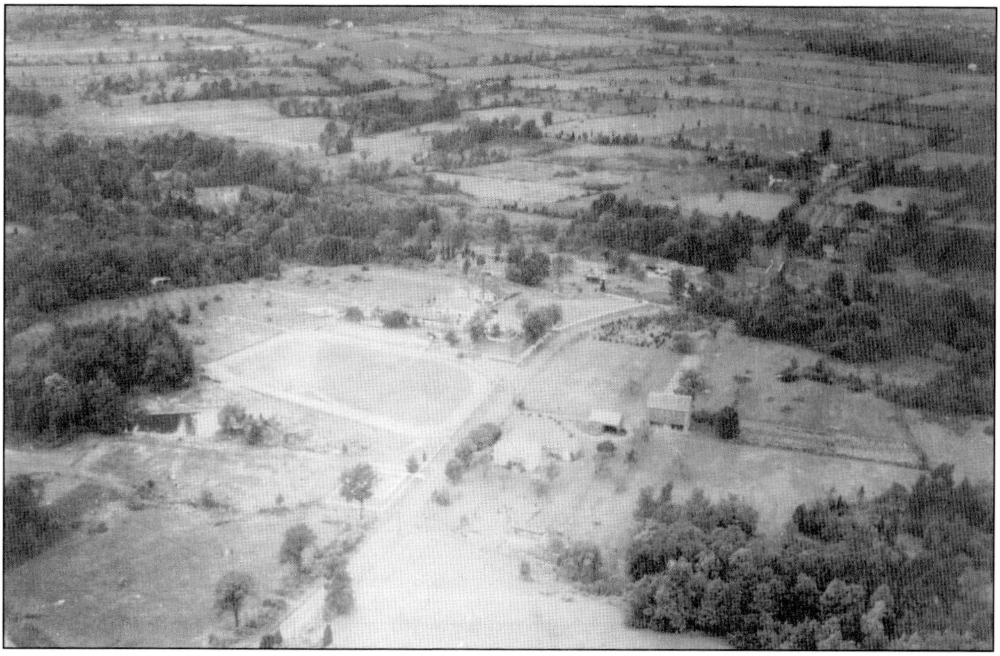

This mid-20th-century photograph is an aerial view of the Homestead Campground and an example of the picturesque beauty of Rockhill Township. The campground consists of a main residence, a tenant residence, a recreational building, a barn, a garage, tennis courts, a swimming pool, and a stream, all laid out on a sprawling estate of 34 acres. (Courtesy of Whitey Hager.)

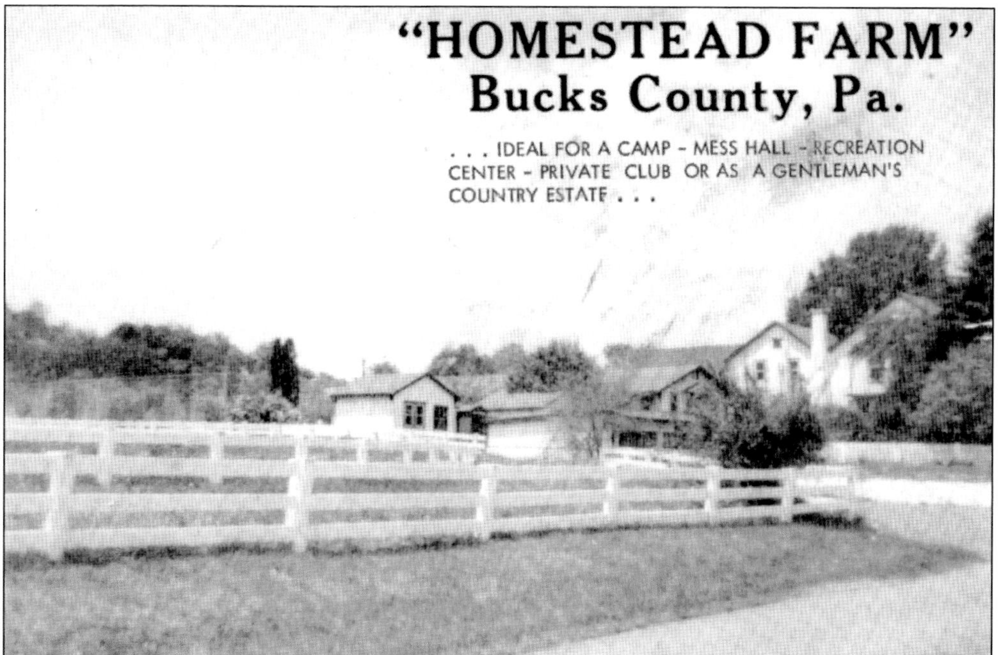

This photograph shows the real estate advertisement of the Homestead Farm around 1967. Homestead Farm was the childhood home of a prominent Philadelphia businessman. He spent 50 years developing and enlarging this beautiful estate. (Courtesy of Whitey Hager.)

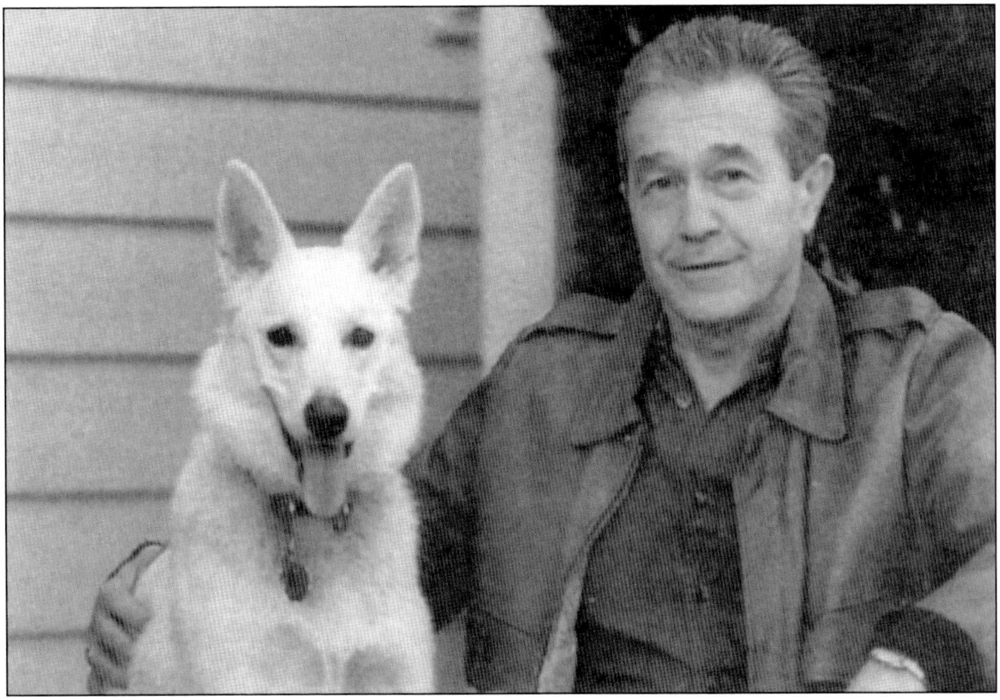

Lee Felbinger is the author of three books about the history and collectibles of the Lone Ranger. Lee is pictured here with his dog Silver that he purchased from Silverdale. (Courtesy of Lee Felbibger.)

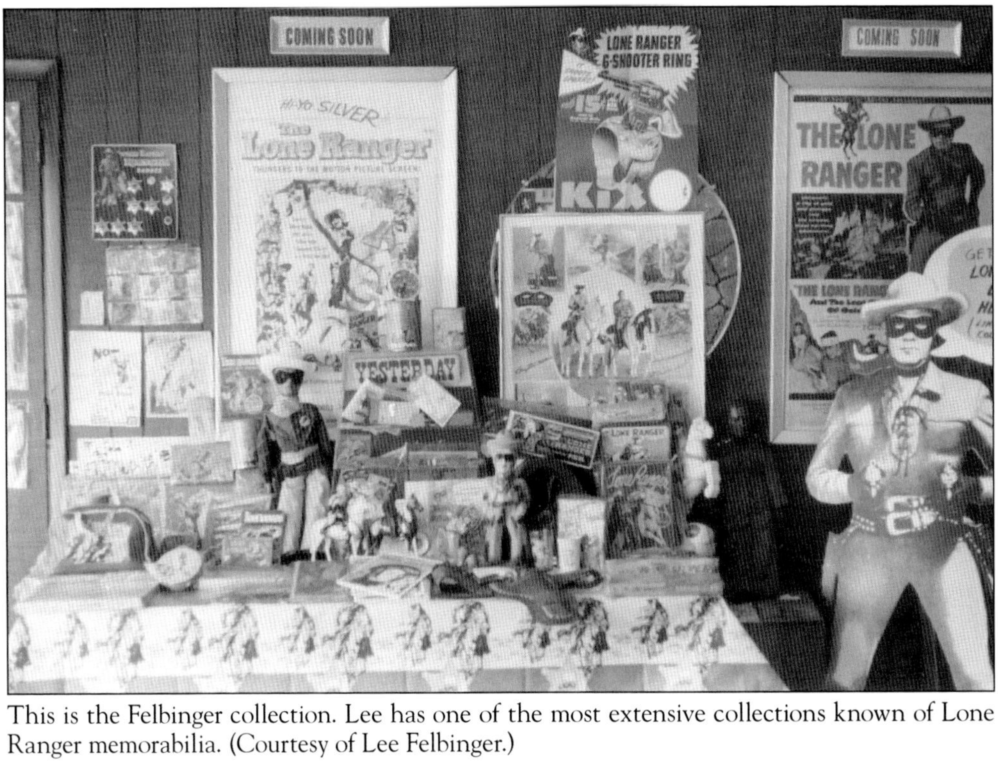

This is the Felbinger collection. Lee has one of the most extensive collections known of Lone Ranger memorabilia. (Courtesy of Lee Felbinger.)

West Rockhill's very own Charlie Guenst played with the Hazelhurst Cardinals, a class D minor league team for the Louisiana Cardinals. Charlie's family has been a fixture is West Rockhill since the 1890s. (Courtesy of Charles Guenst.)

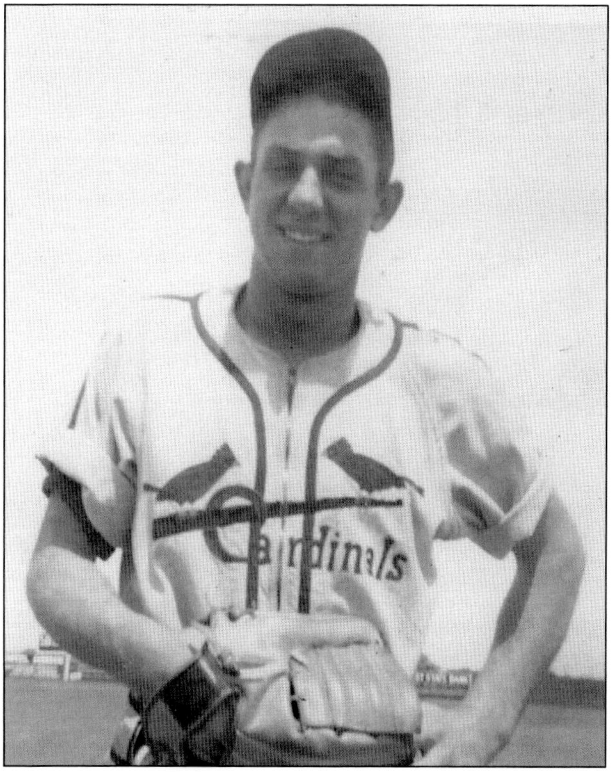

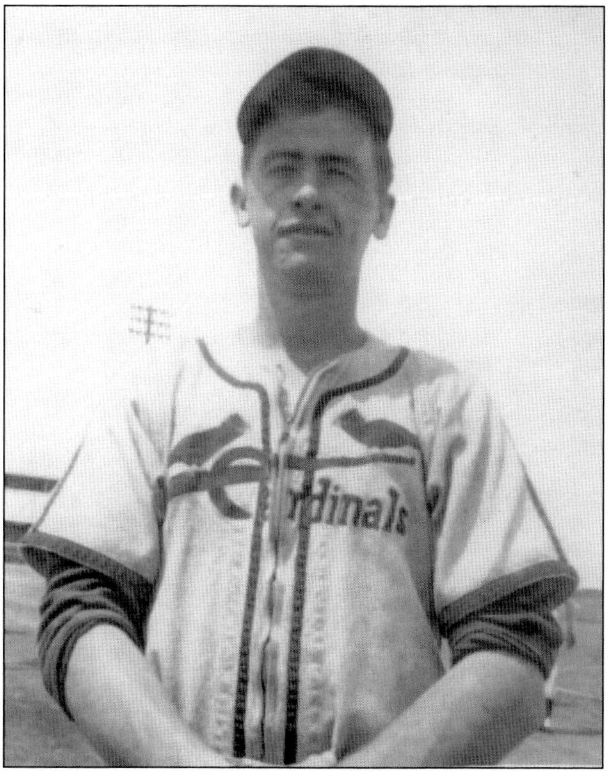

This photograph is of Jim Moyer, who also played ball for the Hazelhurst Cardinals. Moyer is the father of Jamie Moyer, famed pitcher of the Philadelphia Phillies. Although Jim and his son Jamie lived in a neighboring township, many current residents of East and West Rockhill grew up with both Jim and Jamie. (Courtesy of Charles Guenst.)

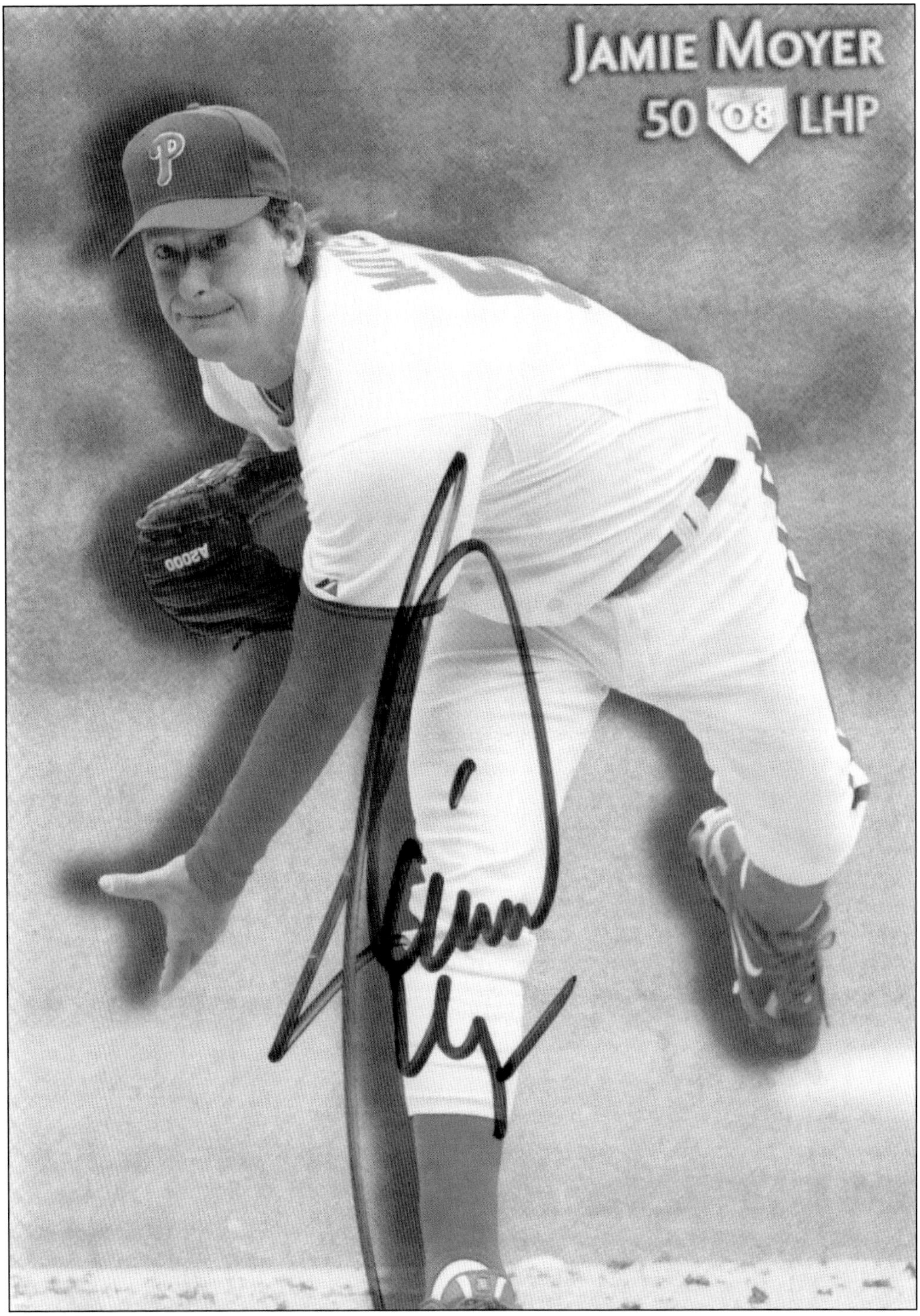

Famed Philadelphia pitcher Jamie Moyer was born in Grand View Hospital, but he grew up in nearby Sellersville. Although he did not grow up in East or West Rockhill, many people from this area attended school with him and knew him well. Jamie started playing professional ball in 1986 and has played 24 seasons. (Courtesy of Charles Guenst.)

RUTH "RICHY" RICHARD • c/of

ALL AMERICAN GIRLS PROFESSIONAL BASEBALL LEAGUE

1943-1954

HGT: 5'4" WGT: 134 BATS: LEFT THROWS: RIGHT BORN: 9/20/28

HOMETOWN: ARGUS, PENNSYLVANIA

COMPLETE MAJOR LEAGUE BATTING RECORD

YEAR	CLUB	G	AB	R	H	2B	3B	HR	RBI	SB	BB	SO	AVG
1947	GRAND RAPIDS CHICKS	47	147	5	26	3	1	0	7	2	4	13	.177
1948	ROCKFORD PEACHES	110	363	30	61	9	5	1	35	11	25	24	.168
1949	ROCKFORD PEACHES	84	265	23	45	0	0	1	20	11	27	14	.170
1950	ROCKFORD PEACHES	95	315	29	79	11	6	1	28	12	25	13	.251
1951	ROCKFORD PEACHES	99	368	34	102	7	3	0	60	6	18	19	.277
1952	ROCKFORD PEACHES	106	394	41	112	14	5	3	46	9	13	12	.284
1953	ROCKFORD PEACHES	92	341	33	86	11	0	2	48	7	15	9	.252
1954	ROCKFORD PEACHES	92	325	42	97	12	0	7	43	14	15	5	.298
	Major League Totals	725	2518	237	608	67	20	15	287	72	142	109	.241

Major League Fielding Totals	G	PO	A	E	PB	PCT.	POS.
	653	2613	603	130	45*	.956	C
*1953 N/A	51	55	2	4		.934	OF

CAREER HIGHLIGHTS

Five time All Start catcher, 1949-1954 . . . Once caught two back-to-back no-hit games in a playoff series . . . Toured Central America with A.A.G.B.L. All Stars, 1949 . . . Played against men's teams with Allington's All Americans after A.A.G.B.L. suspended operations . . . Ruth Richard lives in Sellersville, Pennsylvania and works as a solderer on aircraft gauges . . . She hunts, fishes, plays golf and makes the best pickles in town".

West Rockhill's very own Ruth Richards played for the All American Girls' Baseball League (AAGBL) as the five-time all-star catcher from 1949 to 1954. She once caught back-to-back no-hit games in a playoff series. She toured Central America with the AAGBL All Stars in 1949. She played against men's teams with Allingtons All Americans after her AAGBL career. Ruth was born and raised in Argus and still lives in the house she grew up in. (Courtesy of Ruth Richards.)

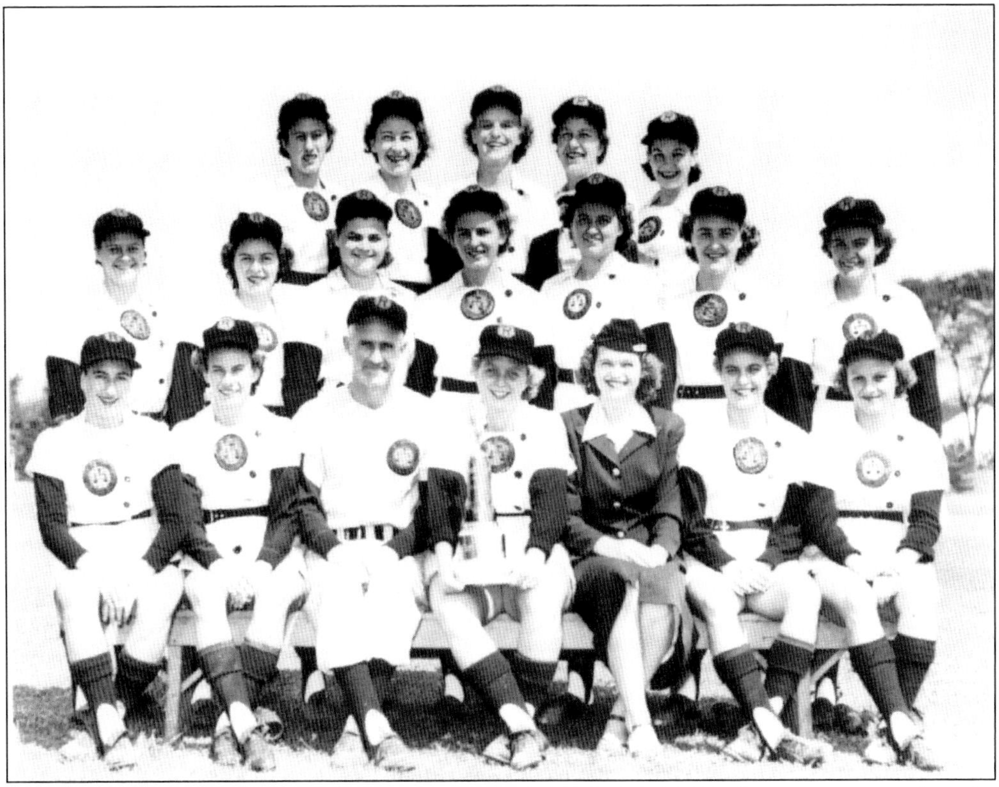

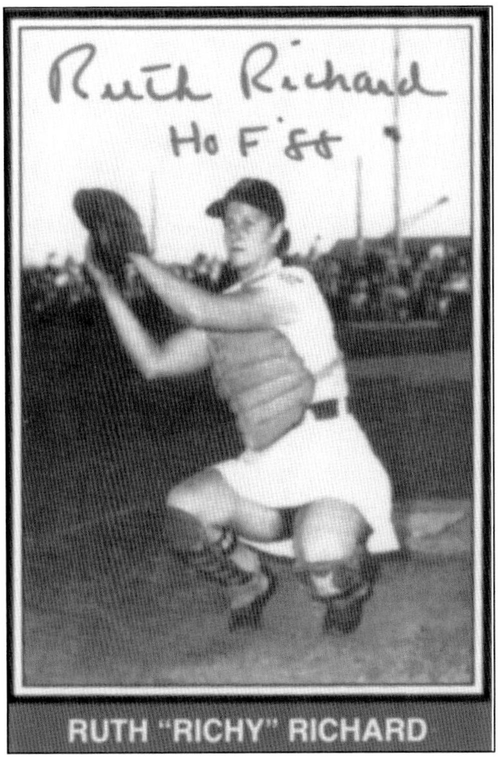

The 1949 AAGBL champions are gathered here. Included in the photograph are, from left to right, (first row) Dorothy Ferguson Key, Melba Alspaugh, manager Bill Allington, Lois Florreich, Dorothy Green, chaperone Charlen Barnett, and Irene Apple Areen; (second row) Ruth Richards, Alice Pollitt, Jean Lovell, Jacqueline Kelley, Louise Erickson, Betty Werfel, and Helen Fox; (third row) Dorothy Karmenshek, Dorothy Harrell Doyle, Elenor Callow, Rose Gacioch, and Doris Neal. (Courtesy of Ruth Richards.)

Pictured is the major league baseball card for Ruth Richards, who played from 1943 to 1954. (Courtesy of Ruth Richards.)

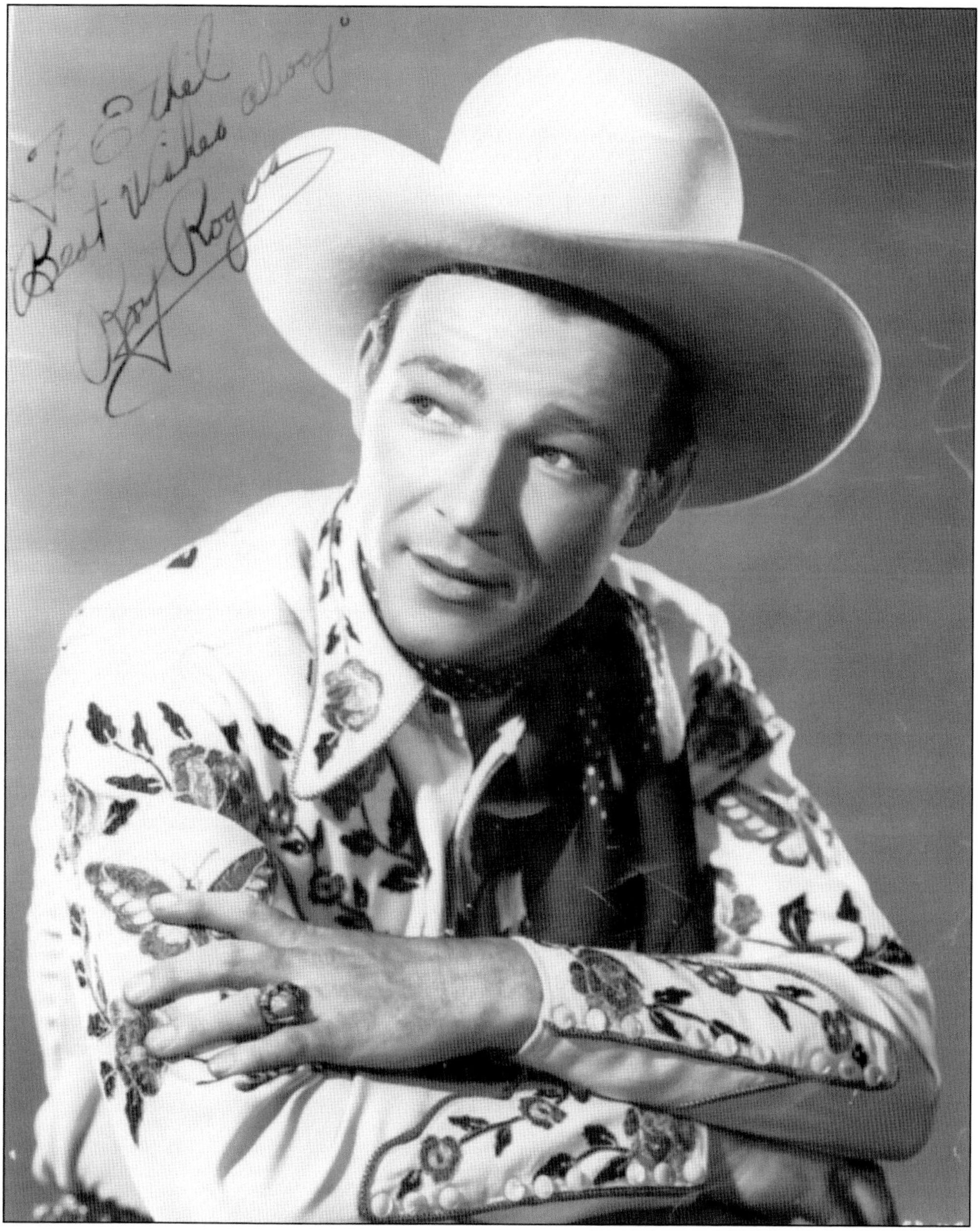

This souvenir photograph of Roy Rogers from the Grand View Hospital collection was signed "to Ethel." Roy Rogers was a frequent visitor at Grand View Hospital's yearly Lawn Fete. He came frequently to visit his friend William Hill Sr., who owned and operated the Palomino farm on Cat Hill Road. Ethel is believed to have been an employee of Grand View Hospital. (Courtesy of Sellersville Museum/GVH collection.)

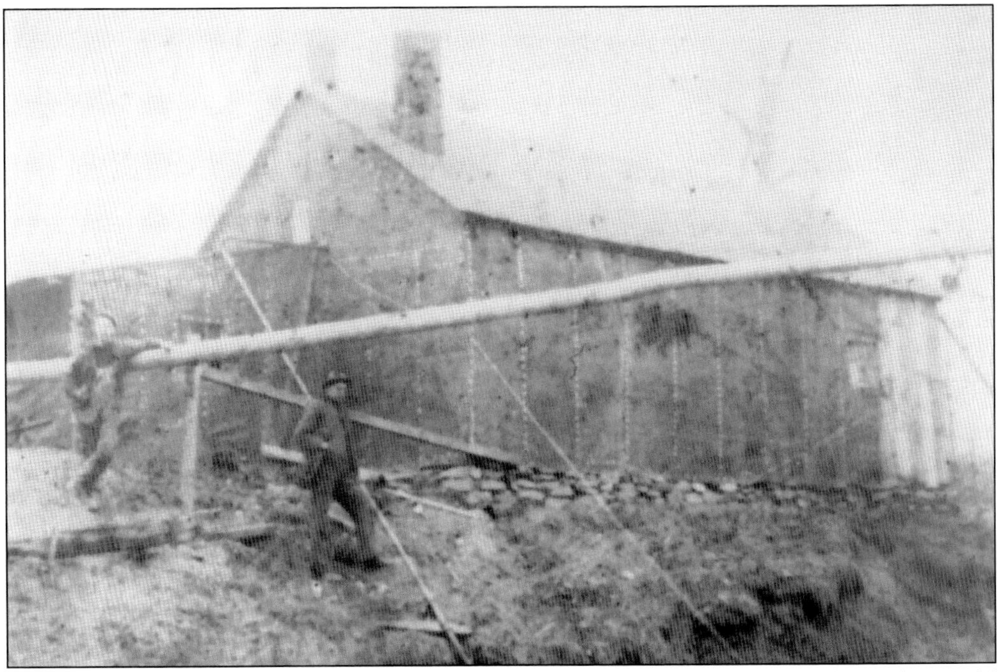

There's gold in them there hills—or maybe not. These photographs of the mine located on Gold Mine Road in West Rockhill were taken in 1905. The mineshaft reached 90 feet into the rocky terrain and was in operation for several years. Jacob Opdyke was the manager of the mine until the early 1900s, when it was flooded after a dynamite charge was set off, and mining operations ceased. A 1908 survey claimed that the rock yielded about $1 worth of gold per ton of rock. Jim Pettie bought the property in 1922. He still owns it today. The mine still exists, and it is still flooded. (Both, courtesy of George DiDomizio.)

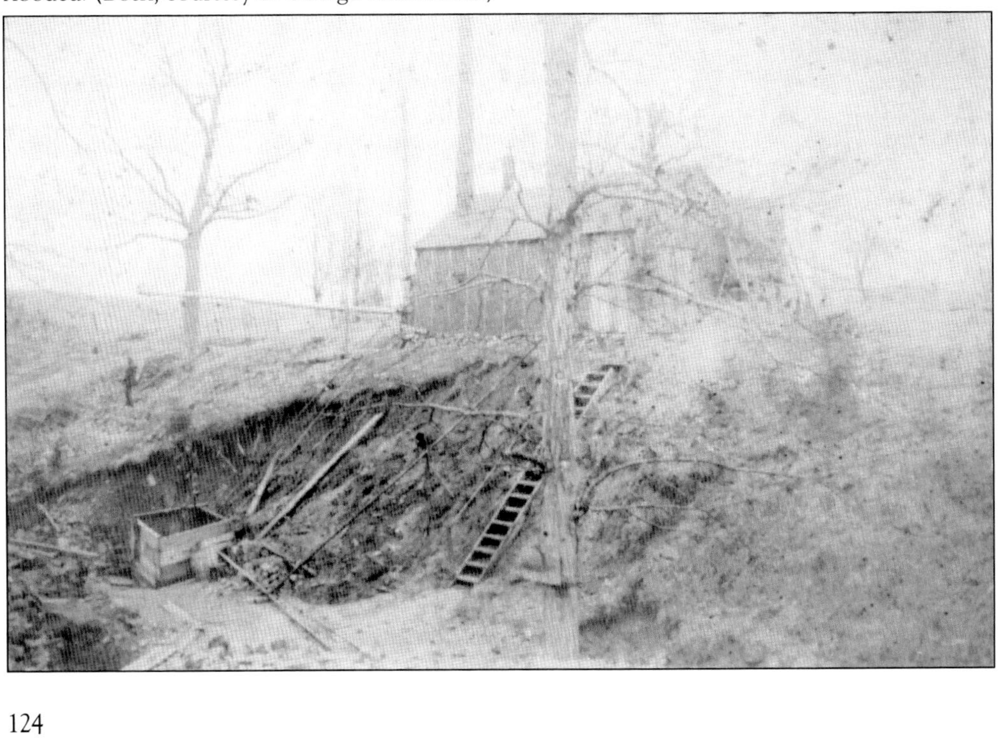

When Roy Rogers starred in the Philadelphia Rodeo, he was introduced to and befriended William Hill Sr. of West Rockhill township. Hill was renowned for his Palomino horses, which he raised on his farm on Cat Hill Road. Rogers came to visit the Hill farm to see the Palominos in 1942, when this photograph was taken. Pictured at right around 1939 is the barn on the Palomino property. (Both, courtesy of WRHS.)

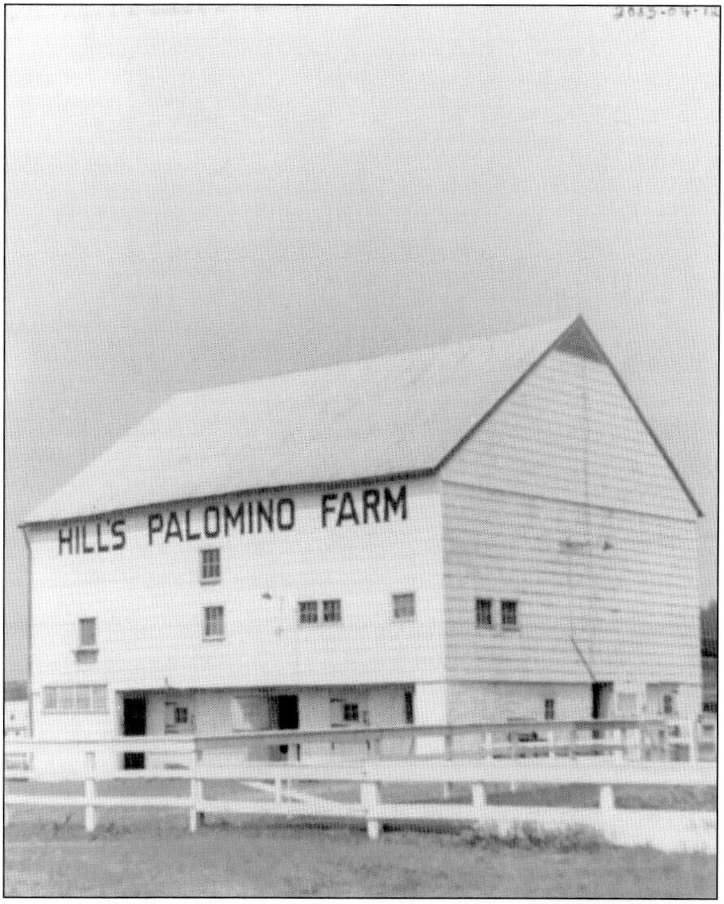

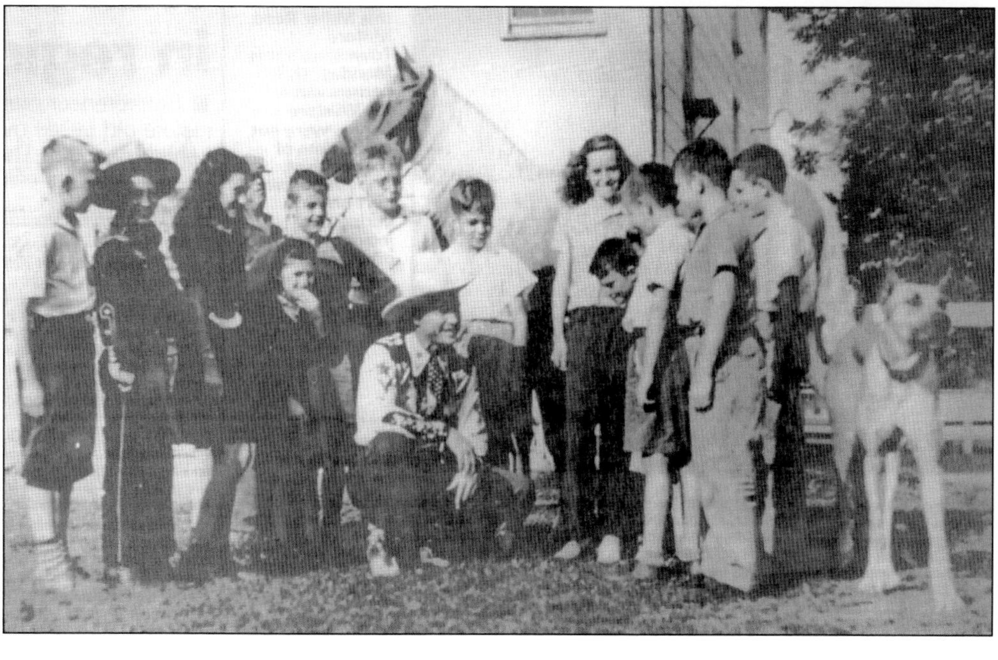

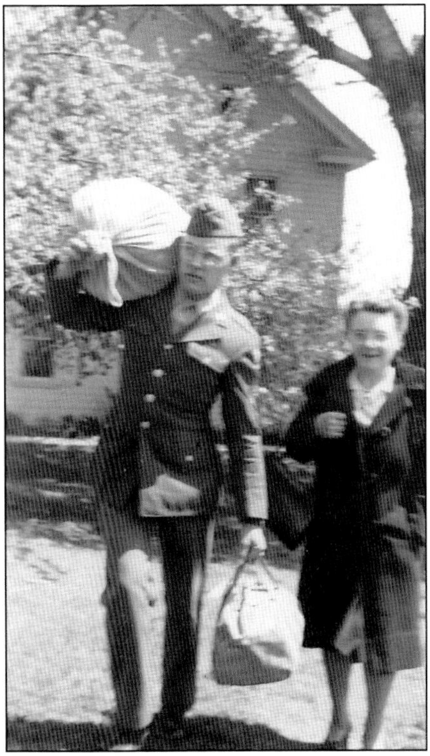

The Charles family sees off their son during World War II in 1944. Charles Guenst served with the 37th Division Tank Company, 148th Regiment in Camp Poke in 1954. The residents of East and West Rockhill want to take a moment to thank all those who served and died for our country. There are many residents who have served in many conflicts, beginning as early as the Revolutionary War. We want to remember and honor them in the last two photographs of this volume. (Left, courtesy of Petrona Charles; below, courtesy of Charles Guenst.)

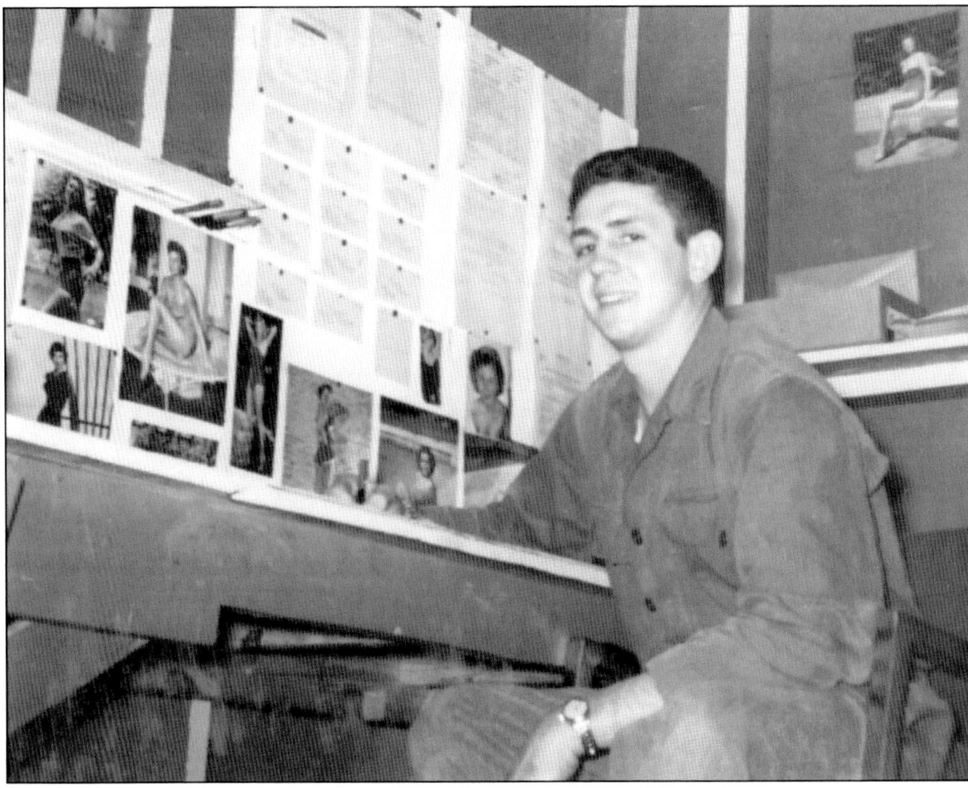

Bibliography

Clemens, S.W. *Faith and Community: A History of Peace-Tohickon Evangelical Lutheran Church.* Indian Valley Printing, Ltd, 1992.

Davis, W.W.H. *History of Bucks County*, vol. I. Lewis Publishing Co., 1905.

Hendricks, W.J. MD. *History of Grand View Hospital: 1913 to 1968.* 1966.

Past and Present. Jerusalem Evangelical Lutheran Church of Almont, PA.

Price, C.H. *A History of Christ Reformed Church at Indian Creek (Indianfield).* Telford, PA, 1966.

Reynolds, M. *Place Names in Bucks County.* The Bucks County Historical Society, 1953.

West Rockhill Historical Society Archives

www.stjohnsridgevalley.com

Yoder, J.D. *The Pennridge Schools Through the Ages: A History of Excellence.* 2004.

www.arcadiapublishing.com

Discover books about the town where you grew up, the cities where your friends and families live, the town where your parents met, or even that retirement spot you've been dreaming about. Our Web site provides history lovers with exclusive deals, advanced notification about new titles, e-mail alerts of author events, and much more.

MADE IN THE USA

Arcadia Publishing, the leading local history publisher in the United States, is committed to making history accessible and meaningful through publishing books that celebrate and preserve the heritage of America's people and places. Consistent with our mission to preserve history on a local level, this book was printed in South Carolina on American-made paper and manufactured entirely in the United States.

This book carries the accredited Forest Stewardship Council (FSC) label and is printed on 100 percent FSC-certified paper. Products carrying the FSC label are independently certified to assure consumers that they come from forests that are managed to meet the social, economic, and ecological needs of present and future generations.

FSC

Mixed Sources

Product group from well-managed forests and other controlled sources

Cert no. SW-COC-001530

www.fsc.org

© 1996 Forest Stewardship Council